OXFORD WORLD'S CLASSICS

THE OXFORD SHAKESPEARE

General Editor · Stanley Wells

The Oxford Shakespeare offers new and authoritative editions of Shakespeare's plays in which the early printings have been scrupulously re-examined and interpreted. An introductory essay provides all relevant background information together with an appraisal of critical views and of the play's effects in performance. The detailed commentaries pay particular attention to language and staging. Reprints of sources, music for songs, genealogical tables, maps, etc. are included where necessary; many of the volumes are illustrated, and all contain an index.

SHELDON P. ZITNER, the editor of *Much Ado About Nothing* in the Oxford Shakespeare, is Emeritus Professor of English at Trinity College, the University of Toronto.

THE OXFORD SHAKESPEARE

Currently available in paperback

The rest of the plays and poems are forthcoming

OXFORD WORLD'S CLASSICS

WILLIAM SHAKESPEARE

Much Ado About Nothing

Edited by
SHELDON P. ZITNER

OXFORD
UNIVERSITY PRESS

OXFORD

UNIVERSITY PRESS

Great Clarendon Street, Oxford OX2 6DP

Oxford University Press is a department of the University of Oxford.
It furthers the University's objective of excellence in research, scholarship,
and education by publishing worldwide in

Oxford New York

Athens Auckland Bangkok Bogotá Buenos Aires Cape Town
Chennai Dar es Salaam Delhi Florence Hong Kong Istanbul Karachi
Kolkata Kuala Lumpur Madrid Melbourne Mexico City Mumbai Nairobi
Paris São Paulo Shanghai Singapore Taipei Tokyo Toronto Warsaw

with associated companies in Berlin Ibadan

Oxford is a registered trade mark of Oxford University Press
in the UK and in certain other countries

Published in the United States
by Oxford University Press Inc., New York

© Sheldon P. Zitner 1993

The moral rights of the author have been asserted

Database right Oxford University Press (maker)

First published by the Clarendon Press 1993
First published as a World's Classics paperback 1994
Reissued as an Oxford World's Classics paperback 1998

British Library Cataloguing in Publication Data

Data available

Library of Congress Cataloging in Publication Data

Data available

ISBN 0–19–812992–0 (hbk.)
ISBN 0–19–283418–5 (pbk.)

5 7 9 10 8 6

Printed in Spain by
Book Print S.L., Barcelona

PREFACE

I AM greatly indebted to Stanley Wells, who kept me from a hundred errors, as did my colleague Nancy Lindheim, who read a mid-course draft of the Introduction. John Adames, Ron Bryden, Ruth Harvey, Lynne Magnusson, Heather McCallum, Willard McCarty, Helen Ostovich, Frances Whistler and Brian Parker were generous with their time and knowledge; Herbert Weil answered questions about recent productions of *Much Ado*. I have incurred too many other debts to acknowledge all of them here. The deepest, however, is to my daughter Julia.

The Social Sciences and Humanities Research Council of Canada aided my stay at the Folger Library, whose staff was, as always, expert and helpful, as were the staffs of the Library of Congress, the Theatre Collection of the New York Public Library, the University of Toronto and the Trinity College libraries; to all of them my thanks.

Acknowledgement of the receipt of the manuscript of this edition arrived with news of the death of George Hibbard, a good friend and example to everyone concerned with editing Renaissance drama. This edition is dedicated to his memory.

S. P. ZITNER

CONTENTS

Contents

LIST OF ILLUSTRATIONS

GENERAL INTRODUCTION

Much Ado About Nothing *and the Romantic Comedies*

Shakespeare's three great romantic comedies, so widely studied and performed, can easily become too familiar. *A Midsummer Night's Dream* can seem only a fragile artifice, and the lucky marriages of *Twelfth Night, or What You Will* and *As You Like It* too close to the commercial offer to please implied in the titles. In such a mood, one turns to a play which is often grouped with the romantic comedies, *Much Ado About Nothing*. Not that *Much Ado* is unknown or even unpopular, but it is less accessible, less easily pigeon-holed among the reliable expectations of memory. Its characters are more problematic; Beatrice and Benedick must project a harmony amid contention, which the least impression of bickering or incompatibility can vulgarize. Almost as daunting, the actors preparing the roles of Hero and Claudio face epithets like 'peripheral' and 'uninteresting', often applied to what ought to be the central roles of *ingénue* and suitor. Yet such difficulties make *Much Ado* a challenge to the interpretative skills of actors and audiences, and so less likely to cloy.

Like the romantic comedies *Much Ado* has a stagy love-plot that ends in reconciliations. Yet the ensuing marriage of Claudio and Hero is not quite as everyone would like it (nor can we condescend to Elizabethan audiences by assuming it was wholly as they liked it), and both the marriage and the events leading to it are overshadowed by the odd but believable courtship of Beatrice and Benedick. This *is* as we would like it, but more Bloomsbury than Arcadia, promising what Bertrand Russell called 'hilarious Olympian controversy' rather than cosy domesticity.

Much Ado clearly differs from the romantic comedies on the matter of love. It gives us nothing like love at first sight. Claudio made his calculations about Hero before the war and is now only rechecking them. All the lovers are concerned about rank, money, and Society. Hero, primed for a proposal by Don Pedro, accepts one from Claudio without even catching her breath. Jane Austen's Mrs Bennett would have understood, but taken a moment to ponder. Beatrice and Benedick evidently had a hurtful connection some time before and are still smarting from it. Margaret wants to marry above stairs, and Leonato wants his daughter safely bestowed. Benedick's acceptance of Beatrice is also his acceptance of her intellectual superiority and of his lifelong vulnerability to her sexuality, something rather different from romantic stellification of the beloved. Her acceptance of Benedick is guarded and defensive, despite the sonnets which finally have to be snatched from their pockets. The only late-night wooing the play offers is a malicious charade with a wry allusion to *Romeo and Juliet*. There is little romantic love in any of this, unless one takes Claudio's formulaic echoes for the thing itself.

Much Ado has no fairy transformations of lovers or symbolic cross-dressing. Its disguises are plain deceptions, like the tricking of Margaret into aping her mistress. Characters have difficulty in knowing one another face to face, but everyone seems to recognize everyone else through the costumes and visors of a masked ball, though several have wicked or prudential motives for pretending not to do so.

The Messina constabulary is high comedy's obligatory lower-orders turn. But Dogberry and the Watch represent the bungling Law, at which laughter is always warranted. This is somewhat different from the class condescension to the 'mechanicals' in *A Midsummer Night's Dream*. Dogberry's English is an uncultivated variant of the verbal strategies of his superiors, and both his empty proverbial wisdom and the discoveries made by the Watch augment the play's scepticism of human understanding. Dogberry's examination of the conspirators, for example, is the proper gloss on Claudio's inquisition of Hero. Borachio, Shakespeare's alcoholic, has none of the merriment of Sir Toby of *Twelfth Night*. He is as unfunny as Michael Cassio, the poor head for drink in *Othello*, and allowed—despite the brevity of the part—a touch of the pathos granted at the end to Falstaff. Low comedy in *Much Ado* is less opportunistic, less patronizing than in other middle comedies.

Unlike them, too, *Much Ado* is set in a this-worldly Messina. It sits on no fortunate coast of Illyria, borders no fairy-haunted Athenian wood or forest of Arden offering pastoral renewal. Its nature is a rich man's garden, the lessons drawn are political bromides, and its talk is drawing-room banter.

In *Much Ado* no supernatural forces are at work. The ritual at Hero's shrine in 5.3 is neither orthodox nor therapeutic, and it does not cap motifs such as a fairy underworld. Some directors cut it. Nor are there accidents and revelations—as in *Twelfth Night*—suggesting divinity at work. When the Watch blunders onto Don John's plot, it is dumb luck, not the argument from design.

Villains are foiled, lovers wed, and dancing ends the play, but *Much Ado* has broad sunless patches. The romantic plot is overlaid with harsh realism. Hero wed is still something of a sacrificial figure, and at the end the social codes that govern Messina are all in place, not even momentarily shaken as they were in Verona. In addition, Shakespeare insists on determinisms that trivialize human choices. Don John was born a bastard, Conrad under Saturn, Margaret below stairs, and Beatrice, dauntlessly happy, under a dancing star. Common sense (or is it sentimental hope?) tells us that sooner or later a Beatrice and a Benedick would have found each other, but who can swear it?

In *The Whole Journey* C. L. Barber identifies the 'precariousness of mutuality' as the 'subject' of *Much Ado*.[1] The psychological resistance of the lovers to one another implies that the social inequalities imposed on gender may be only the public, historical forms of that precariousness. And after all this it is hardly reassuring to recall that Beatrice and Benedick, who most engage our hopes, are named 'blessed', as if members of a secular elect.

The secular temper of *Much Ado* is reflected in its marriages. In the romantic comedies marriages are also symbolic political settlements. *A Midsummer Night's Dream* founds a dynasty upon former enemies. In *As You Like It* the restoration of a duke, and in *Twelfth Night* a duke's capacity to rule, are secured by marriages between couples also related by blood. Clearly, *Much Ado* has no such dynastic paradigms. Neither Don Pedro's Aragon nor Leonato's Messina is in turmoil or neglected, and Don John's plot is a petty threat. The marriages

---

[1] C. L. Barber, *The Whole Journey* (Berkeley, Calif., 1987), 7.

of Beatrice and Benedick and Hero and Claudio are of interest largely to themselves. Claudio shows no desire to govern anywhere, nor is Don Pedro in a hurry to resume governing at home.

Unlike the romantic comedies, *Much Ado* neither dispels nor masks class divisions by incorporating them in an idealized community. Dogberry is obsequious and unpleasant, at all times an impediment to justice. Leonato is a person of rank but without distinction or obvious ability. Messina has its balls and entertainments. Yet in the play 'degree' is divisive and burdensome. Shakespeare makes little use of the hint in the sources at Hero's low station, but he does use it when Leonato, like Beatrice, scorns the unprincely behaviour of the two princes who have accused his daughter. The contrast between the fates of two gentlewomen, Maria in *Twelfth Night* and Margaret in *Much Ado*, both clever and articulate, both fond of drunkards, is characteristic of the two plays: Maria, marrying happily above her station in part as a reward for her aid in punishing the social upstart Malvolio; Margaret, easily victimized because of her social ambition, and allowed to remain below stairs by grace and favour. Lastly, there is the devolution of Don Pedro. As the play opens he is a gracious and victorious commander. As the play closes, he is like Antonio at the end of *The Merchant of Venice*, an odd man out, the rather diminished object of Benedick's patronizing advice to get a wife, whatever the risks of being cuckolded.

Much Ado is concerned with wooing and bedding as activities, but it also keeps them to the fore as issues. The affinities of the play are with the problematic realism of *The Taming of the Shrew*, *All's Well That Ends Well*, and *Measure for Measure*, and with later plays in which the spirit of their *novellieri* antecedents—especially of the *novelle* or short tales of Boccaccio and Bandello—is more pronounced than it is in the romantic comedies. For all these differences, *Much Ado* shares the ebullience of romantic comedy if not wholly its festive release. In part this ebullience is an effect of romantic plot devices, masked ball and dancing, deceptions in the garden, lovers finally wed. Yet in *Much Ado* the ebullience also comes from language, from pervasive wit that creates a Utopia of discourse. Such language and its melody as repeated in Dogberry's bass are the play's special achievement. The probable

date of *Much Ado* and the play's literary antecedents are what
we should expect from these characteristics.

Date

Much Ado was probably written during the last third of 1598
and completed before the end of the year. The early limit is
set by the entry of Francis Meres's *Palladis Tamia* in the
Stationers' Register on 7 September 1598; the later limit by
the withdrawal of Will Kemp from Shakespeare's troupe, the
Lord Chamberlain's Men, early in 1599. *Palladis Tamia*, the
wit's treasury, was a comparative listing of English, classical,
and Italian literary achievements. Since Meres includes for
praise much slighter Shakespearian comedies such as *The Two
Gentlemen of Verona* and *Love's Labour's Lost*, it is unlikely he
would have omitted *Much Ado* had he known it. His inclusion
of Everard Guilpin's *Skialethia*, a work entered in the Register
eight days after his own, shows that Meres tried to keep up
to the minute.

Will Kemp, the accomplished low-comedy actor, was one of
the original Lord Chamberlain's Men. Shakespeare had him
in mind for Dogberry, as speech-prefixes in the quarto edition
name him in 4.2. From his appearance in the 1598 cast-list
of Jonson's *Every Man in His Humour* and his absence from
the 1599 cast-list of *Every Man out of His Humour*, a play
perfect for his talents, it appears that Kemp left the company
early in 1599 or shortly before. Certainly he had left it by 11
February 1599, when he began his famous month-long morris dance from London to Norwich.

Completion near the end of 1598 is consistent with the
play's style and theme. The rhymed quatrains in *Much Ado*
show its affinity with *Love's Labour's Lost* and *Romeo and Juliet*.
Its double endings and frequent enjambment show its affinities
with the Henry IV plays, *As You Like It*, and *Twelfth Night*.

Thematic resemblances are similarly suggestive. Margaret
seems a step towards the upwardly mobile Helen of *All's Well*,
composed slightly later, as one can demonstrate from the
clown part, which was evidently written with Will Kemp's
gentler successor, Robert Armin, in mind. In both plays
Shakespeare provides sympathetic motives for his subversive

servant-figures, as he does for the yeoman-soldier Williams, who poses awkward political questions in *Henry V*. In *Much Ado*, fragile family and gender relations, a questionable war, and a rivalry for power without serious implications seem a middle term between the disappointments of the history plays and the awkward resolutions of the problem comedies.

Sources

The term 'source' carries implications of derivativeness that even cursory comparison of *Much Ado* with its antecedents (a less tendentious term) dispels at once. That so many antecedents have been suggested is not surprising since the nominal main plot, the indictment and vindication of a chaste woman, was common literary property. The Italian critic Paolo Beni, praising Ariosto's use of it, wrote in 1607 that he doubted 'if there can be found either in ancient or modern literature anything more wonderful and affecting, or better knotted and untied. It could serve as the very Form and Idea of the finest Tragi-comedy . . . ' (quoted in Bullough, ii. 70). What attracted Shakespeare to it, in addition to its structural elegance, was what attracted him to stories as diverse as those of *Othello* and *Cymbeline*, the exculpatory symbolism of the woman wrongfully accused but finally vindicated.

The antecedents of *Much Ado* have been studied exhaustively by Charles T. Prouty, by Geoffrey Bullough (who translates and reprints important passages), and by Kenneth Muir. Of the sixteen antecedents Prouty treats (two of the eight plays he mentions are lost), none of the plays and only four of the non-dramatic works were likely to have actually come to Shakespeare's hand; some of these, such as François de Belleforest's *Histoires Tragiques*, were probably not of much use. Closest to *Much Ado* is a work undoubtedly familiar to Shakespeare, the twenty-second tale of Matteo Bandello's *La prima parte de le novelle*, published in 1554. This version of the Hero–Claudio material was elaborated and moralized in Belleforest's French translation of 1574. Shakespeare probably went directly to Bandello; he was familiar with John Florio's English–Italian dictionaries; in any case, Bandello's Italian prose is hardly insuperable for a competent Latinist.

The twenty-second tale is set in Messina, to which King Piero of Aragon has come with his wife and eldest son, taking control of Sicily at the suggestion of the Pope after the massacre of the island's French overlords and the defeat of King Carlo II of Naples. During the ensuing peace, one of Piero's favourites, the valiant and wealthy Timbreo, falls in love with Fenicia, the beautiful 16-year-old daughter of Lionato, a nobleman of good lineage, but apparently of little wealth or distinction. After a courtship kept proper by Fenicia despite his initial attempts at seduction, Timbreo dispatches a matchmaker to initiate wedding arrangements to which Lionato agrees.

The impending marriage dismays Girondo, a friend of Timbreo, who secretly loves Fenicia and determines to break up the match. Acting through agents, Girondo offers to prove Fenicia's promiscuity, provided Timbreo takes an oath of silence. The 'proof' is a few ambiguous words and the sight of a man climbing a ladder at night into an unoccupied part of Lionato's mansion. This satisfies Timbreo, who sends a messenger to denounce Fenicia and withdraw his offer of marriage. Lionato in turn accuses Timbreo of concealing his true motive, distaste for an alliance with a family not his equal in wealth. (Although Lionato, unlike his counterpart in *Much Ado*, does not doubt his daughter's innocence, his strain of self-pity may have given Shakespeare a further hint for the role.) Fenicia meanwhile is dying of a broken heart, so say her physicians, who give her up for dead. As her body is being washed for burial, Fenicia regains consciousness. Realizing the difficulty of finding her a husband after the scandal, Lionato decides to go through with a mock funeral and to send both Fenicia and her younger sister Belfiore to his brother's country villa, keeping them there until Fenicia has grown up and altered in appearance, thus becoming marriageable again, this time under the name of Lucilla.

After the funeral, Timbreo realizes the flimsiness of the 'proof' on which he acted. Girondo too is overcome by remorse, and confessing his crime to Timbreo in the church containing Fenicia's shrine, he offers Timbreo a dagger with which to take his revenge. Timbreo refuses, stating that had he known Girondo also loved Fenicia he would have withdrawn his own suit to her. Thus honourably reconciled, the two knights visit Lionato and ask forgiveness. Timbreo places himself entirely at Lionato's service, but Lionato asks only that Timbreo consult him before considering marriage again.

At 17 Fenicia is even more of a beauty than before, and though Timbreo does not recognize her on a visit to the villa, Lionato has no trouble persuading Timbreo to marry her. At the ensuing banquet, all is explained to Fenicia, and Timbreo recognizes her at last. Girondo asks Lionato for the hand of Belfiore, a request readily granted. On the return of the marriage party to Messina, King Piero entertains them lavishly, heaping honours and money on the newly-weds. Bandello ends with a roll call of Sicilian, Neapolitan, and Spanish noble families supposedly related to the protagonists, families whose members the narrator, rather self-conscious about turning from story to panegyric, claims to see present in his audience.

The attractiveness of Bandello's tale lay in its twisting plot and suggestions of stageable scenes. But parts of the tale were also irrelevant or uneconomical (the royal group), unstageable (Fenicia's long period of unconsciousness culminating in the washing of her body and her awakening), or off-putting (Bandello's panegyric to Spanish nobility). There were also details that strained credulity. Despite this, the *novellieri*, Boccaccio even more than Bandello, offered a realism of tone, a prose style, and a mode of observation close to the matter-of-fact responses and motivations most readily transferable to the stage. But the central characterizations in this Bandello tale were sometimes glaringly at odds with that realism. Most obviously so were the contradiction in Timbreo between the high-mindedness of the noble and the eagerness of the seducer, between Timbreo's early attempts at seduction and his gullibility and his later good will and intelligence; and in Girondo between the noble friend and the unscrupulous schemer. Such contradictions presented problems less tractable than the possible staleness of the conflicting claims of love and friendship as dramatic themes.

It would have taken more indifference to gender inequality than Shakespeare then possessed for him to deal with the behaviour of Bandello's male paragons in the 'romantic', i.e. relatively unquestioning, manner of the tale. He had tried something like this in *The Two Gentlemen of Verona* and had failed, especially in the last act, when Valentine forgives his treacherous friend Proteus and indeed offers him Sylvia, even after Proteus had tried to rape her—and when Proteus reforms at once upon learning that the page is his supposedly beloved Julia. Convincing words had not come; what one remembers are comic servants and a dog. Convincing words *had* come in the sonnets when the poet apparently surrendered his mistress to the young man, but that was in a genre that justified a unique subjectivity. In any case, the sonnet 'characters' are not left as romance figures; all are finally queried and found wanting.

The Bandello story was obviously acceptable, but not its male protagonists. The transformation of Timbreo and Girondo into Claudio and Benedick implies a rejection of the idea that the seduction and betrayal of women are irrelevant grounds for judging male character, or that the seduction and betrayal of women are merely to be expected, and hence only minor issues compared to the exalted demands of male friendship, however inconsistently those are complied with as, for example, by Girondo. In Benedick and Claudio the relation between Timbreo and Girondo is transformed from a historically backward-looking sexual rivalry to a forward-looking moral distinction. The unfairness of Hero's situation, and by implication its cause, is presented to an audience (already aware of her innocence), through the biased reactions of Claudio, Don Pedro, and Leonato and through Benedick's significant hesitation. Against them are set Beatrice's informed loyalty and the Friar's sensitivity and logic. In Bandello the sympathy of Lionato is only half self-pity and the betrayal of Fenicia is largely an episode in the unfolding of a knightly friendship.

At least as important ideologically as Shakespeare's transformation of Bandello's protagonists was his transformation of the aristocratic and military framework of Bandello's tale. King Piero of Aragon is a presiding figure wholly outside the central story, but making it possible and validating its conclusion. His conquests bring the characters together; he rewards their union, feasts the local honourables, and provokes Bandello's rapturous catalogue of nobility. Elizabethan panegyric could be just as sycophantic as this, especially in literary dedications, and Shakespeare himself had been purposefully complimentary on occasion. But the praise of the young man in the sonnets, for example, does not have to be explained away by anything more than other sonnets, 124 for a start. Shakespeare came to writing *Much Ado* from 1 *Henry IV*, that is, from Falstaff's critique of honour, and was shortly to go on to the mockery of the French nobility and a carefully qualified celebration of even Henry V himself. It would have been easy while in this vein to find Bandello's panegyric of largely Spanish noble families easily disposible.

Shakespeare dismantles Bandello's framework and reassembles it as irony. Shakespeare's Don Pedro is not a king, nor does he have a queen or a male heir. His famous victory is introduced by a caste-obsessed messenger with no concern for the merely common dead. Don Pedro steps off Bandello's pedestal into the midst of the story, and though he woos for Claudio and sets up Beatrice and Benedick, he bungles his way through the play like the others, finally putting up with Benedick's condescending advice on his bachelorhood. In Bandello, hierarchy is a comfortable, secure given. In *Much Ado* it is also a given and secure, but rather less comfortable.

Commentators make much of Shakespeare's apparent equalization of the fortunes and rank of Claudio and Hero, as contrasted with the differences between Timbreo and Fenicia. This is a tricky matter: neither of the Bandello suitors raises the issue. Bandello's Lionato speaks of himself as 'poor', but his circumstances, as Bandello describes them, seem adequate, if insufficient for grand dowries. In any case, Fenicia's birth and wealth are not crucial in Bandello's tale, nor are they in Shakespeare. The raising of class issues here would have blurred the focus on gender issues that are evidently Shakespeare's primary concern. Despite this, *Much Ado* exhibits a lively consciousness of the implications of rank and caste from the first words of the play.

There is perhaps another instance of Shakespeare glancing back ironically at the aristocratic context of Bandello's tale. Bandello follows a description of Fenicia's wedding gown with a lengthy, courtly-erotic account of its occupant. Perhaps Shakespeare recalled the passage, crediting it to the upwardly mobile Margaret. Finally, Shakespeare altered Bandello's tale

·in order to make its events seem more circumstantial or simply to increase their dramatic effectiveness. Timbreo alone sees Girondo's proof of Fenicia's infidelity; in Shakespeare both Claudio and Don Pedro are deceived. Timbreo denounces Fenicia through a messenger; Claudio himself denounces Hero before the altar.

Some *Much Ado* plot elements without antecedents in Bandello may have been suggested by Ariosto's *Orlando Furioso*, published in 1516 and translated by John Harington in 1591. In Ariosto's fifth book, the story of Ariodante and Genevra is told by Dalinda, Genevra's treacherous maid. Genevra, daughter of the Scottish king, is desired by Polynesso, Duke of Albany, who has seduced Dalinda as a means to that end. Genevra, in love with Ariodante, is loved in return. Polynesso, determined to prevent a match, positions Ariodante and his brother Lurcanio so they can see him being greeted by Dalinda wearing her mistress's clothes as he enters Genevra's window. Ariodante, grief-stricken, disappears, sending word that he has committed suicide. Lurcanio denounces Genevra who, under Scottish law, will be put to death unless a champion appears to defend her honour. All is happily resolved with the reappearance of Ariodante, determined to champion Genevra even before he is certain of her fidelity (a glance toward Benedick?). The lovers are reunited; Dalinda's punishment is a nunnery.

The importance of Dalinda, whose fate begins and ends the tale and who narrates it, may well be reflected in the care with which Shakespeare creates the role of Margaret, a less conventional figure than Ariosto's Dalinda. Margaret is handled with as much sympathy but less condescension: in Ariosto she is naïve, all victimized infatuation. Her presence strengthens the charade of 'proof', as does the presence of Lurcanio so the deception is more convincing than it is in Bandello. The character of Polynesso may also have been useful for Shakespeare; Ariosto's Duke of Albany is, save in motivation, pure Don John. Ariosto gives us none of the complications of Bandello's romantic paragons. For all its romance trappings, Ariosto's version is more careful in naturalizing the motivations of its protagonists than is Bandello, hence closer to Shakespeare in this respect.

One or two further hints for *Much Ado* Shakespeare may have found in Spenser's *Faerie Queene*. In the 1596 edition, 2.4.16–38, Spenser tells the story of Phedon, about to marry Claribell. Phedon is betrayed by his supposed friend Philemon, as 'either envying my toward good, | Or of himselfe to treason ill disposed' (22.2–3). Here at last is Don John plain. Philemon courts Claribell's maid Pryene by flattering her with the notion that only fortune (rank), and hence fine clothes keep her from being considered the equal of her mistress. This seems closer than Ariosto's Dalinda to Shakespeare's Margaret. Spenser requires no verisimilitude so there is no window, only an 'appointed place'; the ruse works, as Phedon sees what he thinks is his beloved Claribell in a compromising situation. Enraged, Phedon poisons Philemon, and chases Pryene hoping to stab her, but is overtaken by Sir Guyon and the Palmer, who impart the obligatory Spenserian lesson about moderation.

Another version of the Hero–Claudio narrative appears in George Whetstone's *Rock of Regard* (1576), a collection of moralized tales and poems. The difficulties arising from conversations overheard and misinterpreted make Whetstone's story of Rinaldo and Giletta of some interest. Other versions include Abraham Fraunce's Latin play *Victoria* (*c*.1580–3) and *Fedele and Fortunio* (1585), a play attributed to Anthony Munday. Both attempted to capitalize on the popularity of Luigi Pasqualigo's *Il Fedele* (1579). Shakespeare may have known Whetstone and Munday's imitation of Pasqualigo. It is unlikely that he was acquainted with the original, despite the temptation to see the beginnings of Beatrice in Pasqualigo's servant-confidante Beatrice, who discourses wittily on love and urges her mistress to sham death to gain her lover's sympathy. From Whetstone perhaps Shakespeare may have taken the possibility of scenes of courtly festivity, but he knew their value from earlier plays. From Munday (who follows but dilutes Pasqualigo here), he may have had the idea of comic police making an arrest; in Munday, however, the arrest is not crucial to the main action.

What is of more interest than the possibility of Shakespeare's borrowing bits of the Hero–Claudio plot he could have easily invented is the direction of his alterations. His addition of Beatrice and Benedick, his recharacterizations of the protagonists, and the perspectives the play provides in by-the-by comment, especially by Beatrice, place to the fore the social issues that vindication-plots ignored or obscured in happy endings.

Without Timbreo and Girondo to vie for Fenicia and to confess their betrayal of her, Shakespeare had to invent a Don John to initiate the plot against Hero and a Watch to expose it. The antecedents of the Watch and of the Beatrice–Benedick plot are fewer and less specific. The bumbling of the constabulary was proverbial and easily illustrated; to make them the instruments of justice was a happy if obvious irony. The plays of John Lyly offered some theatrical precedent for Shakespeare's witty lovers, as did Biron and Rosaline in his own *Love's Labour's Lost*. As early as 1901, Mary Augusta Scott argued for the friendly but sharp debates between Lady Emilia Pia and Lord Gaspare Pallavicino in Baldassare Castiglione's enormously popular guide to sophisticated conduct, *Il Cortegiano* (translated in 1561 by Sir Thomas Hoby), as models for the exchanges between Beatrice and Benedick.[1] Perhaps more relevant is the anecdote told by Castiglione's Count Ludovico di Canossa, who recalls an occasion when a woman who had no thought of doing so fell in love with a man merely because she overheard it said that they were in love. The woman in question accepts the man as worthy of her love because she is impressed by 'so general a judgement' (Bullough, ii. 79). This is close but not quite Shakespeare's Beatrice, who is hardly indifferent to Benedick at the outset. For Beatrice one of the issues in her change, not of heart but of her mode of expressing her true feelings, is the overheard allegation of 'cruelty'. The psychological mechanism of her acknowledgement of Benedick is more complex than that in Castiglione's anecdote. It is in fact nearly opposite: Castiglione's anecdote has common opinion overruling individual judgement; Beatrice, however, is ruled by a particular sense of self that leads to a change in conduct. The possibility that Castiglione's work was in a more fundamental sense an antecedent for *Much Ado* has been argued by Barbara Lewalski in her 1969 edition of the play. She finds the play's intellectual

---

[1] M. A. Scott, '*The Book of the Courtier*: A Possible source of Beatrice and Benedick', *PMLA* 45 (1901), 476.

centre in its alignment of modes of desire and modes of knowledge, and hence sees (Lewalski, p. xiv) in *Much Ado* a debt to Neoplatonic philosophizing on love, particularly to Cardinal Bembo's discussion in Castiglione's Book IV.

The Title

Crack Me This Nut, a now-lost comedy of 1595, may be a precedent for the throwaway titles—*Much Ado About Nothing*, *As You Like It*, *All's Well That Ends Well*, *Measure for Measure*, and *Twelfth Night* (more particularly its subtitle, *What You Will*)—that Shakespeare gave the comedies he wrote around the turn of the century. If this was a small vogue, authors (or perhaps booksellers) seem to have been of two minds about it. The *Annals of English Drama* notes that Chapman's 1599 *All Fools but the Fool* had been altered from *The World Runs on Wheels*, and Dekker's *Bear a Brain*, of the same year, from the equally unforthcoming *Better Late Than Never*. Both titles, however, may refer to either *The Shoemaker's Holiday*, or *Look About You*. Shakespeare used enough of them to suggest that such titles had a particular attraction for him. Their teasing playfulness shows his confidence in his relations with his audience; apparently he felt no need to promise them *The Insatiate Countess*.

Frequent scenes of 'noting' and some passages of word-play in *Much Ado* have encouraged critics to tease significance from its title. Toward the end of 4.1 Beatrice and Benedick try to shield themselves from the consequences of love by equivocal declarations that they love 'nothing in the world' so much as each other: either nothing else so well, or mere nothingness as much. More trivial is Don Pedro's pun on 'nothing' and 'noting' as musical notation in 2.3. In his 1883 edition, R. G. White applied the noting-nothing pun to the scenes of 'noting' that generate both plots.

As a euphemism, 'nothing' may also have some claim. Adrian Colman argues that there is no way of proving Shakespeare intended a sexual meaning in the title, or that he did not[1]. 'Thing' and 'nothing' are the all-purpose sexual

---

[1] E. A. M. Colman, *The Dramatic Use of Bawdy in Shakespeare* (1974), 15–19.

signifiers, and Elizabethan writers played regularly with their off-colour connotations. 'You are naught, you are naught', Ophelia chides Hamlet when he talks smut. 'I think nothing', she had just said. 'That's a fair thought to lie between maids' legs', Hamlet had replied. 'Nothing' can refer with equal warrant to the male or female genitalia. The word and its opposite are used in both senses elsewhere in Shakespeare; so concludes David Willbern—who refers to *Much Ado* only in passing.[1] *Much Ado* looks often and askance at sexuality. The male obsession with sexual betrayal underlies the violent jealousy of Claudio and, supposedly, the militant bachelorhood of Benedick, as it does most of the play's jokes. Sexuality itself, its powers and delights, is hardly devalued in the play, but the conventional—that is the vaginal—basis of male 'honour' is; and with it the consequent male fear and the hatred of the women charged with guarding men's honour between their legs. Claudio understands nothing of the implications of such notions for his experience, but the advice to Don Pedro suggests that Benedick does. Finally, there is the possibility that the application of 'nothing' is more general, a sharp dismissal of wedding and bedding as pursued among Messina's gilded youth.

Perhaps more important is what *Much Ado About Nothing* has in common with titles like *As You Like It* and *What You Will*. They are light-hearted and teasing, but self-withholding. What *you* like and will, as the titles imply, may be quite different from the author's preferences, and some degree of alienation is implicit in an author's undertaking to elaborate mere nothing. This is notoriously the case in the mordant nihilism of the Earl of Rochester's poem 'Upon Nothing'. An intellectual reserve, a refusal to evoke romance as the prime mode of the play, are evident in Beatrice's word-play, often subversive of the givens of rank and gender, in Leonato's painful distrust of Hero, and in the qualified gaiety of the ending.

[1] D. Willbern, 'Shakespeare's Nothing', in M. Schwartz and C. Kahn (eds.), *Representing Shakespeare* (Baltimore, 1980), 244–36.

Place and Setting

Unlike many of Shakespeare's plays, *Much Ado* does not create a strong sense of place. Shakespeare's Messina, as Mario Praz observes, is 'senz'altro una città imaginaria'.[1] It bears no resemblance to Renaissance Messina or any other Italian city of the day. What it does resemble, however, is an Elizabethan town with a simple municipal organization operating under royal charter. Shakespeare's Messina is something of a social backwater; compare the gorgeous wedding gown of the Duchess of Milan with Hero's modest wedding dress which, according to her fashionable gentlewoman, is appropriate to the occasion. There is a provincial overtone in the strain felt by Leonato on receiving Don Pedro and his party; the formality is excessive and observed to be so. Leonato is unused to such exalted guests or to such entertaining. Public rooms, evidently not often open, must be perfumed by specially hired staff (Borachio); for music Leonato must depend on the Prince's man Balthasar. This is hardly Bandello's upscale Messina of the banquets. What Leonato *is* used to are easy, informal relations with townsfolk such as Dogberry, whom he can address as friend and neighbour. Evidently he is also used to a household without a wife's control, hence to a rather permissive domestic scene dominated by his teenage daughter, Hero, her two gentlewomen, and the unconventional Beatrice. This makes easier Don John's plot to discredit Hero, something that could have taken place only with difficulty in *All's Well*, whose household organization left no wall without ears.

In other plays the impression of place derives from mutually defining contrasts; town against country, court against tavern, and from evocative scene-setting. *Much Ado* has little of such poetry—Hero's description of her garden, a few words from Don Pedro on the beauty of the night—and no great removals of the action from place to symbolic place, to a Dover Cliff or a forest of Arden, for example. Social rather than physical ambience concerns the dramatist, but picturesque settings blur rather than clarify that ambience. As a text *Much Ado* implies a classical spatial economy and a radically stylized

[1] M. Praz, *Shakespeare e l'Italia* (Florence, 1963), 91: 'above all, an imaginary city'.

1. A renaissance garden, or 'orchard', including a 'pleached bower', from *Hortus Floridus* (1615), by Crispin van de Pass.

setting. With the exception of the church scene in which Claudio denounces Hero, and possibly the supposed penance in 5.3, the action takes place in or near Leonato's mansion.

Earlier editors often attempted to locate the action of individual scenes in the play, usually following Capell, Theobald, and Pope. Of the play's seventeen scenes, at least nine are localized differently by different editors. Generally the issue is whether to place the scene inside Leonato's house, before it, or in the adjoining garden. In only a few instances does the choice seem significant. For example, the depth of Leonato's anxiety and of the deference he shows Don Pedro can be indicated to some extent by the choice of locale: a public room in the governor's house, with its suggestion of Leonato's status, or a more deferential welcome outside.

How casual Shakespeare could be about location unless it affected meaning is clear from 1.2 and 1.3. Scene 1.2 opens with Antonio's second-hand account of Don Pedro and Claudio speaking of Hero when walking 'in mine orchard'. Thus we also ought to locate all of 1.1 in Antonio's orchard, an unlikely place for receiving the Messenger, unless we think

Pedro and Claudio repeated elsewhere their exchange of twenty lines earlier in 1.1. In 1.3 Borachio also claims to have overheard Claudio and Don Pedro discussing the proxy wooing, this time in a musty room. These are knots to be cut by directors, not untied by editors.

Where there is a need to define a place, it takes only a few descriptive lines (Hero's in her garden), minor props (trellis and tree for arbour and concealment), or only the stage architecture itself—as in 3.3 when Borachio and Conrad shield themselves from the weather under a 'penthouse', presumably the canopy over part of the stage. The action of *Much Ado* takes place largely in virtual rather than 'real' space, and the properties Shakespeare required for *Much Ado* were all on hand, an indication of his professional concern for easy transfer to different venues.

Organizing the Dramatis Personae

The story of Hero and Claudio does not require the whole cast of *Much Ado*. Hero and Claudio yes, but why Beatrice and Benedick? Leonato, but why Antonio? Margaret, but why Ursula? And why both Conrad and Borachio? Characteristically, the Shakespearian dramatis personae goes beyond the necessities of narrative, constituting a system of contrasting dyads and triads (Hal and Hotspur, Lear's three daughters), and even more sophisticated thematic variants (Hotspur as Time's fool, Hal redeeming it, Falstaff wasting it, Henry IV 'serving' it). In part, this systemic pairing reflects a view of character, specifically the Pauline voluntarism that prompts us to 'look here upon this picture and on this' in order to judge the characters resulting from the life-choices of Claudius and Hamlet's father.

There are further consequences arising from this process of doubling and tripling. In 'Emotion of Multitude', his seminal remarks on *Lear*, Yeats observes that the reverberations of parallel lives suggest to the audience the universality and hence the likelihood of what is occurring on stage. Shakespeare does with character what he does with scene and incident, maximizing the differences, here between characters brought together by incident (Leonato and Dogberry) or family or occupation (Hero and Beatrice, Dogberry and Verges). The result is vivid delineation, not only for its own sake, but for rapidity in orientating audience attention and easing the writer's task of generating dialogue.

Finally, the playwright is something of a company manager. In writing the play Shakespeare distributes the burden of work so as to sustain the enterprise, demanding of actors only what they can perform, bringing along novices by creating parts that stretch their talents.

Lovers

Hero and Leander, with George Chapman's continuation of what Christopher Marlowe had left undone, was published in 1598. Even without this jog to memory, Shakespeare might have named his *ingénue* Hero after the faithful young woman whose lover is drowned swimming to an assignation. Benedick's ironic reference to 'Leander the good swimmer' in 5.2 suggests that allusions to the story would have been widely understood. Shakespeare's dependence on its associations is clear from Claudio's puerile repetition of Hero's name as he denounces her.

The Hero of *Much Ado* is one of Shakespeare's passive young women: obedient, unquestioning, well brought up, thoroughly conventional and rather prudish. As is Polonius speaking of Ophelia, Leonato can be confident when he says of Hero, 'My daughter tells us all'. With the gardener in *Richard II*, Hero can gather politically correct platitudes (hers are naïve and unambiguous) from her garden in 3.1; she is uneasy at the sexual innuendo in Margaret's reference in 3.4 to the coming marriage; in 2.1 she is prudently specific in offering to do any 'modest' office to unite Beatrice and Benedick. In the brief self-defence she makes in 4.1, she responds with delicate obliqueness to the implicit charge of fornication, but directly to the apparently mentionable charge of conversation 'At hours unmeet'.

Shakespeare seems at times to do everything but make Hero disappear; unlike Beatrice, this is a part requiring only a second-best boy actor. In 1.1, in answer to Claudio's request for an opinion of her, Benedick, an admittedly unreliable judge of women, finds Hero merely Leonato's 'short daughter', 'too low for a high praise, too brown for a fair praise, and too little for a great praise'. Even Hero's most intense reactions (she blushes and goes pale) are conveyed by someone else, by the Friar, who describes her innocence, her shame, and her rage. Later in the scene it is the Friar who provides an apologia which invents more than describes the 'lovely' life of a Hero who speaks so little in her own right. No wonder Shakespeare chose a name that was a label. But even so evocative a name as Hero could not compete in implication with 'Beatrice', yet another indication of Shakespeare's curious reversal of traditional priorities in subordinating his 'main plot.'

Shakespeare's Hero is both a foil for Beatrice and a partial explanation of her character. In 2.1 Antonio asks Hero if she will be ruled by her father in the choice of a husband. Beatrice intervenes, saying that it is Hero's duty to curtsy and act as it pleases her father—adding however, that if the man chosen for her is not handsome, Hero should curtsy again and say ' "Father, as it please me" '. Beatrice, unlike Hero, is not a highly placed heiress. Older, with no father, and moving toward what was thought an unmarriageable age, she has developed tough—if not single-minded—views which question the constraints imposed on women. She tries to stake out a position of modified obedience for Hero, a position hardly radical when *The Miseries of Enforced Marriage*, to use the title of a popular play performed by Shakespeare's company in 1607, had long been acknowledged. For Hero, however, Beatrice's compromise might have been unsustainable. The instant change from Hero's preparation for Leonato's 'dream' of a match with Don Pedro to her acceptance of Claudio suggests complete pliability.

Yet Hero's loyalty is not witless acceptance. Like her discreetly flirtatious responses to the Prince during their turn around the dance floor, her answer in 3.1 to Ursula's question, 'When are you married, madam?' shows some wit: 'Why, every day, tomorrow.' Perhaps this also hints at a long-prepared dedication to the social role that might make her ultimate marriage to Claudio plausible. However, Hero is not all conformity and quiet. Beatrice is a fool and you're another, she tells Margaret after Margaret questions her taste in clothes, a matter not of prime interest to Hero. Perhaps the outburst is pre-nuptial jitters. Hero obviously looks to Beatrice as to an older sister, but there may be truth as well as feigning in the critique she makes of Beatrice when trying to trick her into accepting Benedick. Beatrice, Hero says, is 'self-endeared'; her being 'so odd from all fashions' is not commendable; her spirits are as coy and wild as the haggard of the rock.

From the perspective of conformity those who forsake it must always seem to assert an egotistical superiority. Looked at positively, Hero's choice is to be 'other-endeared', and so she can be portrayed but this, one can argue, is precisely the self-sacrifice that has been imposed on her. Hero's reference to the 'haggard', the female falcon in the wild, need not mean that she accepts a wholly instrumental role. In *Shakespeare and His Social Context*, Margaret Loftus Ranald, who discusses the term 'haggard' in relation to *The Taming of the Shrew*, points out that the art of falconry distinguished between training and taming, and recognized that training altered both master and bird, whose native wildness it sought to preserve if only for the sake of the hunt.[1] The analogy reduces a human to an animal relation, an exploitive one at that, and encourages the male master's illusion that women can be 'mastered' without 'breaking their spirit'. Yet to deny the distinction that was made through the analogy is to ignore a small, ameliorative point of argument in the current discussions of marriage.

By the turn of the century matches like that between Hero and Claudio were already looking out of date or at least rather high aristocratic. Shakespeare had been on safe ground with social opinion in questioning parental interference with a love-match, even in the society of *Romeo and Juliet*. Yet it was (and still largely is) thought unlikely that a Hamlet would 'carve for himself'. The matching of a governor's daughter and a count—especially a young count so near a prince—comes close enough to a power transaction to 'place' if not extenuate Leonato's heavy-handed management and Hero's acquiescence.

The frequent appearance of dukes and counts in Elizabethan drama may lead to underestimates of the steepness of fortune's

---

[1] M. L. Ranald, *Shakespeare and His Social Context* (New York, 1987), ch. 4.

hill. Sir Thomas Wilson, describing 'The State of England' in a contemporary treatise,[1] estimated that in 1600 there were only 60 peers, 500 knights, and 16,000 lesser gentry in a population of 4,000,000. It would have been easy enough for an Elizabethan audience to set the Hero–Claudio match to one side, accepting its rather bloodless quality as highly probable and well observed. The situation of Beatrice and Benedick, unusual as the two and their wooing were, would have seemed closer to courtships the audience actually knew.

At least some of those courtships were influenced by a degree of clerical support for more latitude for women in the conduct of marriage, though not for their parity. Paul's often quoted Letter to the Ephesians 5: 22 ('Wives, submit to your husbands as to the Lord') could be countered with Galatians 3:28 in which Paul himself had said that 'in Christ there is no male or female'. But popular sermons teased an appropriate moral from texts with more picturesque images: Eve was created not from Adam's foot but from his rib, and so it was the divine intention that she walk by Adam's side, not be trodden underfoot. The term 'helpmeet' suggests both the limitations and advances implicit in the sermons. Milder attitudes toward women were reflected in the sentimental *Frauendienst* of romantic plays and poems, more substantially in sermon and homily and, some speculate, in individual marriages, particularly among couples with puritan sympathies.

It is unlikely, however, that Elizabethan marriages were any closer to the norms of advice and preachment than are marriages now. A passage from I. G.'s 1605 *Apologie for Women-Kinde*[2] seems plausible if only because it seems familiar. According to I. G., women gave way to their husbands' authority 'Only for order', but 'the authority is vain' as 'every one can tell'. Though clearly partisan, I. G. believes that the God who refrained from casting Eve into slavery or servility also 'left her guidance to her husband's will'. The result is a familiar blur. The kind of marriage it implies is hardly egalitarian, but as a formula it probably represents, historically, a

---

[1] Edited by F. J. Fisher for the *Camden Miscellany*, 3rd ser., 52 (1936), pp. i–vii, 1–47.
[2] Quoted in L. Woodbridge, *Women and the English Renaissance* (Brighton, 1984), 76.

turn for the better. Progressive humanists could be even more optimistic about the possibilities for mutual contentment in the sexuality and companionship of marriage, as was Erasmus in *A Ryght Frutefull Epistle in Laude and Praise of Matrimonie*, written about 1530. The actualities of Elizabethan marriage in general are impossible to know and, as Carol Thomas Neely points out,[1] there is inadequate evidence for choosing among contradictory assertions about women's improved or worsened lot during the period.

If we are to draw conclusions from what we know of Hero's off-stage aristocratic sisters, it is doubtful that Hero could even look forward to the kind of marriage I. G. described. Don Pedro, a bachelor, had to remind Claudio of the minimal behaviour expected of a husband. In *English Society* 1580–1680, Keith Wrightson describes the marital fate of young women of the high aristocracy.[2] Their lives could be quite empty, and they themselves merely 'ornamental and idle' as they stitched away solitary hours while their husbands warred or governed.

Shakespeare has given us a submissive Hero, yet he has also given the actor enough to create a more subtle role. Neither her apparent enthusiasm for her 'own dear Claudio', nor her conformity precludes apprehensiveness and regret. When her gown is praised in 3.4, Hero replies, 'God give me joy to wear it, for my heart is exceeding heavy'. This can be played as virginal jitters but, alternatively, it can also express a pang of resignation to a narrow fate. Hero's answer to Margaret's question about when she is to be married, 'Why, every day, tomorrow' may be spoken with grim anticipation, a tone Leonato's heavy-handedness could easily motivate.

Hero's vulnerability is due as much to youth as to social status. Shakespeare remembered Bandello's adolescent heroine in creating what Don John sourly calls this 'forward March chick' and in matching her with a 'start-up' suitor. Extreme youth is not unusual in engaged couples of the high aristocracy. There is one other young Claudio in Shakespeare, the unfortunate prisoner of *Measure for Measure*. The two Claudios share only their ordinariness and lack of moral distinction.

---

[1] C. T. Neely, *Broken Nuptials in Shakespeare's Plays* (New Haven, Conn., 1985), 1–23.

[2] K. Wrightson, *English Society* 1580–1680 (1982), ch. 4.

(The Claudios of the *commedia dell'arte* were young lovers; perhaps Shakespeare recalled them wryly.) In *Much Ado* Claudio is addressed as 'young Claudio', 'Lord Lackbeard', and 'boy'. He does not bridle at epithets that would have drawn Coriolanus' sword, for the epithets are undeniable.

Immaturity explains and extenuates Hero's passivity, as it does Claudio's too-quick suspicions and his ready acceptance of Don Pedro's offer to woo Hero in his stead. Even Claudio's military prowess, like that of Bertram in *All's Well*, seems connected with immaturity; indeed, Claudio is a first sketch for Bertram. The Erasmian scepticism about war Shakespeare develops in *All's Well* through Parolles' follies and Bertram's astounding feats as a teenage Alexander touches Beatrice's tart comments on killing and eating in 1.1 and her deprecation of Benedick's need to associate with some 'young squarer', some precocious master of brawling like Claudio. Through Bertram's career Shakespeare will imply that war is as much a boy's as a man's game; Claudio's victory over Don John suggests that the idea was already formed.

Alone onstage at the start of 2.3, Benedick tells us that Claudio in love has 'turned orthography' and that his words are a 'very fantastical banquet'. No one familiar with the play will believe it. Having denied Claudio the sighing and sonnet-eering of the conventional stage lover, Shakespeare repeats the strategy he used in creating Hero. He makes Claudio in love the matter of someone else's virtuoso soliloquy. The description is a rehearsal of the Benedick-to-be who speaks it. It applies to no Claudio we have seen and it only underscores what he lacks. Claudio does make a brief declaration in 2.1, just after Leonato has offered him Hero in marriage. 'Lady,' he says to Hero, 'as you are mine, I am yours. I give away myself for you, and dote upon the exchange.' The speech is provoked by Beatrice's prodding of the lovers to declare themselves. It is weakened rather than justified by Claudio's insistence that his silence is 'the perfectest herald of joy', and by two rather cool formulations: '*as* you are mine' and I 'dote upon the *exchange*' (italics mine). Why posit what sounds like a condition, and why not dote on the lady herself?

Anyone unfamiliar with Elizabethan marriage laws and customs would not realize that the words Claudio speaks constitute, as do the two other such exchanges in the last scene, espousals *de praesenti*, a form of union then considered virtually indissoluble. Thus there may be some slight extenuation for Claudio's later misbehaviour in the legal character of the commitments here, in the handfast—a probable piece of stage business—and the kiss. But Shakespeare does nothing to underline the point. Later he will neglect it again in the case of the Claudio of *Measure for Measure*, where the stakes are even higher.

As aristocratic suitor, if not as young lover, Claudio is highly plausible. He consults his elders, Benedick and the Prince, describing to his commander his subordination of his initial 'liking' of Hero to the 'task in hand'. Now that 'war-thoughts | Have left their places vacant', 'soft and delicate desires' have 'come thronging' in, 'All prompting me how fair young Hero is, | Saying I liked her ere I went to wars'. This is a report to a superior rather than a confession of love; Claudio's thoughts and feelings come curiously self-propelled and nicely prioritized; nor do they overflow their categories. It is tempting to imagine Don Pedro with tongue in cheek when he warns Claudio that he will be 'like a lover presently, | And tire the hearer with a book of words'. Don Pedro's offer to intercede with Leonato has the right cachet, and Claudio does not hesitate. Nevertheless he is still concerned about appearances: 'lest my liking might too sudden seem, | I would have salved it [prepared for his declaration of love] with a longer treatise'.

Claudio can hold his own in scenes of soldierly ragging (indeed he must if Shakespeare is to write them without introducing more characters), but the verbal leanness of a minor part accords with this limited sensibility whose thoughts and feelings come from narrow conceptions of soldierliness and personal honour. As David Cook points out, in both 1.1 and 2.1 Claudio is on stage for sixty lines before he speaks a word.[1] But when he thinks that his honour is at stake, as in the church scene, he can find words enough.

---

[1] D. Cook, 'The Very Temple of Delight: The Twin Plots of *Much Ado About Nothing*', in A. Colman and A. Hammond (eds.), *Poetry and Drama* 1570–1700 (1981), 41.

When he does speak at length, Claudio is unsympathetic. Like his mentor Don Pedro and some of Shakespeare's other command-figures (Henry V, the Duke in *Measure for Measure*, Prospero), Claudio is an instigator of spectacle. An unpleasant self-satisfaction prompts both his decision to denounce Hero before all the congregation and the denunciation itself. 'But fare thee well, most foul, most fair; farewell | Thou pure impiety and impious purity': the rhetoric is mechanical and absolute. That it has as its primary aim the advertisement of Claudio's own still spotless honour only makes it worse. However, Don Pedro and even Leonato accept the charges as proved. This may not be the exoneration of Claudio for which T. W. Craik argues,[1] but at least it demonstrates that Claudio is not unique, not exclusively the 'hateful young cub' Andrew Lang thought him. However, the Friar's plan to lead Claudio to remorse through Hero's supposed death simply fails, as his behaviour and the Prince's in 5.1 show. Any expression of remorse has to be projected into the two lines (5.1.245–6) in which Claudio tells of the return of Hero's image 'In the rare semblance that I loved it first'. No matter how impressive the ritual at Hero's shrine, wishfulness cannot explain away Claudio's defects, but criticism that isolates Claudio overlooks the ideological breadth of Shakespeare's unpleasant portrayal of Hero's accusers.

Propriety, plausibility, laconic speech and cliché, absence of intimate feeling, a touchy concern for (male) opinion—in all these Claudio exemplifies the social style of Honour. Add to this his youth, and his ready suspicion first of Don Pedro and then of Hero becomes 'natural'. Yet both suspicions are suspicions of Hero, not 'natural' but exaggerations of accepted misogynist absurdities, here given a romantic coloration: if Don Pedro has betrayed him it is not because Don Pedro is disloyal but because, as Claudio bitterly observes at the ball after being taken in by Don John's lies, 'beauty is a witch | Against whose charms faith melteth into blood', blood being our common sexuality. W. H. Auden wrote that had Claudio's love been 'all he imagined it to be, he would have laughed in Don John's face'.[2] But Claudio loved honour, not only more, but almost exclusively.

[1] T. W. Craik, '*Much Ado About Nothing*', *Scrutiny* (1953), 314.
[2] W. H. Auden, *The Dyer's Hand and Other Essays* (New York, 1962), 518.

Yet even with honour as a motive for his blindness, can one accept Claudio's excuse, 'sinned I not | But in mistaking'? And does his response to Leonato's second offer of a bride ('Your over kindness doth wring tears from me') give us at last a Claudio 'fit' for marriage; or only a Claudio grateful for any way out of a situation in which his honour is at risk? Auden, already generous to Claudio even in condemnation, thought him fit, as have others, if only because exonerating Claudio, according to Robert Grams Hunter, allows audiences to have the 'comic experience'.[1] Yet the question is not whether 'we' exonerate Claudio, although we are free to do so. We can find him innocent and Don John the only guilty party, as does Craik.[2] We can forgive his youth; view the death of Hero as a symbolic purging of Claudio's offence, as does David Cook;[3] or stage it, as did Trevor Nunn, so that 'Claudio's penance at the tomb [would] not be undervalued'.[4] Or we can take our cue from Leonato and Hero. But if the plot 'forgives' Claudio, the script seems less ready to do so. How is the actor to speak and behave in 4.1 and 5.1? How make his eagerness to wed even an Ethiope contrition rather than only care for his honour, which marriage into Leonato's family will clear? The treatment of Claudio in performance is a measure of how far directors are willing to risk the dark side of the play.

It is a mistake to dismiss Hero and Claudio as merely 'ordinary' and 'uninteresting'. The ordinary has its own interest; it is where nature puts her bets on survival. Further, Hero and Claudio are painful historical portraits, and if their attitudes are commonplace they are necessarily so in order to define the rare luck of their quarrelsome intellectual superiors. There is, in addition, a canny irony in Shakespeare's enlisting such agents in a romantic plot. As John Russell Brown observed, *Much Ado* will not 'betray its secret to . . . piecemeal criticism'.[5]

---

[1] R. G. Hunter, *Shakespeare and the Comedy of Forgiveness* (New York, 1965), 108.

[2] Craik, '*Much Ado About Nothing*', 314.

[3] Cook, 'The Very Temple of Delight', 35.

[4] R. Berry, *On Directing Shakespeare* (1977), 71.

[5] J. R. Brown, *Shakespeare and His Comedies* (1957), 121.

Beatrice and Benedick are older, more experienced, less constrained socially and intellectually, more sensitive and more expressive. They were also intended to be more active physically. In her book *On Some of Shakespeare's Characters*, one of the great nineteenth-century Beatrices, Helen Faucit, conceived of Beatrice as 'tall, lithe, quaint and sportive'.[1] The parcelling out of traits among the lovers is a nice instance of theatrical pragmatism. An older (and taller) boy would have been needed for the older, more difficult role of Beatrice; hence a diminutive Hero for the sake of contrast as well as the impression of extreme youth. A tall Benedick was needed as a physical match for Beatrice, and further attributes, such as his being a 'valiant trencherman', followed. Beatrice's remark in the last scene that she had been told that, for love of her, Benedick was 'in a consumption' may be a joking allusion to the actor's size. Perhaps Thomas Pope, the large comic actor who played Falstaff and Sir Toby Belch, created the role.[2]

Beatrice and Benedick are more than unconventional contrasts to the younger couple's conventionality. They are blessed, not in being the Perfect Conduct-book Couple, but as individuals singled out for unusual gifts, among them their talents, their second chance, and each other. Beatrice, however, is more thoroughly blessed; the gift to Benedick seems centred on words. Appropriately, his name entered the language as a now obsolete generic term for newly married bachelors of long standing; it served as a compliment in the days when that status had a sentimental import.

Beatrice and Benedick are best remembered as linguistic marvels. For aspiring actresses, the role is a pinnacle, like the role of Hamlet for men, and for the same reason: there are so many fine things to be said, and in the theatre the play stands or falls on the role. Beatrice's first words, like Hamlet's, have a tart, cryptic quality that sets her apart as distinctly an individual with private concerns, *with* a public group, but not *of* it. From then on she too is a social critic, orientating our understanding, expressing herself through irony, and, at a crucial moment, regretting her inability to act.

[1] H. Faucit, *On Some of Shakespeare's Characters* (Edinburgh, 1885), 376.
[2] As suggested by T. W. Baldwin, *The Organization and Personnel of the Shakespearean Company* (Princeton, NJ, 1927), 246.

Helen Faucit, who preferred the gentler role of Rosalind, nevertheless inveighed against the 'heresy' of Mrs Pat Campbell's portrayal of Beatrice as a tomboy, a shrew, and in general an 'odious woman'.[1] The heresy still surfaces in the theatre as an apparent confusion between *Much Ado* and *The Taming of the Shrew*, although there are few similarities between 'curst Kate' and Beatrice. Indeed, after overhearing Hero's Kate-like 'character' of her in the arbour scene, Beatrice is appalled. In any case, 'curst'—for Antonio at least—is a code-word for Beatrice's failure to obey her male relatives. Ellen Terry took pains to indicate from the beginning that Beatrice was half in love with Benedick; her devotion to the single life is queried before it is expressed since her interest in Benedick is obvious from her first words, despite their sarcasm.

As Helen Faucit observed, there is an edge to Beatrice's wit that 'sorrow and wrong', far from removing, had sharpened. The resistance Shakespeare attributes to Beatrice is not the soft-spoken resignation Faucit tacitly accepts as the proper feminine response to adversity. Despite this verbal edge, a star danced at her birth and she has been thoughtfully amused ever since. Inevitably her thoughts have centred on the situation of women, and her amusement on men, whom she finds both intolerable and desirable.

An intellectual history can be gathered from the order of the topics on which Beatrice exercises her wit. In 1.1 her initial target is Benedick as lady-killer (he 'challenged Cupid at the flight'), then Benedick as courageous soldier ('a good soldier to a lady'), Benedick as intellectual opponent ('four of his five wits went halting off'), then Benedick as faithful companion ('O Lord, he will hang upon [a male friend] like a disease'). A little later Beatrice calls him 'a pernicious suitor'. Decoding these complaints requires only Don Pedro's statement that Benedick had 'cut Cupid's bow-string', or Beatrice's that Benedick had won her heart 'with false dice'.

Evidently Beatrice thinks the barrier between them is Benedick's commitment to the all-absorbing male cults of war, comradeship, and honour. It was the assurance held out by

---

[1] Faucit, *On Some of Shakespeare's Characters*, 364.

those cults, an assurance of a nobler intimacy and of protection from enervating sentiment and sexual betrayal that prompted the cutting of Cupid's bow-string and led him to become 'a professed tyrant to women'. Benedick is not so much older than Claudio as to be free of the adolescent fears, so evident in his misogynistic wit, that lead to false idealisms such as those of the young men in *Love's Labour's Lost*. Against such cults Beatrice has set her wit: for Beatrice war is what riding to hounds was for Oscar Wilde, a hunt for the inedible; male alliances are mercurial and superficial, with 'every month a new sworn brother'; honour is the treacherous 'princely testimony' of the likes of Claudio and Don Pedro. For these Benedick has rejected all that women offer with marriage, which is in every way superior. From hurt and self-concern Beatrice develops both targets and a mechanism of wit.

Yet Beatrice is neither a malcontent nor a radical. Her 'How long have you professed apprehension?' is a self-serving bit of class condescension to Margaret. Beatrice, about whose personal fortune we learn nothing (some productions suggest she is an heiress; Michael Langham's tried her as a poor relation), is as keen as the other lovers on remaining in the circle of privilege. Messina as it is—this is the world in which she has given her heart and in which she must live. There is no *contemptus mundi* in her, no generalized vituperation, no pining; she will enjoy even leading apes to hell, should it come to that.

The role is frankly physical. In her exchange with Benedick when they are alone after the denunciation in church, the kinetic energy that generates her brief, probing sentences, as much as her cause and her love, is irresistible. Benedick is overwhelmed. According to the *Personal Reminiscences of Henry Irving* by the creator of Dracula, Bram Stoker, Ellen Terry played the scene 'striding to and fro with long paces';[1] Helen Faucit combined forthrightness with delicacy. One wonders what in the world Dorothea Jordan did on stage that led her to say, admittedly after ten years of acting it, that the role was 'a very easy quiet part'.[2] Beatrice has little of Hero's

---

[1] B. Stoker, *Personal Reminiscences of Henry Irving* (1906), i. 101.
[2] Quoted from B. Fothergill, *Mrs. Jordan* (1965), 181.

maidenly reserve. She wants as handsome a man for herself as for Hero (a claim she makes for all women), and she can trade off-colour repartee with Margaret while keeping her moral distance. Shakespeare may be taking a certain risk to make a point when Beatrice says of Benedick 'I would he had boarded me.' The sexual innuendo is now diminished, but it could hardly have been lost on the audience.

Beatrice's mode of wit is typically ironic, though she is neither afraid to strike nor unwilling to wound. Indeed at one point she seems willing to kill. Yet irony itself, with its cryptic quality that forestalls reaction and its flattering appeals to laughter and intelligence, indicates that Beatrice speaks under constraint. Despite her position in Leonato's household and the latitude granted her as an amusing 'original', she is 'merely' a woman. Antonio and Leonato, even Benedick, simply leap away (the 'jade's trick') when they've had enough. To be listened to at all, a woman must amuse, or at least observe limits. Her engaging self-deprecations—Beatrice leading apes to hell, sunburnt Beatrice crying 'heigh-ho for a husband'—these are Beatrice's recognition that she understands the game. But the self-deprecatory element in Beatrice's wit also reflects long-term anxieties. If Beatrice fears marriage she is also fearful and chagrined at being single: on the one hand she faces the prospect of being 'overmastered'; on the other the pains of rejection, sexual denial, and exclusion from what was, outside the church, the only career with status open to women.

Though Beatrice objects to much of what men have made of themselves and of society, she also accepts much of it. She wants to marry Benedick, and when this seems possible after the deception in the arbour, she falls at once into the wildness-taming clichés of marital submissiveness. Typically, however, it is Beatrice herself who will do the taming. From her intellectual and moral domination of the play and from the parody obedience test of 5.2, we can guess that Beatrice's obedience will be qualified at best, and that it is not a sentimental anachronism to see the play hinting at something for Beatrice rather different from strictly patriarchal marriage.

In the modern theatre these issues can rarely arise; audiences sense the future of fifth-act marriages as happy or unhappy according to current standards. Criticism, however, puts the question of Beatrice's future on the agenda of inter- pretation. Beatrice's language and behaviour argue that her view of marriage is not extreme. Men are valiant dust (no cleric would quarrel), but women *are* overmastered by them nevertheless. (Even Goneril will legitimize male rule when she speaks contemptuously of her husband as a fool who 'usurps' her body.) Beatrice says she would have women exert power through a veto, and then during courtship, but Beatrice would not be the first of Shakespeare's characters to present ortho- dox credentials and then speak, act, or simply be in ways that question convention. An elegiac tone enters criticism that sees 'the masculine world' of *Much Ado* 'unquestioned from within' or sees Beatrice entering a repressive patriarchal marriage. Carol Cook's article is instructive on this point.[1] Yet though the play does more, only to have created a Beatrice questions her future total subordination, and her mental force, which brings Benedick to some understanding, suggests a continuity of instruction beyond 'I do'.

Yet if the marriage of Beatrice and Benedick may not be conventional, it is unlikely to outrage opinion. Beatrice's strictures against 'honour' rest on scepticism born of the violations of the code. In 4.1 when Benedick seems to defend his comrades, Beatrice scorns Claudio as 'a sweet gallant', and deplores the decline of manhood, which has become only 'curtsies' and compliment; 'men are only turned into tongue, and trim ones, too.' It is the conventional ideal that Beatrice admires; moreover it is a conventionally aggressive 'man of honour' that she wishes she were: 'O God that I were a man! I would eat his [Claudio's] heart in the market place.' (This echo of Beatrice's scornful offer in 1.1 to eat anyone Benedick killed in war is awkward.) Perhaps Beatrice's wish 'to be a man' reflects a self-denigrating accommodation to the idea of male superiority; more likely it is simply an outraged recog- nition of the way things are. Though something of the femin- ist that Ellen Terry, truly a feminist and perhaps the greatest of Beatrices, praised her for being, Beatrice is of her class and

---

[1] C. Cook, 'The Sign and Semblance of Her Honour: Reading Gender Difference in *Much Ado About Nothing*', PMLA (1986), 186–202.

2. Ellen Terry in the 'overhearing' scene (3.1).

day. Occasionally her statements have connotations that time has made more radical than the character.

This tug of motives dictates the strategy of her wittiest remarks, which mock conventional ideas, especially those on the role of women, by appealing to conventional sources that usually support those ideas. The strategy allows for both the thrust and the drawing back that comprise irony. Beatrice, still 'orthodox' in objection, will not marry because Adam's sons are her brothers and she refuses to violate the Anglican Table of Affinity by a 'match in [her] kindred'.

Inevitably, we take Beatrice's wittiest remarks less seriously than those—such as her sharp thrusts at Benedick in the first scene—in which the balance tips from ingenuity toward scorn. Her manifestos of bachelorhood come from too lively and sexually inclusive a sensibility not to undermine themselves, at least in that historical context. She proposes to remain single because of the imperfections of men. But she concludes by acknowledging that, like Adam's sons, she too is a kind of valiant dust, so her demand for male perfection is suspect. The acceptance of mutual imperfection, necessary to sustained love, is already implicit in her continuing interest in Benedick, despite his past errors. Before the play ends that acceptance becomes explicit. 'For which of my bad parts didst thou first fall in love with me?' Benedick asks in 5.2. 'For them all together', Beatrice replies.

In phrases like 'valiant dust' and 'wayward marl', with the amusing metaphysical upset of noun by adjective, and the repetitions that suggest opulent verbal resources, Beatrice's wit comes close to Benedick's. Freud's *Jokes and the Unconscious* reworks traditional distinctions between humour and satire as distinctions between innocent and tendentious wit. Humour, Freud argues, has no reformist tendency, accepting its nominal object as it is. Misogynist jokes are an attractive store of wit to some of those otherwise underendowed who would regret losing them through changes in the condition of women, even though they might welcome those changes. Jokes generate a minor interest in their survival somewhat apart from their social origins or social effects. Shakespeare makes us aware that Benedick, who is not underendowed, has none the less assumed misogyny as a persona, in part as a thematic aid to his wit. When solicited for an opinion of Hero, he asks Claudio, 'Do you question me as an honest man should do, for my simple true judgement, or would you have me speak after my custom, as being a professed tyrant to their sex?' Apparently Benedick thinks himself capable of providing true judgements of women apart from his 'tyrannical' comic turn. Yet when Claudio asks him to speak 'in sober judgement', he does not. His negative portrait of Hero is a witcracker's set-piece directed not at her intellect, where a charge of mediocrity might have held, but at her physical appearance—against the evidence of the play. Benedick's mask of misogyny is evidently difficult to remove, a telling observation. His consciousness of his self-division, acknowledged in the mocking word 'tyrant', is small excuse, though it does prepare us for his later turnabout.

Anyone fed up with girl-friend, wife, and mother-in-law jokes will no doubt bridle at the notion that Benedick's wit is self-protective and largely of the 'innocent' sort. It takes the rapid elegance of a Gielgud or the *brio* of a Sinden to focus attention on Benedick's language as adroit performance rather than on its social implications. But marriage and Beatrice are as much its occasions as its targets. It is a rhetoric of masked fear, and it flourishes where there is no opposition to query it, as in soliloquy or in the extended treatment of a single subject to which there is no reply; otherwise it would collapse at once. Beatrice, however, is at her best in contention, and always victorious.

Typical of Benedick's good moments are his ingenious variations on the theme of Beatrice's attacks on him. His exotic offers to go to the ends of the earth to avoid her say less about Beatrice than about Shakespeare's store of picturesque allusion. None of this lessens our (or Benedick's) admiration of the lady who can inspire such distinguished nonsense. What gives the game away—in addition to Benedick's sheer extravagance—is his repetition of Beatrice's description of him as 'duller than a great thaw'. The comparison is suggestively different in its homeliness, yet so much in his own vein of witty metaphor that he cherishes it verbatim.

Most innocent of his 'innocent' witticisms is an exemplary sentence in Benedick's soliloquy after the deception: 'When I said I would die a bachelor, I did not think I should live till I were married.' The gentle self-mockery of this verbal sleight suggests how Benedick's tyranny to women is to be taken. When his guard is down Benedick reveals a saving modesty. Beatrice is wise, he says, 'but for loving me'. This prepares for the self-questioning in his question to Beatrice: 'Think you in your soul the Count Claudio hath wronged Hero?' Knowing what the audience knows, the question must seem naïve, but it shows why Benedick has no need of the tendentious and reformist strategies of Beatrice's wit. Frustration and disadvantage are obviously not his themes.

Yet 'language is always a matter of force; to speak is to exercise a will for power; in the realm of speech there is no innocence'—so Barthes observed.[1] Finally Benedick's wit rests on the self-serving clichés of male victim and persecuting virago. These are, however, qualified by the intimation that

---

[1] See R. Barthes, in S. Sontag (ed.), *A Barthes Reader* (1982), 381.

they are not deeply held, and mask both his fear of marriage and an attraction to Beatrice so great as to need disguising, especially from Benedick himself.

Another strain of wit in *Much Ado* deflects its social implications almost as well as does Benedick's. Dogberry's rationales for avoiding police duties are impeccable: contact with criminals defiles, and so the police should avoid it; only those subject to police jurisdiction may be arrested, so those who refuse arrest are obviously not subject to it. This logic recalls Beatrice's strategy for marshalling conventional morality and legalism to mock both. Dogberry's physical prudence is matched by his judicial caution. Of Conrad and Borachio, by now clearly guilty, he says that they are '*little better*' than false knaves, or at least '*will go near*' to being thought so (italics mine). The Dogberry scenes are hardly intended to prompt reform, and Dogberry droll is only perfected by being also Dogberry insufferable. What he is and his not knowing what he is flatters the observer, and for a moment rights the social balance. The presence of the Watch alone is proof that crime does not pay in Messina.

The almost constant wittiness of *Much Ado*—even Conrad and Borachio execute multiple puns as they are led off by the Watch—has been judged a defect, making Messina a cold and artificial place where what Johnson called the 'reciprocation of smartness' seems to some critics to dampen authentic passion and justify cruel remarks. It is difficult to convey cleverness as an index to feeling, and actors sometimes manage only half the task, in itself a considerable achievement. Yet read backwards from the moment when Beatrice and Benedick are alone after the denunciation of Hero, *Much Ado* hardly fits the charge. Moreover, as Rossiter[1] observes, 'It is a notable point in Shakespeare's contrivance that he gives both wits their off-day, as soon as love [which Rossiter sees begun only after the deception scenes] has disturbed their freedom.' It is only a step to recognizing earlier connections between wit and love. The wit serves as shield against vulnerability; when the shield is less needed, it can be lowered.

---

[1] A. P. Rossiter, *Angel with Horns* (1961), 69.

Like Dogberry, Beatrice and Benedick are vain of their wit. Wit is their mode of being and since it allows so epicurean a response to life, evidently something of a *raison d'être*. Through their rhetoric we come to know a great deal about Beatrice and Benedick, especially about their self-deceptions and vulnerability. Their instant capitulation to the plots to unite them is a sure-fire cliché of comedy, but nonetheless psychologically sound. We learn just enough about their earlier estrangement to make sense of this mutual capitulation in their 'merry war'.

Explaining his determination not to marry Beatrice (but how did marriage to her pop up on his agenda? or to him on hers?), Benedick says that 'She would have made Hercules have turned spit . . .'. Is this fear of domination only another patriarchal conceit? The context here is the story of Hercules' three years' expiatory bondage with Omphale. (Benedick unwittingly states not only his fears but his guilt.) Yet Beatrice seeks no expiation. For all her condemnation of Benedick's male alliances, Beatrice is also solicitous of them. When the need to right the wrong done Hero arises in 4.1, Beatrice answers Benedick's question, 'May a man do it?' with 'It is a man's office, but not yours.' I do not think that Beatrice's answer turns only on Benedick's extra-familial status. Not until the two have made their mutual declarations of love and she has a right to assume that Benedick's alliance with Claudio is now secondary is she free to say 'Kill Claudio'. But such alliances are not broken in an instant. To Beatrice's credit she persists after Benedick's initial refusal, and to his credit he soon recognizes the absoluteness of the new commitment he has made.

For all their sophistication, the most likely cause of their obscure earlier difficulties is a common one, consistent with the text: a woman ready for marriage, a man for courtship. Yet the two continued to care for each other as is indicated by the mutual resistance it requires all their wit to sustain. Most of Benedick's wit has this resistance as its obvious theme; Beatrice's confession of love in 4.1 barely pierces an armour-plate of equivocation. But if words obscure their love, words—their matched sonnets—finally reveal it. Their resistance breached, what we know of them promises the self-completion that comes from mutual acceptance.[1] In this lies their difference from Hero and Claudio who, as Joan Rees observed, 'seem to have no principle of growth in them'.[2]

Brothers

The two pairs of brothers, Don Pedro and Don John, Leonato and Antonio, are as ingeniously differentiated as the two pairs of lovers: Don Pedro and Don John noble and powerful bachelors with no significant age difference, both of them initiators of spectacle and intrigue, assured, intelligent and formal in speech, at odds—one apparently trusting, the other full of the dangerous discontent attributed to illegitimacy; Leonato and Antonio both apparently widowers, privileged but in a lesser sphere, older and with a pronounced age difference between them, slightly inept and provincial in manner, deferential and unable to act as they would like, eloquent but in an old-fashioned idiom, mutually supportive and loyal.

Shakespeare evidently wasted little thought on the names themselves. Leonato he inherited from Bandello; Antonio is Shakespeare's common name for fathers or father figures. In any case, he abandoned Q's 'Old Man' only when it became useful to do so. In the speech-prefixes Don John is plain English, as was Don Peter (Bandello's King Piero) before Shakespeare Hispanicized the name.

Leonato and Don Pedro are the significant members of the two pairs. Antonio is necessary as brotherly support and intensifier; a younger man could not have served these ends. Confronting Claudio and Don Pedro alone in 5.1, Leonato would have elicited a pathos Shakespeare thought undesirable; or so the caricature dialogue for Antonio seems to demonstrate. Antonio's description of errant youth is yesterday's Letter to the Editor, doubly amusing if Antonio were

---

[1] The style of this mutuality may be suggested in a passage from a 1992 *Observer* interview: '[The author and his wife] have a specialized Darby and Joan act all their own, a continuous line in back-chat—mutually solicitous, happily contradictory. You can see that they're sufficient social life for each other most of the time.' This is what Leonato had in mind when he predicted in 2.1 that if Beatrice and Benedick 'were but a week married, they would talk themselves mad'.

[2] J. Rees, *Shakespeare and the Story* (1978), 29.

played by a boy, as was quite possible. Elsewhere he is a convenient voice for exposition, as in 1.2; and in the ball scene exchange with Ursula for some of the geriatric humour that Shakespeare had used in *Richard II*.

Don John is necessary but not important; his fate and nature are clear at once. Defeated rivals for power had no future, as Machiavelli and the history plays demonstrated, and Don John's illegitimacy is as much a marker as Hero's name. Although we do not learn of it until 4.1, Shakespeare's speech-prefixes show what was uppermost in his conception of the character. Don John is a plausible, 'plain-dealing villain', something he tells us 'must not be denied'. The actor is helped to create the proper effect by portentous runs of monosyllables like, 'I know not that when he knows what I know', spoken just before Don John slanders Hero. There is a sturdiness in his determination to 'claw no man in his humour', but a sinister undertone in the violence of 'claw', which in this context should mean 'stroke gently as if to placate'. Just the sight of him gives Beatrice heartburn. John Russell Brown relates how the Prospect Company's 1970 production of the play in Edinburgh dealt with the villain.[1] Don John was brought onstage at the very end and shot by Don Pedro just before the jolly command, 'Strike up, pipers.'

Don Pedro himself is another matter: legitimate, triumphant, honourable, helpful, well-spoken—if rather formally so—and on occasion humorous. Yet his share in the denunciation of Hero, his proxy courtship, his stage-management of the deceptions, his trial offers of a husband to Beatrice—all these add up to a less competent figure than his entrance or the sources promise. *Much Ado* ends with Don Pedro, like his brother, an odd man out.

Shakespeare often dissociates power from sexual intimacy and makes the point in plays as different as *1 Henry IV* and *Antony and Cleopatra*. But Don Pedro is not as limited a personality as a Henry IV or an Octavius and in *Much Ado* the point is made in a way that suggests loss rather than tacit choice or native coldness. His 'Will you have me, lady?' in 2.1 may be interpreted as only a light-hearted rejoinder, but

---

[1] J. R. Brown, *Free Shakespeare* (1974), 39.

Beatrice is taking no chances. Yet Don Pedro's later declaration that, were Beatrice interested, he would have 'doffed all other respects and made her half [him]self' can be spoken truly, even though it is intended for the eavesdropping Benedick.

More revealing is Don Pedro's readiness to 'win' Hero for Claudio. Neither Claudio's youth nor the political importance of the alliance are invoked overtly in the play as reasons for Don Pedro's offer. The possibility that Don Pedro woos for himself is taken seriously by Leonato and by Benedick, as well as by Claudio. When Benedick's rather callous hints draw an explanation from Don Pedro, his 'I will but teach them to sing, and restore them to the owner' suggests that the Prince, if unwittingly, may be doing something more than eliciting a simple yes.[1] At the ball Don Pedro's ambiguous introduction of himself to Hero as 'your friend' sets a flirtatious tone she then maintains and he does nothing to correct. Hero has every reason to believe that the Prince is approaching her on his own behalf.

Yet Shakespeare's handling of the Don Pedro–Hero material is not loose or careless. The speech that ends 1.1 is further evidence of a strategy to cloud intention. Don Pedro tells Claudio that he will 'assume thy part', 'tell fair Hero I am Claudio', and 'take her hearing prisoner' with his 'amorous tale', all of which seems uncomfortably like an anagram of Don John's later deception. Don Pedro's efforts to help his juniors are to his credit, but some lack in him feeds vicariously on the courtships of the four lovers. This is preferable to his brother's preying on them as 'medicinable' to his 'sick . . . displeasure'. Yet against the glitter of the double wedding the figure of the Prince can seem rather sad.

Leonato is more recognizably literary (an echo of Kyd's anguished elders), more commonplace (the stock father of a marriageable stock daughter), and more surprising (a father who immediately accepts his daughter's guilt). There is a congenial side to Leonato, who can address the Watch as 'friend' and 'neighbour', appreciate Beatrice, forgive Margaret, and raise a laugh at the end with his vain effort to ensure that his daughter is safely off his hands before the

---

[1] The sexual overtones of 'sing' are clear in the example from *Troilus and Cressida* cited by Eric Partridge in *Shakespeare's Bawdy* (1947), 187.

dancing begins. He can make a snappy reply in 1.1 to Benedick's uncalled-for query about cuckolding, but this is the familiar men's-club topic and everyone knows the jokes. Yet in the deception of Benedick Leonato's awkward turning to others when he cannot think of useful lies is amusing.

The rest is unpleasant *senex*. Leonato's welcome to Don Pedro is sycophantic. The rhetoric of Elizabethan formal greeting of superiors *was* sycophantic, but here the excess is underlined by the Prince's dry response: 'You embrace your charge too willingly'. Later in 1.1, the Prince tells Claudio and Benedick that he has told Leonato they will stay in Messina at least a month, and that Leonato 'heartily prays some occasion may detain us longer'. This is said in Leonato's presence, and whether delivered as an intended small cruelty or as matter of fact, reflects well on no one. Such entertainments were a notorious burden.

Leonato's response to Hero's distress is a disaster. Treating her as an appendage, he has little sense of Hero as a person, hence nothing of Beatrice's—or even the Friar's—grounds for thinking Hero innocent. Leonato depends on what he thinks he knows, that princes and counts are men of honour and women sexually unreliable. When Claudio has finished his accusations, Leonato wonders why no one has stabbed him, wishes Hero dead, regrets her birth and nurture, insists that two princes would not lie, rebukes the Friar, relents only when Benedick accuses Don John, then claims he will avenge Hero and boasts of his wealth, strength, friends, and 'policy of mind'. His last speech in the scene insists on the extremity of his grief. This theme is congenial; he elaborates it in a thirty-line speech at the start of 5.1. It is as though Shakespeare were determined to forestall audience sympathy for him. Leonato's confrontation of Claudio and Don Pedro later in that scene goes some way to redeeming him, but in the offer of another bride to a chastened Claudio, Leonato as a character succumbs to the necessities of the romantic plot.

Clearly, such speeches as Leonato's are as little to the modern taste as the attitudes they express. Productions generally trim them. However, Shakespeare's audiences enjoyed grand declamation and sententious wisdom. The tawdriness of what grand declamation could express, here as in *Hamlet*,

3. 'They know that do accuse me' (4.1.177). Beatrice (Eileen Herlie), Leonato (Mervyn Blake), and Benedick (Christopher Plummer), look on as the Friar (Powys Thomas) comforts Hero (Diana Maddox): Michael Langham's production (Stratford, Ontario, 1958).

must not have been lost on the author or on the 'wiser sort'. But the primary implications of Leonato's speeches are ideological rather than literary. The deliberate organization of the negative reactions to Hero emphasizes their common misogynist premisses. Against an indifferent Don John, a benighted, self-centred Leonato, and both Claudio and Don Pedro, Shakespeare poises Beatrice, a humane Friar—remote from gender alignments yet a male, hence authoritative voice—and a Benedick slowly able to believe in the criminality of a prince and, later, in a close friend's outrageous behaviour, inexcusable though the friend has been duped.

Gentlewomen, Conspirators, and Others

Ursula and Margaret, and Conrad, Borachio, and Balthasar have in common their consciousness of social position. Ursula 'knows her place' and forgets it only once; Margaret cannot forget hers and would like to leave it. Conrad insists he is a gentleman; Borachio is critical of gilded youth and reveals qualities above his conspiratorial calling; Balthasar is a minor retainer whose forte is apology for being less than he thinks he ought to be.

To Hero, Ursula and Margaret are Ursley and Meg. The homely English intimate forms suggest an easy-going relationship between a young mistress and what, despite the title of 'gentlewoman', were essentially upper servants. (The social origins and social prospects of gentlewomen were various, as the Marias and Helens in Shakespeare's plays can testify. In effect, their title was a reflection of the rank of their mistresses. A suggestive modern analogy is the notion of 'assimilated rank' given temporarily to certain civilians on military assignment during wartime.)

Ursula and Margaret are rough parallels of Hero and Beatrice; Ursula apparently the more sober of the two, less imaginative and less articulate. Oddly, it is Ursula who is the more active in helping Hero in the deception of Beatrice. Claudio states in 3.2 that it was Hero and Margaret who 'played their parts with Beatrice'. This accords with the ingenious character of Margaret. Perhaps making Ursula Hero's co-conspirator was a simple error, perhaps a mis-step taken in an effort to balance two minor roles.

Both women fetch and carry for their betters. The contrast lies in social attitudes. Ursula seems to have accommodated herself to her place; not so Margaret. At the masked ball, Ursula partners old Antonio, saying that she knows him by his dry hand and tremor. Antonio denies his age. When Ursula persists, he becomes testy. She backs off at once, prudently admiring Antonio's wit. Dressing Hero for the wedding, Margaret criticizes her mistress's rebato. Hero, for once, rebukes her sharply. Margaret mollifies her mistress by praising Hero's new head-dress but, unhappy in retreat, risks wishing the 'tire' were 'a thought browner'.

Margaret is one of a trio of aspiring gentlewomen Shakespeare created—all of them sympathetically—at about the same time. Margaret is less fortunate than either Maria in *Twelfth Night*, who marries Sir Toby Belch, or Helen in *All's Well*, who is presented as at once manipulative and sub-

43

missive. Like Helen and Maria, Margaret is a woman of superior intelligence and wit and, like Helen, she can be frank, though at times also tasteless and ill-considered about sexual matters. Indeed, Shakespeare seems to pit Margaret's innuendos in 3.4 and elsewhere against Hero's prudish reticence in order to locate Beatrice's views on sex as a proper mean. But Margaret's situation is hopeless. During the exchange that opens 5.2, Benedick praises Margaret's wit and beauty, but when she asks if she will always 'keep below stairs' for want of a proper husband, he provides more compliments but no reply. In addition to coveting status obtainable only through a husband, Margaret covets pretty things. Her description of the Duchess of Milan's gown is detailed and enthusiastic; her opinions on 'rebatos' and 'tires' have the assurance of envious observation. Such a Margaret would have been delighted to serve unwittingly in Borachio's plot, playing the engaged heiress and in her mistress's gown. Leonato's forbearance toward her is gracious, but it consigns Margaret, as before, to living below stairs on grace and favour. In the last scene she says nothing. Perhaps she should not be present at the wedding at all, but the scene would be poorer without her pathetic silence.

Margaret's unwillingness to take up with Balthasar is to her credit. Balthasar emerges from Shakespeare's early false starts with possible relatives for Leonato (see the Textual Introduction below). Balthasar apparently becomes a member of Don Pedro's retinue. His precise social status is unclear, but he seems to have aristocratic pretensions, or so commentators conclude from his disclaimers of musical ability before he sings in 2.3. Such disclaimers follow the advice of Castiglione, among others, against being vain of talents for which one can hire clerks and fiddlers. But Balthasar's disclaimers are so excessive as to be ludicrous; hence Don Pedro's punning rebuke.

There is no reason to disbelieve Benedick's comparison of Balthasar's singing to a dog's howling. Benedick is hidden and has no one on stage to amuse. In a neat comic manœuvre Shakespeare has Don Pedro respond to this criticism by addressing Balthasar as though Benedick were not in hiding: 'Yea, marry, dost thou hear, Balthasar? I pray thee get us some excellent music' for serenading Hero, clearly a rebuke. Balthasar's talent is apparently too small to warrant so great a disclaimer. If he sings again in 5.3, he can be neutralized by other voices. There is some slight evidence that this may have been the case. The attribution of the song at 5.3.12 is Dover Wilson's; Q has only the introductory title 'Song'. Margaret's rejection of Balthasar during their turn at the ball prepares for this comedy; his first words to her are the pathetic, 'Well, I would you did like me'.

Don John's tools, Conrad and Borachio—after the Spanish for wine-flask—are a complementary pair. Conrad functions as an ear for Don John's complaints in 1.3 and for Borachio's commentary in 3.3. His birth under Saturn presumably induced the sullen manner that sets off Borachio's tipsy energy. Conrad's initial advice to his master is intelligent and moderate, but his loyalty, 'To the death, my lord', has no reservations. Beyond this, his behaviour in resisting the Watch at the end of 4.2 shows him more pugnacious than Borachio, and when aroused by Dogberry's 'sirrah', Conrad insists that he is a gentleman, another marker for Messina's social dimension.

Borachio is more interesting. His response when called to account in 5.1 is full acceptance of his guilt: 'Yea, even I alone', and a generously specific exoneration of Margaret. His insistence on paying for his villainy with his death recalls his earlier moralizing on the subject of fashion. There is a hint of the *déclassé* in the attitudes and circumstances of both Conrad and Borachio. Like Margaret, Borachio is one of a group of related characters Shakespeare created within a few years of one another. With Falstaff, Sir Toby, and Michael Cassio, Borachio is a difficult alcoholic; the others have fallen socially or are in the course of doing so. In his case alone (Sir Toby is universally incontinent) is drink made the central attribute, and so something of an explanation for his circumstances. In *Shakespeare and the Experience of Love* Arthur Kirsch details the sacred allusions in Borachio's speech to baptism, redemption, and idolatry.[1] The passage has been cut or played as merely tipsy chatter, but Kirsch is right about the seriousness of the moment. It is a brief lifting of the curtain on a

---

[1] A. Kirsch, *Shakespeare and the Experience of Love* (Cambridge, 1981), 53.

4. Officers of the Watch (with pikes) escort a tailor (with shears) to prison, from *The Counter-Scuffle*, by Robert Speed (1628).

possibly unelected anguish different from the self-chosen unhappiness of love and politics elsewhere in the play.

Borachio's strictures against that 'deformed thief' Fashion in 3.3 were conventional, and would have have elicited agreement. The application of those strictures to both sexes precludes misogynist inferences from the discussion of women's fashions in the scene that follows.

The Textual Introduction below discusses the logistics and individuation of the Watch, whose prime figures are Dogberry and Verges. 'Dogberry' can refer to either the red European dogwood or to its berry, or it can be an excremental metaphor. Verges may refer to the 'verge' or staff of office, and 'verjuice', the sour-tasting juice of unripe fruit such as grapes. The names suggest the hearty ordinariness and the 'verjuice face' (*OED sb.* 2b cites the phrase from Marston's 1598 *Scourge of Villainy*), respectively of the popular comic actors Will Kemp and Richard Cowley (see Commentary 4.2.1, 2). Dogberry provides Verges with sufficient occasion for sourness. The Watch appears in the nick of time, and Borachio's slightly vain observation that 'what your wisdoms could not uncover these shallow fools have brought to light' becomes a sobering mockery of comedy's artifice of Utopian endings.

5. Dogberry (David Waller, bemedalled) and Verges (Jeffrey Segal), in Di Trevis's production at the Royal Shakespeare Theatre, Stratford-upon-Avon, 1988.

Amusing as he is, Dogberry is also arrogant, smug, and sycophantic. His patronizing of Verges is dismaying as well as sadistically funny. When Leonato ironically praises Dogberry for his superior wit, Dogberry's delicately modest, 'Gifts that God gives', is delicious. The Dogberryism from whose practical consequences its fictionality protects us is recognizably one of the nastier faces of minor authority. Yet Dogberry's confident, unearned jollity is something like the wonderfully cosseted omnipotence of infancy. What need for such vanities as reading, and writing? All one needs is to be 'a rich fellow enough' with 'two gowns and everything handsome about [one]'. Is there perhaps an explanatory personal survival hinted at in Dogberry's proud reference to his 'losses' and in his surprising and funny response with the traditional beggar's thanks, 'God save the foundation', when Leonato gives him money?

Finally, the roles of Messenger and Friar fix the moral boundaries of male Messina even more clearly than do more important characters such as Don John and Benedick. The Messenger begins the play with news of victory, but he defines a formal, hierarchical male world in which birth, rank, and military prowess are of supreme importance, and a common soldier counts for nothing, even in death. At the opposite end of male moral possibility is the Friar, urging moderation, reason, and faith, but within the bounds of custom. That this requires yet another lie is a sombre qualification, as is (feminists would insist), his vow of celibacy.

Plot Construction

In his *Multiple Plot in English Renaissance Drama*, Richard Levin has a detailed analysis of the formal connections between the two plots of *Much Ado*.[1] The Hero–Claudio courtship is initiated by Don Pedro, who also proposes the deception to unite Beatrice and Benedick. Hero and Claudio help in the deception, and in the last act their evidence finally seals the match. The crisis in both plots occurs at almost the same point for it is the plight of Hero after the denunciation that leads Beatrice and Benedick to their declarations of love. Moreover, Benedick's commitment to Beatrice and her acceptance of him are predicated in part on his understanding of Claudio's behaviour. Without the intervention of the Watch, of course, neither marriage might have taken place.

In addition to these causal connections, the two plots are bound by formal devices, the most important of which are the variant scenes of deception and 'noting', deliberate eavesdropping or casual overhearing. Leonato and Antonio receive a false idea of Don Pedro's intentions toward Hero. Claudio thinks he has overheard proof of Hero's infidelity. Beatrice and Benedick accept without question deceptive (yet not unfounded) accounts of their feelings for one another, and the Watch overhear Conrad and Borachio discussing Don John's plot against Hero and Claudio. The device pervades even details: in 5.1 Don Pedro mishears Benedick's *sotto voce* challenge to Claudio. These instances of noting occupy the spectrum of possibility: speakers without motive or malice or deliberately deceptive; hearers merely unfortunate in mishearing, naïve, or perverse in interpreting, or—like the Watch—

[1] R. Levin, *Multiple Plot in English Renaissance Drama* (Chicago, 1971), 90–3.

6. Conviviality in a garden (cf.2.3), from Thomas Hill's *The Gardener's Labyrinth* (1577).

just lucky; and information conveyed that is disastrous or happy in its effect.

The three narrative centres are connected and contrasted by their distinctive social ethos. The Claudio–Hero courtship is conventional, upper-upper-class, and thoroughly serious. These two are handbook personalities caught in a romantic plot. Beatrice and Benedick are a notch lower socially—she no governor's heiress, he no count; both are rather unconventional high-comedy sophisticates with a rather commonplace story. The Watch are predictably farcical low-comedy proles.

Taken together, the lovers exemplify the alternatives of gender behaviour: female passivity and female assertiveness, male control and male concessions to power-sharing. At the end of the play extremes are, however briefly, suspended, or seem to be so: a subdued if not chastened Claudio is on good behaviour that Hero need not assert herself to demand;

Beatrice seems only nominally and humorously 'obedient', and Benedick may dwindle gracefully to a husband. Fears that his assertiveness in demanding dancing before the wedding may signal a second tyranny seem exaggerated.

Act, Scene, and Pace

The Quarto is printed without act or scene divisions; the Folio supplies the division into five acts, and subsequent editors generally follow Capell's division into seventeen scenes. Different divisions have been proposed, and modern productions of the play routinely vary the number and position of intervals. The Variorum *Much Ado* (pp. 363–7) reprints an 1850 *Gentleman's Magazine* article by James Spedding proposing alternatives to the Folio's act divisions. Spedding ended Act I after the first scene because he thought audiences would doubt that the inaccurate report of Don Pedro's proposal of a proxy wooing could reach Antonio so soon after the end of 1.1. This objection arises less from concern with what audiences find acceptable than from a concern with verisimilitude as conceived of in the context of the elaborate settings of the nineteenth-century theatre. Spedding attributes the audience's incredulity to their having to imagine that the inaccurate report reached Antonio while 'the scene was merely shifting'. In the Elizabethan theatre the scene did not shift save in the most perfunctory formal sense. Capell locates the first scene before Leonato's house, the second inside it, but neither location is specified by the text, nor is a change in location required. Unencumbered by furniture-realism, Elizabethan staging had a fluidity that emphasized contrasts between scenes other than their changed setting.

Scene progression embodies a sequence of expectations aroused and either satisfied or reinforced through postponement. 1.1 leads us to expect a wooing. That it is a wooing by proxy leads audiences (modern audiences more than Elizabethan) to expect complications. In the last lines of 1.1 Don Pedro speaks of raising Claudio's suit with Leonato, who will, he is certain, agree. The scene leaves one expecting the encounter but not its unalloyed success. To hear in the next scene the false report that Don Pedro will woo for himself makes the promised wooing more eagerly awaited—and with it the prospect of mischief. A 'realistic' interruption (whose absence bothered Spedding) would only weaken the effect of the sequence.

Again, although 'real' time has elapsed (for dinner and for the preparations to fool Beatrice in the garden) between 2.3 and 3.1, a 'realistic' gap in stage time between the gulling of Benedick (2.3) and the gulling of Beatrice (3.1) would be intrusive. After Benedick has taken the bait, one wants to see at once if the clever Beatrice will also be fooled. Proximity here provides more than formal pleasure; it underlines a social contrast. The deception of Benedick works because it takes the form of needed male reassurance; if Beatrice loves him, he can relax his fear of domination or rejection. The deception of Beatrice works because it takes the form of doubts by other women of her capacity to love, doubts she can dispel only by once again risking rejection. Their friends are indeed love-gods, who find the most vulnerable spots for their arrows: the socially imposed fears of inadequacy characteristic of each sex. Despite the diptych formality of soliloquy, impassioned prose, and verse, the twin deceptions have a psychological authenticity.

Spedding's complete scheme for revising the Folio act divisions required a second act ending with 2.2 as Borachio and Don John plot against Hero; a third act ending with 3.3, in which the Watch apprehend Borachio and Conrad; a fourth act ending with 4.2, in which Dogberry and Verges examine the culprits; and a last act unchanged.

Two conclusions follow from Spedding's proposals. Despite the unusually long scenes that begin all but the third act, the act as such was probably not an important conceptual unit in composition for Shakespeare. The second is that the play's flexibility in accommodating alternative interval placements allows later productions a variety of effects probably not sought in Elizabethan performance. Not only Spedding's, but other act divisions can be staged. The emphasis in Shakespeare's composition seems to have been on contrasts between adjacent scenes or incidents, and the emphasis in Elizabethan production on a complementary, rapid sweep of narrative, rather than on the suspenseful contrasts underlined by intervals between acts. Having none, Elizabethans were little concerned with effective 'curtains'. Elizabethan performance could be nearly continuous, and there are few points in *Much Ado* that suggest the appropriateness of discontinuous performance.

Estimates of length vary when the play in question is largely in prose, as is *Much Ado*. Alfred Hart concluded that it was only thirty-five over the canonical 2,500 lines that provided the two to two-and-a-half hours' 'traffic of the stage'.[1] Its high proportion of prose (1808 lines by Hart's count) would perhaps have made it longer in the theatre than plays with a similar line-count but more verse. But prose is generally delivered more rapidly than verse, and the exhilaration of uninterrupted, swiftly moving narrative was a goal reachable with audiences inured to continuous performance of various kinds. (The two-hour glass set at the start of Paul's Cross sermons to remind preachers to consider the temporal condition of their audience is a symbol of Elizabethan endurance.) In addition, the Elizabethan actor's delivery was probably more rapid than that encouraged by later acting styles with their elocutionary or psychological pauses.

The remarkable language of *Much Ado*, with its plethora of Good Things might prompt one to suppose actors ought to linger over the lines. On this point Ellen Terry is instructive: 'I have played Beatrice hundreds of times, but not once as I know she ought to be played. I was never swift enough, not nearly swift enough at the Lyceum where I had a too deliberate, though polished and thoughtful, Benedick in Henry Irving.'[2]

Contrasts and Links between Scenes

If only for pragmatic reasons Shakespeare's adaptation of non-dramatic narrative was parsimonious with representation, resorting to it only when there was a clear theatrical need. He eliminated 'ghost' characters (e.g. Innogen, once intended as Hero's mother); reported Claudio's deception by

[1] A. Hart, 'The Number of Lines in Shakespeare's Plays', *RES* 8 (1932), 19–28.
[2] E. Terry, *Four Lectures on Shakespeare* (1932), 97.

Borachio (usually an incident in the sources); but he staged Claudio's denunciation of Hero (sometimes only told or effected through agents in the sources). The reasons, practical, theatrical, and ideological, for such changes are not hard to find. Economical disposition of narrative into scenes, the 'treatment' as it is called in film work, requires a basic theatrical competence only, and E. A. J. Honigmann thinks that the mature Shakespeare did not even bother to work from an 'author plot' or treatment.[1] It is the contrast and linking of scenes that shows the subtler aspects of Shakespeare's dramaturgy.

Scenes and the incidents that comprise them are primarily sequences of expectations generated by the narrative and then satisfied by it. One is led to expect a wooing—two take place; to expect trouble—Don John obliges. 'Let us to the great supper', says Don John to his confederates at the end of 1.3. The next scene opens with Leonato's question 'Was not Count John here at supper?' Antonio's answer: 'I saw him not', signals trouble to come.

Some links between scenes are unrelated to the progress of the narrative. Leonato ends 5.1 determined to quiz Margaret on her involvement with that 'lewd fellow' Borachio. 5.2 opens with Benedick's mock-gallant courting of Margaret to help him in his suit to Beatrice. Margaret's name is the last and the first to be spoken, and the witty, off-colour exchange tells an audience more about Margaret than Leonato could ever find out, let alone understand. It answers his question about her connection with Borachio by leaving unanswered her question about herself: will she never marry out of her station? These opening speeches of 5.2 do nothing to further the plot of *Much Ado*, but they tie up what some critics have thought the 'loose end' of Margaret's motivation, and provide a sombre counterpoint to the imminent marriages. Another relevant linkage with implications for character occurs between 3.3 and 3.4. The first scene presents Borachio's tipsy diatribe against the 'deformed thief' Fashion and its effect on the young. This prepares for the contrast in 3.4 between Margaret, absorbed and as we know literally 'corrupted' by

---

[1] E. A. J. Honigmann, *Myriad-Minded Shakespeare* (Basingstoke, 1989), 193.

fashion, and Hero, not at all 'deformed' by it. Hero's lack of affectation intensifies the pathos of her circumstances and, by the contrast between the women, Borachio's success with Margaret is explained further.

Expectations and hence scene linkages arise from the givens of genre and from the increasing definition of character. The oncoming shadow of Shakespeare's problem plays is the clash of such expectations. The genre leads us to expect a rehabilitated Claudio, a proper fifth-act bridegroom. But such a Claudio cannot be produced so late in the play without violating the character we know. Hence the ritual lamentation of 5.3, which provides externally the contrition which the genre demands but the character cannot convincingly express. For the moment the problem of conflicting expectations is finessed. Or is it? Ralph Berry quotes Trevor Nunn as warning us that we must take Claudio's repentance seriously.[1] He is not alone in what may well be a futile caution. Does anyone have to plead so for Leontes? Only the dominant presence of Beatrice and Benedick at the end of the play shields Claudio from questions asked more urgently about Bertram in *All's Well*.

Yet *Much Ado* is not quite a problem play; it raises few such conflicting expectations. However, its relatively unsurprising sequence of incidents is rarely bland. Scenes or the incidents that comprise them shift irregularly among the main social groups sometimes using them as complete groups, more often partially or with mediating figures like Benedick.

Shakespeare also uses other variables to intensify contrasts between adjacent scenes or their component incidents. Among these variables in scene composition are length, emotional tone, pace, degree of audience engagement, stage movement, number of characters on stage, verbal texture (e.g. the use of prose or verse), and non-verbal expression (e.g. song, instrumental music, and dance). Rarely (as at 3.1, 3.2, and 3.3) does Shakespeare write adjacent scenes of roughly similar length. Scenes with logically clustered incidents recur through the play (e.g. 1.1, 4.1). Each is at least three times as long as the scenes that follow. Typical of such contrasts is the opening scene, which begins in stiff officialese, runs through

---

[1] Berry, *On Directing Shakespeare*, 71.

Beatrice's tart wit, Claudio's naïvely confessional prose and Benedick's flip responses, and ends with Don Pedro's stodgy stage verse. Its component incidents are distinguished through character grouping, language, and tone.

Shakespeare's most telling variations are the three incidents of 4.1. The denunciation of Hero begins with Leonato's ominously amusing misinterpretation of Claudio's intent. This only sharpens expectation, soon satisfied as prose shifts to versified denunciation. The second incident, also in verse, centres on Leonato's self-pitying condemnation of Hero, which he alters to self-congratulatory if conditional outrage as Beatrice and the Friar come to Hero's defence and suggest her mock funeral. In the last incident Beatrice and Benedick are alone on stage. Speaking now in prose, Beatrice and Benedick exchange understandings in sometimes flat, uncharacteristically direct sentences, the most notorious of which is Beatrice's imploring two-word command. 'What a strong conflict of emotions used to come over me when acting this scene', wrote Helen Faucit, who analyses its moving interplay of hesitation and commitment.[1] As J. F. Cox tells us, for other Beatrices too this was the great moment of the play, though occasionally undercut, as was evidently done by Dorothea Jordan with a casually hearty 'Kill Claudio'.[2]

Not surprisingly, as the numbers on stage decrease, depth and immediacy of feeling increase. The denunciation of Hero is exciting enough, but extreme audience reactions are held in abeyance (T. W. Craik calls it comic detachment), since Claudio is deluded and will not be sustained. Moreover, audience engagement must be saved until after Beatrice and Benedick are alone.

Sympathy is what we might have expected to begin the second incident. What we get is Leonato's self-pity and denunciation of his child, surprising yet clearly in character. He gives us twenty-four lines of this in the formal manner that Jonas Barish found typical of the role.[3] Leonato's chain of

[1] Faucit, *On Some of Shakespeare's Characters*, 37.
[2] J. F. Cox, 'The Stage Representation of the "Kill Claudio" Sequence in *Much Ado About Nothing*', *Shakespeare Survey 32* (1979), 27–36.
[3] J. Barish, 'Pattern and Purpose in the Prose of *Much Ado About Nothing*', *Rice University Studies*, 60 (1974), 19–30.

rhetorical questions: 'Grieved I'?, 'Chid I'?, 'Why had I'? (twice), and several variants—is a creaky echo of Kyd, or at least the textbook rhetoric of Leonato's youth. The Friar's sententiousness is also lengthily self-conscious, conveyed in long-breathed Miltonic syntax and run-on lines. His advocacy of deception and lying in a good cause has a precedent in Friar Laurence, and his rhetoric is a way of dealing with Leonato on Leonato's own terms.

Finally Beatrice and Benedick are alone. Benedick's failure to leave with Claudio and Don Pedro is an augury that his 'Lady Beatrice, have you wept all this while?' promises will come true. For the play's most intense moment Shakespeare employs prose, and of the prosiest sort: ellipsis, interjection, sentences of two and three words. It was for this disclosure of passion ('Not an *emotion*. A *passion*', was Ellen Terry's marginal note), that the false or inappropriate feelings and the contrived rhetoric of the earlier incidents, and even the verse of Beatrice's soliloquy after the deception scene, prepared us. Rhetorical ornament is not in itself a cue for audience disengagement. The whole stylistic spectrum of a play determines the effect.

Local Effects

During actual performance, however, some of the most telling strokes of dramaturgy are small and local, among them the artful release or withholding of information, the management of pace, the canny suiting of word to action. *Much Ado* is a treasury of such local effects. To place an audience in a position of superior knowledge prompts a self-congratulatory attention. Bertrand Evans has studied this 'discrepant awareness'—his term.[1] Obviously angling for audience amusement are Don Pedro's slow twigging to the significance of his brother's flight from Messina, and the initial inability of both Claudio and the Prince to understand Benedick's hostile attitude to them after his 'conversion'.

Three distinctive instances deserve notice. During the masked ball, the blocks of dialogue assigned to the dancing

---

[1] B. Evans, *Shakespeare's Comedies* (Oxford, 1960).

7. The masked ball (2.1) in John Gielgud's production at the Shakespeare Memorial Theatre, Stratford-upon-Avon, 1950.

couples last the length of a 'bout' or turn around the dance floor—except in the case of Beatrice and Benedick, who speak at greater length and so must 'follow the leaders' to catch up; follow them only 'in all good things', says Benedick, suspicious of the relation between the 'leaders', Don Pedro and Hero, and wary of a similar alliance with Beatrice.[1]

Second, in the denunciation scene, as in any scene of prolonged seriousness, the playwright (and the audience) are at the mercy of the easiest raised guffaw in the house. The playwright's task is to draw off incipient laughter. In *Much Ado* Shakespeare inserts verbal lightning rods in the denunciation scene: Benedick's citation of grammar book interjections, such as 'ah, ha, he' is grotesquely out of place, as is his choice understatement, 'This looks not like a nuptial', which always gets a preventive laugh.

Third are Shakespeare's apt uses of echo and allusion. Not the least of his advantages as a playwright for a repertory company was an audience which could remember at least the great successes, such perennials as Kyd's *Spanish Tragedy*, and

[1] Such small but elegant artifices of dramaturgy are illuminated by Alan Brissenden's *Shakespeare and the Dance* (1981), 49–50.

such recent plays as Shakespeare's own *Romeo and Juliet* and *The Taming of the Shrew*. There are evocations of all three in *Much Ado*. Leonato and Antonio seem to have wandered out of the old tropes of *The Spanish Tragedy* into a language whose sparkle makes their deep distress seem quaint and, like the creaky rhetoric of Hamlet's 'Murder of Gonzago', a generational distancing device that encourages condescension. We are, no doubt, to take Leonato's speeches as heartfelt, but among the perversities of 'honour' they are clearly outmoded.

In 3.3, when Borachio relates his wooing of her as Hero, he describes Margaret as bidding him 'a thousand times good night'. To a careful memory the tag from the balcony scene of *Romeo and Juliet* would suggest an ironic contrast in occasions. More securely, *Much Ado* echoes *The Taming of the Shrew*. Beatrice has been reduced to shrewishness in some productions. She seems to invite the description in order to refute it. In 5.2, having confessed himself unable to celebrate his love for Beatrice adequately in rhyme, Benedick greets her entrance—he has just asked Margaret to fetch her—with the question: 'Sweet Beatrice, wouldst thou come when I called thee?' The public proof of the 'taming' of Kate is Petruccio's hundred-crown bet that she, of all the wives present, will come soonest at her husband's call. Kate alone appears, and at once. Beatrice also answers the Petruccio-Benedick question with a dutiful, 'Yea, signor, and depart when you bid me.' Benedick, enchanted, says, 'O, stay but till then', whereupon Beatrice says, ' "Then" is spoken. Fare you well now'. Having made her point, she asks whether Benedick has actually challenged Claudio. Shakespeare's allusion to the earlier play's test of subjugation forces a comparison, and both raises and makes problematic the view that *Much Ado* casts only a sugaring of wit over the male domination apparently acceptable in the *Shrew*.

Stage History

Although the record is all but blank, there is no reason to doubt the Quarto title-page: *Much Ado* was 'sundrie times publikely acted' by the Lord Chamberlain's Men. *The Shakespere Allusion-Book* identifies some significant references to the play.[1] On the evidence of several stage echoes of Benedick and one of Dogberry in Thomas Heywood's *Fair Maid of the Exchange* (1607) the play was apparently popular before the Restoration. In the dedication to *The Italian Tailor* (1609), Robert Armin, who had played Dogberry, mentions a beggar who 'hath been writ downe for an Asse', and in lines printed in a 1640 edition of Shakespeare's poems, Leonard Digges equated the popularity of *Much Ado* with that of the Henry IV plays: 'let but Beatrice | And Benedicke be seene, loe in a trice | The Cockpit[,] Galleries, Boxes, all are full'. Taking advantage of the flexibility of Elizabethan syntax, Digges runs the last phrase into a reference to *Twelfth Night*, thus again suggesting a popularity for *Much Ado* comparable to that of Shakespeare's better-documented successes.

Of actual performances before the Restoration we have only the evidence of the Quarto and the Lord Chamberlain's accounts of expenditures on the marriage of Princess Elizabeth to the Elector Palatine in May of 1613. For fourteen plays at Whitehall, among them '*Much Adoe abowte Nothinge*', John Heminge received £93. 6s. 8d. on behalf of the company. The documents[2] record a further payment of £40 for six additional performances, one of them for 'Benedicte and Betteris'.

After the Restoration, the Lord Chamberlain parcelled out performance rights to Shakespeare's plays. *Much Ado* went to William Davenant and the Duke of York's Company. Davenant promised to 'reform and make [Shakespeare's work] fitt' for Restoration tastes. One such reformation was Davenant's *The Law Against Lovers*, performed on 15 February 1662. Davenant's play—so it was considered by his contemporaries—was a pastiche that used a quarrelsome Beatrice and Benedick as sub-plot to a sentimental romance between *Measure for Measure*'s Isabella and a merely prudent Angelo, who was only 'testing' her virtue. Benedick became Angelo's brother and Beatrice a great heiress, but her baby sister Viola stole the show (so Pepys thought), with the songs and dances Davenant added. In addition, Davenant cleared the dialogue

---

[1] *The Shakespere Allusion-Book*, ed. J. Munro (1909, reissued 1932), i. 45, 178, 194.

[2] Reprinted by E. K. Chambers in *William Shakespeare: A Study of Facts and Problems* (Oxford, 1930), ii. 343.

of off-colour remarks. Only two performances of the play are known.

Much Ado continued to flesh out adaptations. Charles Johnson's *Love in a Forest* (1723) was a *mélange* of *As You Like It* with insertions from *A Midsummer Night's Dream*, *Love's Labour's Lost*, *Twelfth Night*, and, from *Much Ado*, some forty lines of Benedick's witty resistance to love from the end of 1.1. James Miller's *The Universal Passion* of 1737 mixed Molière's *Princesse d'Élide* with *Twelfth Night* and *The Two Gentlemen of Verona*. The play has clear echoes of the major figures in *Much Ado*, but is disorganized, trivial, and on occasion misogynistic. What slight success it had may be attributed to Kitty Clive as Liberia, the play's Beatrice. Clive was noted for low comedy, which suggests what became of the role in this adaptation.[1] The last of the eighteenth-century adaptations was Robert Jephson's *Law of Lombardy* in 1779.

Much Ado itself was revived by John Rich in February 1721 after 'Not [being] acted these Thirty Years', and again by Rich at Covent Garden, running for three nights in 1737 and 1746, and for a benefit night in 1739. From 1748, when David Garrick first acted in it—after two months of rehearsals —until he retired in 1776, Garrick's Benedick was a mainstay of Drury Lane. He was so successful that he revived the play yearly, and went on to take the role about a hundred times in all. Garrick had a succession of Beatrices, of whom Hannah Pritchard, the first, and Elizabeth Pope were perhaps the most capable. Frances Abington, who played Beatrice during the last two years of Garrick's Benedick, continued as a successful Beatrice, taking the role for the last time in 1798 at the age of 61. Garrick's interpretation of the play comes through the observations in Thomas Davies's *Dramatic Miscellanies* (1783– 4). Evidently Garrick's staging made every scene between Beatrice and Benedick 'a continual struggle for superiority'

---

[1] See C. B. Hogan, *Shakespeare in the Theatre 1701–1800* (Oxford, 1952), i. 341. The following remarks on the 18th-century stage are indebted to Hogan, H. Spencer, *Shakespeare Improved* (Cambridge, Mass., 1927), G. C. Odell, *Shakespeare from Betterton to Irving* (New York, 1920), to the Cambridge edition of the play (1923), to *The London Stage: 1660–1800*, pt. 3, *1729– 1749*, ed. A. H. Scouten (Carbondale, Ill., 1961), pt. 4, *1747–1776*, ed. G. W. Stone (Carbondale, Ill., 1962), to the Variorum *Much Ado*, and to Cox, 'The Stage Representation of the "Kill Claudio" Sequence'.

that left the audience unable to decide who had won the battle. Garrick must have conveyed a great force of character to achieve equality with Beatrice despite the text. Yet one wonders what nuances of hidden sympathy may have remained hidden beneath the more accessible delights of draw and rematch.

Garrick's successes at Drury Lane left his Covent Garden rivals little appetite for *Much Ado*, which they mounted for only four performances during his reign. After Garrick, performance during the rest of the century was dominated by the role of Beatrice: Frances Abington played Beatrice against several Benedicks until 1798; in 1779 Sarah Siddons appeared as Beatrice in Bristol; Elizabeth Farren first took the role in 1787 and played it the following year against John Philip Kemble's Benedick and in revivals until 1797. Also playing Beatrice against the older Kemble was Dorothea Jordan, the last of the century's notable Beatrices. The theatrical history of *Much Ado* effectively divides at mid-century. Before Garrick in 1748, the unadapted *Much Ado* was revived only rarely; the Beatrice–Benedick material appears largely in fancified, moralizing adaptations. During the second half of the century, however, there were slightly fewer than two hundred performances of the play itself, about half of them by Garrick.

Much Ado was increasingly popular during the nineteenth century. The main features of its history during the period are frequency of performance; the continuity of actors associated with the play and hence the growth of traditions of performance; the distinction of two 'serious' Beatrices, Helen Faucit and Ellen Terry (both long-lived in the role), as against a variety of merely comic or trivializing interpreters; and finally the subordination of the text to spectacular sets and comic business, tendencies culminating in Beerbohm Tree's production of 1905.

Charles Kemble began playing Benedick in 1803 opposite Anne Brunton (who managed to giggle through her indignation), Fanny Kemble (who marred her restraint elsewhere by throwing herself on Benedick during her confession of love), Louisa Nisbett (who not only fell upon Benedick but broke into loud sobs at 'Kill Claudio') and—in contrast—Helen Faucit, whose delicacy and intelligence in the role, which she first played at 19 when the 61-year-old Kemble chose her for his last season in the role of Benedick in 1836, made hers one of the defining interpretations. Writing in 1847, George Fletcher (quoted in Variorum, 386–7), indicted the mid-century stage for 'the prevailing misconception' of Beatrice as 'either a hoyden or a vixen, or . . . a compound of the two', exempting only Helen Faucit. She played the role for forty-three years, giving her last performance as Beatrice at the opening of the Memorial Theatre, Stratford-upon-Avon in 1879.

Nineteenth-century Beatrices were not alone in falsifying their roles. At Beatrice's confession of love, Charles Kemble tittered, provoking audience laughter before kissing her. In a Drury Lane revival of 1843 Macready conveyed 'the pride of successful love' in his exchange with Beatrice, and further cheapened its final moments with sentimental interpolations. Evidently a Benedick for whom love was not a barnyard triumph was as difficult to imagine as a self-possessed Beatrice. Among a variety of alternatives to productions featuring Helen Faucit were those of Samuel Phelps at Sadler's Wells in 1848, 1850, and 1858, with Henry Marston as Benedick and a different Beatrice for each revival; and Charles Kean in 1858, with Kean as Benedick and his wife as Beatrice.

In 1880, the year after Helen Faucit retired, Ellen Terry played Beatrice opposite her second husband, Charles Wardell. The experience led her to deepen her conception of the role. When she played it in 1882 she was 'not the same Beatrice at all'.[1] In that year Irving revived *Much Ado* at the Lyceum with Ellen Terry as Beatrice and, according to George C. Odell, excellent interpretations of Hero (Jessie Millward) and Claudio (Johnston Forbes-Robertson), and magnificent sets and costumes. Over Terry's objections, Irving altered the play to achieve effective 'curtains', and retained some traditional stage business demeaning to Beatrice. Despite his playing the role of Benedick for light comedy, Irving seemed to Terry rather too deliberate a Benedick, although she was to judge him much 'improved' in a later revival. Her Beatrice was more fiery and physical than Helen Faucit's, but Terry found equivalents for Faucit's bright humour and principled thoughtful-

---

[1] E. Terry, *Memoirs* (1933), 127.

ness. The production ran for 212 performances, had a successful American tour, and returned to London for 31 more performances. It was revived in 1891. Terry continued in the role after her association with Irving. In 1903 she played Beatrice in a brief London production notable for the then shocking, simplified sets designed by her son Gordon Craig; the production went on three provincial tours.

There were, of course, other productions during the period, but Cox,[1] for example, cites some of them largely as illustrative misinterpretations: the cock-of-the-walk Benedick of Walter Lacy in the Haymarket productions of the 1850s, and the complementary distortion of Beatrice in the stagy outbursts of sobbing by Julia Neilson at the St James' in 1898.

Sets became increasingly lavish as the century progressed. Charles Kean's farewell season production of 1858 opened on the harbour of Messina, with gradually illuminated noble houses and the Mediterranean glowing under a rising moon. Irving's Lyceum production was similarly elaborate, with a cavernous church interior impressively recorded in the painting by Johnston Forbes-Robertson, Irving's Claudio. 'Expensively mounted and superlatively dull' was Shaw's verdict in the *Saturday Review* of 25 May, 1885, but Shaw, who ought to have recognized his own material in Beatrice (or perhaps because he did), thought *Much Ado* a 'shockingly bad' play. This theatrical grangerizing of *Much Ado* culminated in Beerbohm Tree's 1905 production, which supplied '(all) the lovely things Shakespear dispensed with'. So wrote Shaw in the *Saturday Review* of 11 February 1905, adding a catalogue of scenic excess and half-seriously recommending Tree's 'endless larks in the way of stage business'. Shaw's warning that his readers would never have the chance to see this sort of entertainment again was prophetic. Gordon Craig's stark sets of two years before signalled the passing of Victorian rococo. 'Larks' were soon to fall out of favour as William Poel and others rethought the Elizabethan platform stage and searched out 'Shakespeare's' meanings in the text.

In the twentieth century, productions of *Much Ado* are numerous enough to warrant an independent study, indeed

[1] Cox, 'The Stage Representation of the "Kill Claudio" Sequence', 30–1.

so numerous that striving for differentiation, with inevitable lapses into empty novelty, is a motif of recent performance. Another is the awareness of what may be learned from the Elizabethan stage and, more recently, from academic interpretation. Like all Shakespeare, *Much Ado* has been internationalized, and performed in translation not only into other languages, but into cinema and television. And especially since the Second World War important productions have tended to explore the play's darker themes.

Comparative figures in J. C. Trewin's *Shakespeare on the English Stage: 1900–64* (1964) show that West End productions of *Much Ado* lagged behind those of the vastly more popular *Twelfth Night*, and numbered little more than half those of the other two romantic comedies. Much of this discrepancy dates from the first two decades. Sprague and Trewin date the absence of *Much Ado* from the West End during the nearly two decades beginning in 1905.[1] But the play was performed elsewhere during the 1920s by touring companies such as Frank Benson's, and it was mounted regularly at Stratford, 'where it was something of a mascot', and occasionally at the Old Vic. At Stratford it had 35 productions, roughly the same as *Twelfth Night*'s 39, but fewer than *As You Like It*'s 43. Since the 1960s the play has been performed regularly by professional, amateur, and especially academic casts.

The number and variety of twentieth-century productions preclude more than suggesting a few directions and achievements. William Poel's 1904 London School Board *Much Ado*, with period music directed by Arnold Dolmetsch, an advocate of music played on original instruments, and a scholarly talk by Dr Furnivall, was thought by the *Times* reviewer (quoted Mares, 20) as of antiquarian interest only. But Poel's historical concern spread.

There was no lack of distinguished acting in *Much Ado* before the end of the Second World War. Among others, Sybil Thorndike played Beatrice at the Old Vic in 1915, and again in 1927 with Lewis Casson as Benedick; in 1925 Edith Evans played Beatrice opposite Baliol Holloway as Benedick, and in

[1] A. C. Sprague and J. C. Trewin, *Shakespeare's Plays Today* (1970), 12.

1930 Gielgud played Benedick with Dorothy Green as Beatrice. In 1938 and 1945 Donald Wolfit played Benedick, the second time with Rosalind Iden.

Yet it was a 1949 Stratford production with Gielgud directing Diana Wynyard and Anthony Quayle that influenced later conceptions of the play. Gielgud revived this production in 1950, 1952, 1955, followed by European American tours. In these revivals Gielgud himself played Benedick opposite Diana Wynyard, Peggy Ashcroft, and, for the American tour, Margaret Leighton. Wynyard he thought of as grand in the Terry manner, Ashcroft as downright, cheeky, and at times, like himself, a dropper of bricks. In *Stage Directions* Gielgud describes how his interpretation of Benedick altered over time from the comic-dandy wearer of funny hats to the bluff soldier.[1] What was constant was Gielgud's tight rein on the serious elements in the text, his elegant, rapid projection of the play's wit, and his refusal to vulgarize the relation with Beatrice, especially at the end of 4.1. Benedick's observation of her tears became, properly, a turning point in the play. Gielgud had also learned the production lessons of Poel; the costumes were colourful but of the Renaissance ('Boccaccio' had been requested), and the sets handsome but ingeniously flexible. Typically, Gielgud could not see the point of setting a play with so much sexual innuendo in periods that balked at the sight of a woman's ankle. If any fault could be found with his production it lay in a stylistic elegance that gave undue weight to romance and artifice.

Two notable productions of the 1970s anchored the play in social particulars. J. J. Antoon's production ('naughty but endearing' according to Clive Barnes in the *New York Times* of 13 November 1972), opened in Central Park with Sam Waterston as a boyish and romantic Benedick and Kathleen Widdowes as a sharp-tongued but 'feminine' feminist, both of them confused but madly in love. The setting was the American heartland before World War I, shortly after a successful campaign against a vaguely Spanish enemy. (The play suggests the Teddy Roosevelt era, one of America's several Golden Ages.) The Messenger becomes a reporter, the Watch Keystone

---

[1] J. Gielgud, *Stage Directions* (1963), 39.

Kops, and Benedick paddles a canoe. Reviews[1] record almost universal delight in the straw-hat, shirt-sleeve costumes and Antoon's ingenious historical transformations. But reviewers also noted that the production ignored Claudio's jealousy and transformed Don John into an 'almost Hitlerian' villain. John Simon, writing in the *New York Magazine*, was scathing at the production's superficiality; the play was not, Simon insisted, 'about nothing'. 'Barren of essentials' agreed Harris Green in the *New York Times* of 14 January. Antoon's production suffered a peculiarly modern fate. Promising commercial success, it moved to Broadway, but had to close nine days after the production was shown, to a fatally enthusiastic response, on television.

John Barton's 1976 Stratford production was set in a garrison town in late nineteenth-century British India. A reserved but surface-merry Judi Dench played Beatrice; Donald Sinden (as ever) was irrepressibly humorous as a 'bachelor under siege'. The two were finely matched. Like Antoon, Barton sought historical equivalents for Shakespeare's Messina. Beyond its picturesque delights, Barton's India invoked the dangerous leisure of the garrison, in which casual violence can seem natural (gunshots fired as if into the audience by Don Pedro and Claudio signal a transition to the darker second half of the play), fantasies of honour and rank can flourish, and the 'natives' (here John Woodvine's near-Sikh Dogberry) can manage as they will. Barton's historical imagination and the critical scholarship of Anne Barton, who wrote the programme notes, evoked for modern British audiences a historical moment in which the play's destructive codes of conduct seemed plausible, yet not as foreign as the Elizabethan. A false note in the production, according to reviewers,[2] was the whimpering, sex-starved Don John, for whom no historical equivalent was possible. Another was the 'too un-elaborate' church scene, according to Roger Warren[3] in his full account of the production.

---

[1] As abstracted in W. Babula's *Shakespeare in Production, 1935–1978* (New York, 1981), 232–5.

[2] Ibid. 236–7.

[3] R. Warren, 'Theory and Practice: Stratford 1976', *Shakespeare Survey 30* (1977), 171–2.

8. 'I will go with thee to thy uncle's' (5.2.99–100): Judi Dench (Beatrice) and Donald Sinden (Benedick) in John Barton's production, Royal Shakespeare Theatre, Stratford-upon-Avon, 1976.

There were of course other productions. Among interesting leads were Michael Redgrave and Googie Withers (Stratford, 1958), and Christopher Plummer and Geraldine McEwan (Stratford, 1961), directed by Michael Langham. McEwan's Beatrice was a rather brittle, thoroughly up-to-date woman. Zeffirelli's super-inventive 1965 National Theatre production, with Maggie Smith as a 'somewhat waspish' Beatrice and Robert Stephens as a Benedick vain of his waxed moustaches, returned to the larks of Beerbohm Tree. Don Pedro became a nervous giggler and Dogberry no more than a comic foreign accent.[1] Despite the appropriateness of nineteenth-century Sicily as a context for the male honour of the text, apparently Zeffirelli wanted to avoid the text, not dramatize it. He is supposed to have thought the play 'very dull'. *Faute de mieux*, Albert Finney's Latin dictator of a Don Pedro was considered outstanding. Helen Mirren's Hero is particularly remembered from Trevor Nunn's Stratford production of 1968, apparently

[1] Babula, *Shakespeare in Production*, 230–1.

unsuccessful despite the talents of Janet Suzman and Alan Howard, thus illustrating again the trickiness of the necessary match between Beatrice and Benedick.

In 1982, Terry Hands produced the play, first at Stratford, then at the Barbican in London, now with a stylized set and costumes suggesting Restoration glitter. Nicholas Shrimpton found Sinead Cusack as Beatrice a fine actress but 'not a comedienne', at home only in the play's gloomy moments and so unable to match the comic charm and psychological detail of Derek Jacobi's Benedick.[1] If the play did not please it was for subtly instructive reasons. Emrys Jones in the *TLS* of 16 April 1982 saw in Ralph Koltai's remarkable set of perspex panels with their 'kaleidoscopically dissolving images' the suggestion that the evidence of the senses was not to be trusted. With this theme constantly to the fore, the production lost emotional depth and seemed to some an illustration of the modern critical view that *Much Ado* was clever, but essentially cold and empty. A gaunt and disillusioned Don John (John Carlisle) was a portentous index to the interpretation.

Much Ado is performed regularly in North America, most often in an academic context or at one of many New World Stratfords. In 1977, for example, the play was performed by the Folger Theatre Group (associated with the Folger Shakespeare Library) in Washington, DC; at the Colorado Shakespeare Festival; the New Jersey Shakespeare Festival, and the Shakespeare Festival of Dallas; the following year it was performed at the North Carolina Shakespeare Festival. Two American productions of particular interest are the indefatigably comic Tex-Mex production of the 1957 Stratford, Connecticut, Shakespeare Festival with mariachi bands, and Alfred Drake and Katharine Hepburn as Beatrice and Benedick. Dogberry as a confused sheriff was somehow unassimilable into even this loose interpretation. The second is Joseph Papp's highly colourful Goyaesque New York Shakespeare Festival production of 1961. The interpretation turned on the difference between the helpless passion of the lovers and the absurd impression they made. A 1992 production of the new

---

[1] N. Shrimpton, 'Shakespeare Performances in Stratford-upon-Avon and London, 1981–2', *Shakespeare Survey* 36 (1983), 153.

Shakespeare Company, formerly at the Folger Library, was praised on 15 March in a *New York Times* feature article 'as eminently satisfying on its own sunny terms', but since Michael Kahn, the director, had interpreted the play as moving from the comic to the serious, the performance was labelled a disappointing 'Bard Without Laughs' by the *Washington Post* of 4 March.

Stratford (Ontario) Canada has a consistent record of good productions of *Much Ado*, among them Michael Langham's of 1958 with Christopher Plummer; a 1971 production, praised for its picture postcard elegance and queried for the 'unreal' relation between Beatrice and Benedick; and two accomplished productions of 1977 and 1980, with Martha Henry and Alan Scarfe in the first and Maggie Smith and Brian Bedford in the second. A junior production was presented on the 'Third Stage' in 1983. The most recent *Much Ado*, in 1991, directed by Richard Monette, was pretty and sunny, with Goldie Semple as Beatrice and Colm Feore as Benedick.

Dennis Bartholomeusz traces 'Shakespeare on the Melbourne Stage'[1] and records a performance of *Much Ado* with Edwin Booth and Laura Keene, the second after an inaugural *Hamlet* at the Queen's Theatre as early as 1843. Other performances there and elsewhere in English-speaking areas are numerous.

A token instance of the many performances of *Much Ado* in translation deserves mention. Recounting his 1897 production of *Much Ado*, Stanislavski observed (as might Beerbohm Tree), that 'I didn't need scenery and costumes for a play, I needed a play for the scenery and costumes.' He then 'thumbed through Shakespeare' and hit on *Much Ado* as 'a vehicle for medieval Italy'. In *Stanislavski's Encounter with Shakespeare* Joyce Morgan describes the reconstruction of a Turin castle on the stage of the Hunters' Club in Moscow.[2] For Stanislavski the sets clarified the play; what he learned from the production was the importance of external characterization (e.g. setting) in 'defending myself from harmful theatricality in acting'. Among the directors and producers of

---

[1] *Shakespeare Survey* 35 (1982), 38.
[2] J. Morgan, *Stanislavski's Encounter with Shakespeare* (Ann Arbor, Mich., 1984), 26–8.

the later nineteenth century, this was hardly classified information, but it was information that Stanislavski would
have to forget. He was to regret having been over-impressed
by the Meiningen ensemble and other exponents of the dogged
naturalism that once led Chekhov to swear he would write a
play and specify that, no matter what, no birds were to sing.

From Text to Prompt-Book

Difficulties in understanding *Much Ado* can result from Elizabethan idiom and topical allusion. Many such difficulties are
lessened by the method of incremental repetition Shakespeare
developed to match the release of information with the rate
of its reception by outdoor audiences, and by the parcelling
of plot into scenes that such audiences could both anticipate
and distinguish. Adjacent phrases explain one another, and
difficult scenes are clearly 'placed' in the action by scenes that
come before and after. Each play is its own best gloss, yet
successive prompt-books show a history of minor alterations
to adjust the text to changing audiences.

The second volume of William Halstead's collation of eight-
eenth-, nineteenth-, and early twentieth-century prompt-
books[1] provides a historical overview of stage alterations of
the text, and evidence of how few major changes have been
made. This testifies to the play's brevity and construction.
Only 1.2 and 5.3 have been often cut radically. As Stanley
Wells remarks,[2] 5.3 is scenically awkward, requiring props
and stage movement at odds with the rest of the play. Yet
the willingness of directors to cut this 'penance' scene suggests that many did not share Trevor Nunn's view of its
importance, perhaps thinking Claudio's penance hopeless or
the momentum toward double happiness all the purification
Claudio needed.

Halstead's collations show a great deal of minor tinkering,
but frequently adopted cuts occur where one would expect:
in obscure allusions, scene-setting description, and long
speeches. There is also some elimination of minor parts such

---

[1] *Shakespeare as Spoken* (Ann Arbor, Mich., 1979), ss. 111b–134b.
[2] S. Wells, 'Editorial Treatment of Foul Paper Texts: *Much Ado About Nothing*
as Test Case', *RES*, NS 31 (1980), 1–16.

as the pert Boy who fetches Benedick's book, and the Messenger who tries to speed Leonato to church. Leonato himself emerges as more sympathetic for the shrinking of his self-pity. Tedium, however, is part of the effect, and the extent of Leonato's self-obsession emphasizes its tawdriness. The comic business of Balthasar's poor singing is often precluded by cutting the negative remarks of Benedick and Don Pedro. Evidently, fine singing provided atmosphere needed for staging *Much Ado* as romantic comedy. Hero's critical remarks about Beatrice are often cut, as are Beatrice's satiric allusions, among them her scorn of Benedick's supposed challenge to Cupid.

After Garrick many directors cut Don Pedro's misguided banter with the reformed Benedick, improving our impression of the Prince. Claudio's allusion to the 'horn madness' that would afflict Benedick if he married is also often cut, as is some of Benedick's teasing of Claudio in 1.1. Another loss is Benedick's fifth-act advice to Don Pedro to marry despite the risk of being cuckolded. This—with the removal of Claudio's prediction of Benedick's probable post-marital 'horn madness'—cuts the two allusions that bracket the development of Benedick's thinking about women and marriage: the fear of sexual betrayal that supposedly estranged him from women, and his acceptance of cuckolding, however jokingly, as both thinkable and worth risking. Recent productions sometimes depart from the generally conservative earlier treatment of the language of the text, but at some peril; the search for Dogberryisms in the American South-west of the 1880s met with little success.

In addition to excisions, there have been interpolations, perhaps the most offensive and long-lived of which was an addition to the end of 4.1 in frequent use from the Kembles through Irving and designed to provide a more 'theatrical' end to the scene. Ellen Terry deplored the muscle-flexing vulgarity of Benedick's repeated assurances that he would fight Claudio and 'Kill him'—'Dead—as sure as I'm alive I will', but Irving insisted. Gielgud trusted the text, however, moving toward 'a falling close', grave and resolute.[1]

---

[1] Cox, 'The Stage Representation of the "Kill Claudio" Sequence', 35.

Some Problems of Staging

The most obvious difficulty in staging *Much Ado* is casting Beatrice and Benedick. Claudio and Hero are secondary roles, but require the actors to make bricks with little straw, another difficulty. The difficulty of casting the major roles is reflected in their stage history, a succession of commanding individuals rather than balanced pairs. Either a Faucit or a Terry, a Garrick or a Gielgud dominates the stage. Frances Abington, a considerable Beatrice, did not shine until she left Garrick. Rarely has it been the case that a Judi Dench and a Donald Sinden are, conspicuously, matched.

A central difficulty of interpretation threads through the play's history. *Much Ado About Nothing* is a play about gender differences, and since women have acted in it, productions of the play have not only interpreted but exemplified those differences. Box office and the psychological baggage that actors (like all of us) bring with them have served as surrogate Messinas with all the attendant social pressures. Hoyden, tomboy, vixen, shrew, virago; flirt, clinging vine, weeper, hysteric—someone has apparently seen grounds in the text for each of these possible Beatrices. From Miss Reynolds acting Beatrice in 1853 as manipulative and wholly without sympathetic feeling, to Margaret Chatwin sobbing mightily in 1919, most of the variants have been staged. For Benedick the range has been narrower: crude, soldierly, triumphant, smug, elegant, dandified: Gielgud moved from one extreme toward the other.

For both roles the text specifies a broad centre. That so many actors have avoided it is due to reasons other than want of talent—among them personal conviction or lack of it, the views of gender differences then current, and pressure from producer-directors, often the embodiment of those views. Helen Faucit's initial disapproval of Beatrice's 'unfeminine' edge had only to be pushed in one direction to produce a compensatory sentimental dependence thought proper in women during most of the nineteenth century; or, taken in the opposite direction, to produce the will to dominate commonly attributed to women who rejected dependency. Faucit brought to her study of the play intelligence and imagination which overcame the personal and period pressures to act either distortion of the role. Further, to undertake Beatrice at 19 opposite the great old actor of the age argues self-possession and a conviction of personal worth that found echoes in the role. For Ellen Terry neither inner nor outer pressure was as great as it had been for Helen Faucit. Moreover, she was Faucit's immediate heir to the role.

In her memoirs and lectures[1] Ellen Terry detailed her disputes with Irving over the Lyceum *Much Ado*. Superficially these disputes dealt with matters of taste; in effect they turned on how to represent Beatrice as a woman. In support of Irving when Terry objected to putting up a jealous fuss at Benedick's helping the fainting Hero, Walter Lacy, who knew the acting traditions of the play, said that 'it always got a laugh'. Terry was adamant. Further, Terry's refusal to play a vixen Beatrice shows in her dislike of the hectoring insistence of the interpolated 'Dead', 'Dead' ending of 4.1.

Even worse was Tree's vulgarization, including a 'Kill Claudio' spoken while Beatrice (as Lady Macbeth?) is in Benedick's arms. Not all the stage business developed over the years for this crucial scene had the effect of narrowing the character of Beatrice into stereotypes that belied the text, but much of it made difficult the projection of a woman who was neither psychologically dependent nor domineering. Needless to say, dependency and domination were, for many reasons, easier to act. Finally, Terry's situation was much like Beatrice's; when overruled by Irving she considered her alternatives and decided that she had very few.

Inevitably the characterization of Benedick was subject to complementary distortions. A 'reformed' Benedick joining a self-possessed Beatrice was not the norm. Benedick's avowal of love was often acted as a sexual triumph or a grant of protection, sometimes with laughter of the sort Hobbes defined as 'a sudden glory' at Beatrice's expense. Charles Kemble's gentlemanly titters at Beatrice's confession of love also raised such laughter in the audience. Walter Lacy's transcription of

[1] E. Terry, *The Story of My Life* (1908), 163; *Four Lectures*, 96.

the Kemble prompt-book notes that Benedick strutted in triumph about the stage. Since Garrick *Much Ado* had often been revived as a comic set-to, a sunny comedy with avoidable implications. The text allows this, but also more. As Robert Frost said, the poem is entitled to everything in it.

Perhaps the least tractable problem in staging *Much Ado* is the need to clarify yet retain the immediacy of its social premises and—a less difficult task—its psychological insights. No production, however ingenious, can recreate the Elizabethan audience. For them *Much Ado* took place in the present; for us it takes place in an alien past. That love was emasculating and that male honour depended on female exclusivity are ideas that now require (one hopes) as much explanation as the play's allusions to horns and recheats. The violent misogyny that justifies and follows from such ideas appears without warning in unlikely literary and social contexts, something our carefully sanitized classroom literature of the Renaissance does not prepare us for. Accordingly, the men in the play, and to a lesser extent the women, exhibit behaviour and emotions that, while generally understandable, seem at times odd, the justifications for male behaviour having changed more than the situation of women.

The difficulty of finding explanatory contexts for 'the peculiar institution' of Honour in *Much Ado* creates an obvious temptation to play it as costume comedy, since breeches and romance can disguise the peculiar as the picturesque. Yet historical imagination can illuminate the social distance, as John Barton's production showed. The psychological distance, however, is much less, and this aspect of the play's love relations can be conveyed more easily. Benedick's 'tyrannical' wit and Beatrice's sophistry can become metaphors for the common hesitation before the dangers of sexual commitment.

Much Ado ends in two small civil victories, the dismantling of a few barriers to a remarkable intimacy, and the partial relief of one instance of a continuing systemic injustice. That criticism finds both the intimacy and the relief highly problematic says as much about the current contexts of interpretation as about the play. The current immediacy of *Much Ado* is not only a piece of theatrical good luck but a social misfortune.

Some Recent Directions

Scholarship during the last few decades has dealt well with *Much Ado About Nothing,* producing exemplary work on the play's editorial problems, notably by Stanley Wells, and on its stage history, as in the J. F. Cox essay on the acting traditions of the 'Kill Claudio' scene. Pamela Mason has a useful treatment of the play in performance.[1] An ingenious and highly informative theatrical explication is Harold Jenkins's essay on the ballroom scene.[2] For different audiences, J. R. Mulryne's *Shakespeare: 'Much Ado About Nothing'* (1965) has become a standard vade-mecum, and the introductions to school editions of the play are almost without exception worth consulting.

In the main, criticism since the late 1950s has kept to three broad paths. The first of these, which goes back to R. G. White's comments in his 1883 edition of the play, explores the implications of its concern with 'noting', and more broadly with the human incapacity for understanding either the self or others. Perhaps the most forceful interpretation of the play in these terms is A. P. Rossiter's argument that 'misapprehensions, misprisions, misunderstandings, misinterpretations and misapplications are the best names for what the comedy *as a whole* is "about" '.[3] Rossiter's italics allow for his examination of the play's representation of love, among other matters that seem to qualify his conclusion that '*Much Ado* is not a "serious" play'. The play is discussed along similar lines with varying degrees of seriousness and philosophic concern by such critics as Francis Fergusson[4] as a dramatization of human frailty in gathering and judging information; a demonstration of the isolation of individuals in the unique 'reality' that each apprehends;[5] and merely a bright entertainment that exploits the comic side of the unreliability of human behaviour. The difficulty such criticism occasionally

---

[1] In the Macmillan Plays in Performance series (1992).

[2] In B. Fabian and K. Tetzeli von Rosador (eds.), *Shakespeare: Text, Language, Criticism* (Hildesheim 1987), 98–117.

[3] Rossiter, *Angel with Horns,* 77.

[4] F. Fergusson, 'The *Comedy of Errors* and *Much Ado About Nothing*', *Sewanee Review,* 62 (1954), 24–37.

[5] D. Horowitz, *Shakespeare: An Existentialist View* (1965), 19–36.

encounters is the difficulty of isolating misnoting as a theme from the machinery of comic intrigue, which inevitably exploits differences in the information possessed by different characters.

Elizabethan attitudes, especially those bearing on the treatment of Hero, had been discussed in the 1930s and before, but discussions of gender differences in current terms stem from Barbara Everett's seminal article.[1] For Everett the distinguishing quality of *Much Ado* lay in its insistence on the radical difference in outlook and behaviour between women and men. That *Much Ado* is Shakespeare's first play in which 'the women's world dominates' reflects the importance of this difference, as does the symbolic challenge to male solidarity in Beatrice's co-option of Benedick to 'Kill Claudio'. These priorities, which in 1961 Everett saw as the reasons for its lagging behind other plays in popularity, are precisely what made it of interest in the following decades.

Much Ado has rewarded close attention by feminist critics. Carol Thomas Neely's study of the play provides a subtle running commentary on character and event.[2] Neely is particularly acute in her discussion of male animosity to love, and of the function of bawdry, especially jokes about cuckolding, as both implying and protecting male authority, which appears benign in the play largely because it is ineffectual. She is not alone among feminist critics in rejecting a simple affirmative view of the conclusion of the play. Carol Cook concludes that masculine domination is neither changed nor challenged in the play and that in effect Hero remains dead despite her symbolic resurrection.[3] Several critics deal with *Much Ado* in the influential collection, *The Woman's Part: Feminist Criticism of Shakespeare*.[4] Carole McKewin has sensitive readings of intimate conversations among women, particularly of the scene in Hero's dressing-room (pp. 124–6), and Clara Claiborne Park makes some astringent comments on how women like Beatrice are forced to temper their superior

---

[1] B. Everett, '*Much Ado About Nothing*', *Critical Quarterly* (1961), 319–35.

[2] Neely, *Broken Nuptials in Shakespeare's Plays*.

[3] C. Cook, 'The Sign and Semblance of Her Honour'.

[4] C. Lenz, G. Greene, and C. Neely (eds.), *The Woman's Part: Feminist Criticism of Shakespeare* (Urbana, Ill., 1980).

wit in order to protect fragile male egos. The consensus, as Marilyn Williamson puts it,[1] is that *Much Ado* 'reaffirms basic social structures'. How it differs in doing so from a play like Heywood's *Woman Killed with Kindness* is perhaps the next obligatory issue.

Another productive strain in recent criticism examines the society of Messina, at once the scene of deception, intrigue, and the naïve misjudgement of both. Rossiter had characterized Messina as 'no place to trust any man's word' and suggested the upper-class affinities of the play's wit and brittleness. These observations have been elaborated by later critics, among them Elliot Krieger.[2] He defines *Much Ado* as Shakespeare's 'clearest dramatic treatment of the difficulty a ruling class faces in its attempt to isolate itself from inquiry into the traditions and appearances on which it has constructed its scale of values, and of the quantitative loss—on the level of morality and character—that such an isolation entails'. More recent Marxisizing and social criticism continues and refines such themes, as, for example, in Richard A. Levin's *Love and Society in Shakespearean Comedy*,[3] where Messina's shortcomings are analysed in circumstantial detail. It is possible, however, that the specifically political 'decadence' of governing Messina is not foremost among the author's concerns. It is only more easily discussed because of the inherited main plot rather than qualitatively different from the social ambience of Othello's Venice, Hamlet's Elsinore, or even Prospero's island.

An essay that brings together both feminist and more general social concerns is Jean E. Howard's densely argued 'Renaissance Anti-theatricality and the Politics of Gender and Rank in *Much Ado About Nothing*'.[4] Howard thinks of the public theatre as 'one of the chief ideological apparatuses of Elizabethan society'. She goes on to argue, however, that

---

[1] In *The Patriarchy of Shakespeare's Comedies* (Detroit, 1986), 51.

[2] His 'Social Relations and the Social Order in *Much Ado About Nothing*', *Shakespeare Survey 32* (1979), has a convenient review of earlier criticism in this vein.

[3] R. A. Levin, *Love and Society in Shakespearean Comedy* (Newark, NJ, 1985), 86–115.

[4] In the collection J. E. Howard and M. F. O'Connor (eds.), *Shakespeare Reproduced: The Text in History and Ideology* (1987).

'precisely the work's [*Much Ado's*] distance from overtly po-
lemical intent makes it an effective producer-disseminator of
ideology' (p. 174), here the 'male aristocratic theatricality'
legitimated by the final scene. The love of Beatrice and Benedick, Howard continues, 'can be read as encoding the process
by which the powerful determine truth and the way in which
belief depends upon the degree to which a fiction chimes in
with the common sense of the culture' (p. 179). This follows
from an earlier statement that when Beatrice and Benedick
fall in love 'they reveal their successful interpellation into
positions within a gendered social order' (p. 178).

A third direction in recent criticism of *Much Ado* treats what
was once dismissed as the rather hopeless generic mixture
represented by the two plots. Two accomplished discussions
deal with this concern. Alexander Leggatt traces the relation
between realism and convention in the play and uncovers the
parallelism of the two plots.[1] John Traugott traces Benedick's
romance lineage and then turns to a highly sophisticated
discussion of the mutual transformation of the two genres as
it occurs in *Much Ado*.[2]

[1] A. Leggatt, *Shakespeare's Comedy of Love* (1974).
[2] J. Traugott, 'Creating a Rational Rinaldo: A Study in the Mixture of the
Genres of Comedy and Romance in *Much Ado About Nothing*', *Genre*, 15
(1982), 157–81.

TEXTUAL INTRODUCTION

'Staying' and Publication

Later editions of *Much Ado* are based on the Quarto of 1600, first mentioned in a note dated 4 August on a fly-leaf in a volume of the Stationers' Register. (The year 1600, assigned by Edward Arber, the Victorian transcriber of the Register, is not in dispute.) The gist of the note is that *As You Like It*, *Henry V*, Jonson's *Every Man in His Humour*, and '*The comedie of muche A doo about nothinge | A booke*' are 'to be staied'. Both the origin and meaning of the note are unclear. Was it a step to protect plays which Shakespeare's company were not ready to release to the printer? Was publication to be stayed, or only formal entry in the Register? The note is further clouded in such vexed questions of printing history as the validity of 'blocking entries', and the operations of 'pirate' printers, now increasingly doubted.

The struggle against the pirates, if that is what prompted the note, succeeded only in part; an 'illicit' *Henry V* did appear. *Much Ado* was entered in the Stationers' Register on 23 August 1600 in the conventional manner and appeared later that year.

The Quarto title-page offers the reader:

[ornament] | Much adoe about | Nothing. | *As it hath been sundrie times* publikely | acted by the right honourable, the Lord | Chamberlaine his seruants. | *Written by William Shakespeare.* | [ornament] | LONDON | Printed by V.S. for Andrew Wise, and | William Aspley. | 1600.

V.S. was Valentine Simmes, a London printer responsible for the first quartos of Shakespeare's Richard plays and later for the first quarto of *Hamlet*. In 1600 he also printed *2 Henry IV*, whose title-page has standing type which reappears in *Much Ado*. Bartlett and Pollard count seventeen known copies of Q, four defective, the others with five obvious corrections of errors and minor changes in spelling or punctuation from copy to copy. Werstine has made a particular study of the Bodmer Quarto, known but unavailable to Bartlett and

Pollard. The text of this edition derives from the Folger Library copy of Q, which I have collated with Hinman's Oxford Shakespeare Quarto Facsimile, based on the Trinity College, Cambridge, Quarto. Hinman's facsimile records all known quarto variants. First Folio citations are from the Norton Facsimile, also prepared by Hinman.

Setting the Text

Apparently Q was set entirely by Simmes's Compositor A, whose professional fingerprint is the absence of periods after unabbreviated speech-prefixes. Compositor A set a neat page with few obvious errors; even the inverted 'g' in 'Song' (see collation at 5.3.12) seems to have resulted from the inking process rather than from faulty type-setting. Yet modern editors could have been better served by someone less resourceful. A was intelligent enough to make sense of what he set, so he left few anomalies to signal departures from his copy or problems in it. Yet he did make minor omissions, substitutions, interpolations, and transpositions.

The 1600 Quarto was set from the author's manuscript or a transcription of it. Q preserves inconsistent speech-prefixes, 'ghost' characters, missing entrances and exits, and other tell-tales of 'foul papers'. Yet these are mere gnats to vex editors; Q presents only minor problems.

The many characters in *Much Ado* (Beatrice, Benedick, Borachio, Balthasar, Boy, Brother [Antonio], Bastard) whose names begin with 'B' provide clues to how Compositor A set his copy. After exhausting the italic *B* in his case, he substituted roman B and reused italic *B* from the type set for a page just printed. Typographical features like this told John Hazel Smith[1] that Q had been set by formes rather than consecutive pages. It would have followed that anomalies in Q—a crowded page, verse printed as prose—should be attributed to inaccuracies in estimating the copy needed to fill a printed page, rather than to problems in the copy itself. However, evidence drawn from successive positions of distinct-

[1] J. H. Smith, 'The Composition of the Quarto of *Much Ado About Nothing*', *Studies in Bibliography*, 16 (1963), 9–26.

ive pieces of type was used by Hinman (pp. xiv–xvii) to demonstrate that Q was set, not by formes, but seriatim. Hinman's cautious 'for the most part' does not invalidate his conclusion that Q's 'textual peculiarities' are likely attributable to difficulties in the copy. Many editorial problems raised by 'foul-paper' copy have been resolved or clarified by Stanley Wells in 'Foul-Paper Texts', to which all subsequent editors are indebted.

'Ghosts'

Both the first and second acts of the quarto open with a direction for the entrance of Leonato and his wife Innogen. Nowhere does Innogen speak or act, nor is she spoken to or about; she is a textual ghost. Her presence in the directions and her absence from the dialogue prompt different lines of explanation. There is an Innogen-figure in the Bandello story. Yet in the theatre *Much Ado* would be awkward with a fully functioning Innogen. Without her, Hero may be presumed under looser supervision and more vulnerable to social chance, and Leonato more ready to turn on her. More important, maternal protests would have diluted the pathos of Hero's situation and her dependency on Beatrice.

The Innogen puzzle lies also in her inclusion in the entrance direction for the second act. Since she was not needed in the first act, presumably Innogen was unlikely to appear later. Arguing from actors' names in some Q speech-prefixes (now attributed to Shakespeare), E. K. Chambers proposed a 'second hand', the book-keeper's, annotating the copy set by Compositor A. More plausible is Honigmann's suggestion that 2.1 or part of it may have been written before 1.1.[1] Non-serial composition can produce seamless work, yet the chatty character-exposition opening 2.1 seems unlikely as material to be worked up before establishing the plot lines of 1.1. Even assuming that 1.1 *was* the scene written later, why repeat in 1.1 what had been abandoned in 2.1?

Elsewhere too any thought to add visual weight to Leonato's household gave way to the economies of composition. Innogen

---

[1] E. A. J. Honigmann, *The Stability of Shakespeare's Text* (1965), 147 n. 3.

is accompanied in the 2.1 stage directions by a ghost-kins-
man; a ghost-cousin is spoken of as the son of '*Anthonio*' at
the start of 1.2., but his existence is denied in 5.1, where
Hero is presented as the sole heir of both brothers. Of Antonio
himself there have been questions because of the various
speech-prefixes and inconsistent references to the role. And
though they are hardly ghosts, Balthasar and the Sexton
sometimes appear in stage directions yet say nothing in the
dialogue (2.1, 5.1) that follows.

E. K. Chambers suggested that many difficulties could be
resolved if such shadowy junior characters were combined.[1]
Yet whatever uses Shakespeare may have first seen for them,
kinsman, cousin and son were all likely to have been of
duelling age, thus dangerously capable of upsetting the plot
by contesting the insult to Hero more effectively than Leonato
or Benedick.

Speech-Prefixes

Wells observes that five of the Watch speeches in 3.3 (at lines
37, 44, 48, and 53 of this edition) 'could be spoken by the
same man', any one of three Watchmen on stage.[2] Rowe's
allocation of these speeches to Watch 2 looks unsatisfactory
to Wells since it enlarges a part without justification. It also
negates what may have been Shakespeare's decision to leave
the allocation of speeches and the number of the Watch up
to the circumstances of production. A touring cast with several novices and only one comic actor up to playing Watch
2 is one such circumstance, but only one. Flexibility in
allocating minor roles permitted adjusting the burden on
actors of limited ability or experience, and it saved money on
hired men.

Also telling against editorial rationalization of the Watch
speech-prefixes is an inferable pattern of composition. The first
three Watch speeches in 3.3 are allocated as follows: the first
to Watch 1 and the second and third to Watch 2; the nine
which follow are undifferentiated. The last four in the scene

---

[1] *William Shakespeare*, i. 386.   [2] Wells, 'Foul-Paper Texts', 11.

are given alternately to Watch 1 and Watch 2. In 4.2 the first three Watch speeches are alternated, the last given to Watch. Of the twenty speeches assigned to the Watch, then, Q gives five to Watch 1, five to Watch 2, and ten simply to Watch. This shows an initial differentiation that lapses as composition progresses, but is revived toward the end of 3.3, where the last four Watch speeches follow one another. Apart from the allocation of speeches here the speeches show little occasion or substantive need for individuation. The inferable pattern of work parallels the one that produced the ghost figures of Innogen and the kinsman: assembling what might come in handy, using what was needed.

The abandonment of individuated Watch speech-prefixes suggests more than the Law of Least Effort. Consider one alternative to the assumption that Shakespeare intended a consistent attribute (pompous literacy) or a role (leadership) in the Watch characters. A pomposity infecting *all* the constabulary and the conspicuous lack of a proper chain of command can 'play' at least as comically as strict hierarchy and doing the police in several voices. Dogberry has character enough. What Keystone Kops do best is get in one another's way, here perhaps by trying to outdo one another in self-importance.

A possible clue to Shakespeare's conception of the Watch as unindividuated lies in the reuse of the surname Seacoal for both George and Francis, the latter presumably the sexton. This overlap may be a sly allusion to nepotism, but seems to me evidence of imagination choosing to work at a low level of character-specificity, with 'Seacoal' as a mental catch-all for minor officialdom.

Modern editions deal with Q's Watch speech-prefixes in various ways, all defensible, all tending to alter Q's allocations to accommodate some principle of individuation. This edition assigns all the Watch speeches to A WATCHMAN, leaving individuation to the actors. To abandon the First and Second Watchmen is not to abandon Q or its copy, but to follow Shakespeare's treatment of the Watch as illustrative and choral. The change may also further what has in any case been stage practice: varying the number and character of the members of the Watch as each production warrants.

Another textual cat's cradle involves speech-prefixes in the dance sequence of 2.1. After the initial 'bout' between Don Pedro and Hero, Margaret dances forward—with whom? Q's speech-prefixes make her partner Benedick (*Bene.*) for three speeches and then Balthasar (*Balth.*) for two. Capell tried to save the appearances by adding a direction for a change of partners. Dover Wilson rejected both Benedick and Balthasar in favour of Borachio, 'the obvious partner for Margaret'. Theobald allocated Benedick's speeches to Balthasar; most editors agree. Wells suggests palaeographic reasons for Compositor A's possible misreading of hasty script or abbreviations.[1] Compositor A must have found the abbreviated speech-prefixes with their easily misread vowels and appetite for italic *B* a great nuisance.

Wells infers their history from Q's speech-prefixes and 2.1's obviously flawed entrance direction: *Enter prince, Pedro, Claudio, and Benedicke, and Balthaser, or dumb Iohn.* Here *dumb Iohn* seems a misreading of Don John, and the awkward succession of ands and commas looks like second thoughts about likely characters for the scene. Wells conjectures that the speeches attributed to Benedick may have been intended for him at first but, realizing that he could wring a climax from a Beatrice–Benedick encounter later on, Shakespeare continued the Margaret–Balthasar dialogue, allocating subsequent male speeches to Balthasar without correcting the prefixes of earlier ones. Wells's reconstruction frees Compositor A of the onus of misreading.

Yet the Margaret–Balthasar dialogue might have been intended from the outset, and the male speech-prefixes misread. Far from being the obvious partner for Margaret, Borachio is the *least* appropriate. Presumably Borachio is sufficiently in her good graces for Margaret to consent to her unwitting part in his plot against Hero. Yet from the beginning of this exchange Margaret is stand-offish, and her last speech prays God to keep her partner from her sight afterward: hardly the language for flirting with Borachio. However, the ineffectual Balthasar is just right for such treatment. His embarrassment separates the coquetry of the Hero–Don Pedro encounter from

---

[1] Ibid. 8–10.

the tensions of Beatrice and Benedick: a nicely contrasting triad of female self-possession.

Entrances and Exits

A likely intervention of Compositor A in the placement of Q's exit directions occurs at 5.4.12, where '*Exeunt Ladies*' is next to a short line, evidently because there is room for it. Since the stage is not cleared, some specification of the exiting characters might have been expected; available page-space may also dictate '*Ladies*' rather than a naming of persons. If so congratulations go to Compositor A. The exit direction at 3.5.50 seems another instance of placement at the compositor's convenience. Yet, as with other stage directions appearing earlier than they might in a modern edition, the placement may reflect an anticipatory cue for backstage use.

The exits and entrances are what we should expect of foul papers. Exit directions are missing at the end of five of the play's seventeen scenes. The last scene, 3.4, 3.5, and 4.1 have clear verbal cues for closure that might have made exit indications seem unnecessary. Yet mid-scene exits are also inconsistently indicated. For example, there are no mid-scene exits for Don Pedro, Claudio, and Leonato in 2.3, for Hero and Ursula in 3.1, or for Dogberry and Verges in 5.1. Perhaps modern editions, following Cambridge in this last example, take what seems a verbal cue too literally, and so keep Dogberry and Verges from exiting shortly afterward with the Watch. At any rate, in the two other instances the missing exits occur before first Benedick and then Beatrice emerge from hiding, providing the players with physical indications of the staging.

Quarto entrances also ignore the needs and conventions of print. In evidence is Shakespeare's gathering-winnowing method of writing, and his apparent reliance on the actors to pick up or invent details of staging during the collaborative work of performance. For example, Q gives us no entrance for attendants at 1.2.21, or for a messenger at 3.5.51, but these are easily inferred from the text. As we have seen, other entrance directions give us too many characters or, as in the case of Margaret and Ursula in the dance scene, do not clarify their point of entrance. Yet words like 'hasty' and 'careless' have been applied unjustly to the manuscript from which the 1600 Quarto was set. It is a playscript, not intended as the Elizabethan equivalent of camera-ready copy. The dramatist sets down as much as the players need; what questions they have, they can ask him.

The Play in Folio

The 1623 Folio *Much Ado* has no independent authority; it was set from a typographically uncorrected copy of the Quarto which had evidently been lightly annotated after glancing comparison with a prompt-book. F makes some obvious minor corrections, such as 'made an' for Q's 'made and'. But it also introduces minor errors and indifferent substitutions.[1] To editors the usefulness of the Folio lies in its stage directions and speech-prefixes. From the latter we learn that 'Iacke Wilson', of whom little else is certain, was the musician in 2.3. F also supplies some missing exits at the ends of scenes and at mid-scene in 2.3 and 3.1. Yet the Folio seems hardly closer to the stage than is Q. F's business-like *'Enter the Prince'* at 2.1.211 may be nearer to what was staged than Q's prudent inclusion of Hero, Leonato, Don John, Borachio, and Conrad, none of whom speaks until about fifty lines later. Moreover, as Wells points out, F, unlike Q, has Leonato and Hero enter more appropriately at 259 on the same F direction as Claudio and Beatrice. This arrival as a quartet, however, is odd either before or after Don Pedro's 'Look, here she comes'—she being Beatrice. In the old Arden edition Grace Trenery argued that the entrance of Claudio is prepared for, but not that of Leonato and Hero (Trenery, 93). Wells tries to meet this objection by suggesting that the two pairs enter through different doors.[2] This reduces one difficulty but may create another. The artificiality of symmetrical entrances weakens the attempt to naturalize the F stage direction, and having Claudio and Hero on stage together at this point raises expectations of an exchange the writer could hardly postpone.

[1] See S. Wells and G. Taylor, *William Shakespeare: A Textual Companion* (Oxford, 1987), 371–4.
[2] 'Foul-Paper Texts', 6.

The staging remains unclear despite F. I am persuaded that Harold Jenkins's conjecture of an entrance for Hero and Leonato after 261 is not only theatrically effective but likely to have been the historical staging. F's earlier mention of Hero and Leonato may be anticipatory.

That F does not go beyond Q argues that repeated performance of *Much Ado* showed little need for revision, and that, far from being careless, the foul papers had most things right. In an interview Trevor Nunn remarked that 'The text that I didn't trust and should have trusted, was *Much Ado About Nothing*'.[1]

---

[1] Berry, *On Directing Shakespeare*, 70.

EDITORIAL PROCEDURES

Editorial procedures for the Oxford Shakespeare are set out in the introduction to Gary Taylor's edition of *Henry V* and in Stanley Wells's *Modernizing*;[1] Wells's discussion of the editorial treatment of 'Foul-Paper Texts' centres on *Much Ado*. However, a few matters relevant to this edition should be recalled and some others stated.

As stated earlier, the basis of this edition is the Folger Library copy of Q, which has been compared with the Hinman facsimile. However, non-substantive variants or obvious errors in copies of Q have not been collated. F (for which I use the Norton Facsimile) has some useful stage directions and offers precedents for 'modern' spellings (e.g. 'victual') and some minor corrections, yet F does not routinely appear in the collation here as it does in some editions. F's obvious errors are not collated; nor are F's omissions, even when they make sense, as in the dropping of 'up' from Q's 'bind him up a rod' at 2.1.219. One exception occurs at 2.3.43.1, when F's omission may indicate current staging. When F corrects Q, it is of course collated. Although it is probably a compositor's error, F's 'will' for Q's 'good will' at 2.1.216 is among a few readings that suggest nuances of meaning; it is accordingly collated.

F's division into acts has been retained. Scene division and scene location are the work of editors and not collated. All significant departures from the language of Q have been collated. Where an emendation is in dispute as at 2.3.43, the main alternatives appear in the collation. In a few instances, such as Theobald's 'noting' for Q's 'nothing' at 2.3.58, a rejected emendation has been collated because of its scholarly or critical interest.

Modernizations of Q's spelling and diction are typically uncollated except when the modern word might seem remote from Q, as at 1.1.40; or when the modernization is in dispute as at 2.3.171 and 5.1.38; or when, as in the opening stage direction of 3.3, the modernization offered breaks with editor-

[1] S. Wells, *Modernizing Shakespeare's Spelling* (Oxford, 1979).

ial tradition. When modernization would belie Elizabethan usage, forms such as 'holp' (1.1.48) are silently retained. Also kept but not collated are 'an' for the modern 'if' (Q often uses 'and', F. 'an'), 'o' for Q's 'a' (typically F's 'of'), Q's 'a' for the modern 'he', and F's modern 'Count' for Q's 'County'. Quotation marks and apostrophes indicating possession are editorial and uncollated. Q and F are cited in the original spelling.

Q's punctuation has also been modernized. Where this may seem to alter the meaning of Q, which is sometimes ambiguous because of light pointing, or because of Elizabethan conventions such as those governing the use of question marks; or where punctuation is at issue in disputed meanings, the punctuation is collated, as at 2.3.106–7. Dashes replacing Q's periods at the end of incomplete sentences are not collated, nor are dashes collated when used in this edition to signal mid-speech changes in tone, topic, or persons addressed. The punctuation of Q presents problems not to be resolved to anyone's complete satisfaction. An extreme 'modern' lightening of Q's punctuation may hide ambiguities and limit useful indications of meaning and rhetorical phrasing. The alternative, however, may lead to inconsistency and to seeming to direct the play through the punctuation.

Speech-prefixes are collated to record the playwright's shifting emphasis on aspects of the speaker ('brother' and 'old man' for Antonio), his choice of the actor for the role (4.2.2), or to record a speech-allocation in dispute (2.1.101), or a questionable expansion (4.2.62). Excepted are the shifts between 'Prince' and 'Don Pedro', which seem to me of little significance. Disputed speech allocations are signalled in the text by broken brackets around the speech-prefix.

Directions for entrance and exit are collated when they differ from Q in form, substance, or position in the text. In cases where a Folio or an editor has supplied an uncomplicated exit missing from Q, the collation reads only 'not in Q'; changes from 'Exit' or 'Manet' to 'Exeunt' or 'Manent' are collated. Additional stage directions for delivery and stage movement— all but absent in Q—have been introduced for clarity. Most follow from the dialogue and are part of the common editorial legacy; they are rarely collated unless they are in dispute or otherwise problematic, in which case they appear in the text between broken brackets.

Abbreviations and References

The following abbreviations are used in the introduction, collations, and commentary. Unless otherwise specified, the place of publication is London. Abbreviations of the titles of academic journals are those in standard use.

EDITIONS OF SHAKESPEARE

Q	*Much adoe about Nothing*, 1600
F	The First Folio, 1623
F2	The Second Folio, 1632
F3	The Third Folio, 1663
Alexander	Peter Alexander, *Complete Works* (1951)
Boas	F. S. Boas, *Much Ado About Nothing*, Clarendon Select Plays of Shakespeare (Oxford, 1916)
Cambridge	W. G. Clark and W. A. Wright, *Works*, The Cambridge Shakespeare, 9 vols. (Cambridge, 1863–6)
Capell	Edward Capell, *Comedies, Histories, and Tragedies*, 10 vols. (1767–8)
Collier	John Payne Collier, *Works*, 8 vols. (1842–4)
Collier 1853	John Payne Collier, *Plays* (1853)
Dyce	Alexander Dyce, *Works*, 6 vols. (1857)
Foakes	R. A. Foakes, *Much Ado About Nothing*, New Penguin Shakespeare (Harmondsworth, 1968)
Hanmer	Thomas Hanmer, *Works*, 6 vols. (Oxford, 1743–4)
Hinman	Charlton Hinman, *Much Ado About Nothing*, Shakespeare Quarto Facsimiles, no. 15 (Oxford, 1971)
Humphreys	A. R. Humphreys, *Much Ado About Nothing*, new Arden Shakespeare (1981)
Johnson	Samuel Johnson, *Plays*, 8 vols. (1765)
Kittredge	G. L. Kittredge, *Complete Works* (Boston, 1936)
Knight	Charles Knight, *Works*, Pictorial Edition, 8 vols. (1838–43)
Lewalski	Barbara Lewalski, *Much Ado About Nothing* (Dubuque, Ia., 1969)

Malone	Edmond Malone, *Plays and Poems*, 10 vols. (1790)
Mares	F. H. Mares, *Much Ado About Nothing*, the New Cambridge Shakespeare (Cambridge, 1988)
Newcomer	A. G. Newcomer, *Much Ado About Nothing* (1929, rpt. New York, 1967)
Norton Facsimile	Charlton Hinman, *The First Folio of Shakespeare: The Norton Facsimile* (1968)
Oxford	Stanley Wells and Gary Taylor, *Complete Works* (Oxford, 1986)
Pope	Alexander Pope, *Works*, 6 vols. (1723–5)
Pope 1728	Alexander Pope, *Works*, 10 vols. (1728)
Reed–Steevens	Isaac Reed, *Plays*, with notes by George Steevens and Samuel Johnson, 15 vols. (1793)
Riverside	G. B. Evans (textual editor), *The Riverside Shakespeare* (Boston, 1974)
Rowe	Nicholas Rowe, *Works*, 6 vols. (1709)
Rowe 1714	Nicholas Rowe, *Works*, 8 vols. (1714)
Staunton	Howard Staunton, *Plays*, 3 vols. (1858–60)
Steevens	Samuel Johnson and George Steevens, *Plays*, 10 vols. (1773)
Steevens 1778	Samuel Johnson and George Steevens, *Plays*, 10 vols. (1778)
Stevenson	David Stevenson, *Much Ado About Nothing*, Signet Classic Shakespeare (New York, 1964)
Theobald	Lewis Theobald, *Works*, 7 vols. (1733)
Trenery	Grace Trenery, *Much Ado About Nothing*, Arden Shakespeare (1924)
Warburton	William Warburton, *Works*, 8 vols. (1747)
Variorum	H. H. Furness, *Much Ado About Nothing*, New Variorum Edition (Philadelphia, 1899)
White	R. G. White, *Works*, 12 vols. (Boston, 1857–66)
Wilson	J. Dover Wilson and A. Quiller-Couch, *Much Ado About Nothing*, New Shakespeare (Cambridge, 1923)

OTHER WORKS

Abbott	E. A. Abbott, *A Shakespearian Grammar*, 3rd edn. (1870)

Bartlett and Pollard   H. C. Bartlett and A. W. Pollard, *A Census of Shakespeare's Plays in Quarto*, 1594–1709 (New Haven, Conn., 1916)

Bullough   Geoffrey Bullough, *Narrative and Dramatic Sources of Shakespeare*, 8 vols. (1957–75)

Cercignani   Fausto Cercignani, *Shakespeare's Works and Elizabethan Pronunciation* (Oxford, 1981)

Craven   Alan E. Craven, 'Compositor Analysis to Edited Text: Some Suggested Readings in *Richard II* and *Much Ado About Nothing*', *Papers of the Bibliographical Society of America*, 26 (1982), 43–62

Jenkins   Harold Jenkins, 'The Ball Scene in *Much Ado 'About Nothing*', in B. Fabian and K. Tetzeli von Rosador (eds.), *Shakespeare: Text, Language, Criticism* (Hildesheim, 1987)

Prouty   Charles T. Prouty, *The Sources of* 'Much Ado About Nothing' (New Haven, Conn., 1950)

Sipe   Dorothy Sipe, *Shakespeare's Metrics* (New Haven, Conn., 1968)

Thirlby   (Styan Thirlby provided notes for Theobald's editions.)

Tilley   M. P. Tilley, *A Dictionary of the Proverbs in England in the Sixteenth and Seventeenth Centuries* (Ann Arbor, Mich., 1950)

Werstine   Paul Werstine, 'The Bodmer Copy of Shakespeare's *Much Ado About Nothing* Q1', *Notes and Queries* (Apr. 1983), 123–4

Much Ado About Nothing

THE PERSONS OF THE PLAY

DON PEDRO, Prince of Aragon

BENEDICK, of Padua ⎫
CLAUDIO, of Florence ⎭ lords, companions of Don Pedro

BALTHASAR, attendant on Don Pedro, a singer

DON JOHN, the bastard brother of Don Pedro

BORACHIO ⎫
CONRAD ⎭ followers of Don John

LEONATO, Governor of Messina

HERO, his daughter

BEATRICE, an orphan, his niece

ANTONIO, an old man, brother of Leonato

MARGARET ⎫
URSULA ⎭ waiting gentlewomen attendant on Hero

FRIAR Francis

DOGBERRY, the Constable in charge of the Watch

VERGES, the Headborough, Dogberry's partner

A SEXTON

WATCHMEN

A BOY, serving Benedick

Attendants and Messengers

Much Ado About Nothing

1.1 *Enter Leonato, governor of Messina, Hero his*
daughter, and Beatrice his niece, with a Messenger

LEONATO I learn in this letter that Don Pedro of Aragon
comes this night to Messina.

MESSENGER He is very near by this. He was not three
leagues off when I left him.

LEONATO How many gentlemen have you lost in this 5
action?

MESSENGER But few of any sort, and none of name.

LEONATO A victory is twice itself when the achiever
brings home full numbers. I find here that Don Pedro
hath bestowed much honour on a young Florentine 10
called Claudio.

MESSENGER Much deserved on his part, and equally
remembered by Don Pedro. He hath borne himself
beyond the promise of his age, doing in the figure of
a lamb the feats of a lion. He hath indeed better 15
bettered expectation than you must expect of me to
tell you how.

LEONATO He hath an uncle here in Messina will be very
much glad of it.

MESSENGER I have already delivered him letters, and 20

1.1] *Actus primus, Scena prima* F; *not in* Q   0.1–2] THEOBALD; ~ *Innogen his wife,* (*after*
'*Messina,*') Q   9 *Pedro*] ROWE; Peter Q

1.1.0 On the 'ghost' figure of Innogen see
   Introd. p. 81.
3–4 **three leagues** about nine miles or
   fourteen kilometres
6 **action** battle
7 **sort ... name** high social rank ... personal celebrity. 'Sort' still implied the
   'select', e.g. *Measure* 4.4.19, where,
   speaking of noblemen who are to meet
   the Duke, Angelo tells Escalus to
   'give notice to such men of sort ....'
   Presumably the death of common
   soldiers did not matter; hence the
   callousness of 'full numbers' (9) and

'sort' again (32).
8 **achiever** winner
12–3 **equally remembered** appropriately
   rewarded
13–16 The alliteration, antithesis, allusions to natural history, and coy denials of rhetorical adequacy here recall
   the affected courtliness encouraged by
   John Lyly's *Euphues* novels. Leonato
   matches the style in 21–3.
18 **uncle** Claudio is well connected in
   Messina, already a basis for the match
   with Hero; the uncle is not mentioned
   again.

there appears much joy in him, even so much that
joy could not show itself modest enough without a
badge of bitterness.

LEONATO Did he break out into tears?

MESSENGER In great measure.   25

LEONATO A kind overflow of kindness; there are no
faces truer than those that are so washed. How much
better is it to weep at joy than to joy at weeping!

BEATRICE I pray you, is Signor Montanto returned from
the wars, or no?   30

MESSENGER I know none of that name, lady. There was
none such in the army, of any sort.

LEONATO What is he that you ask for, niece?

HERO My cousin means Signor Benedick of Padua.

MESSENGER O, he's returned, and as pleasant as ever   35
he was.

BEATRICE He set up his bills here in Messina, and
challenged Cupid at the flight; and my uncle's fool,
reading the challenge, subscribed for Cupid and challenged him at the bird-bolt. I pray you, how many   40
hath he killed and eaten in these wars? But how
many hath he killed? For indeed I promised to eat
all of his killing.

LEONATO Faith, niece, you tax Signor Benedick too

40 bird-bolt] Q (Burbolt)

23 **badge ... bitterness** The badges worn
by servants of noblemen were signs of
their inferior position; hence the
uncle's tears ('bitterness') absolved
him of an immodest sharing in Claudio's success. The Messenger's tortured
formality puzzles even Leonato.
26 **kind ... kindness** banal word-play on
kind = natural and = humane
26-7 **there ... washed** A common moral
notion; the Countess praises Helen so
in *All's Well* 1.1.44-5.
29 **Montanto** ironic, taken from the fencing term for an upward thrust; also
by extension 'aspiring', or social climbing, both with an unmistakable sexual
reference. Adventurous Beatrices, following Kathleen Widdowes, who
played the role in J. J. Antoon's New
York production of 1972, pronounce
it 'Mount on to', with a sexual allusion

to the common male position in inter-
course. Beatrice's impolite interruption
shows that Benedick is very much on
her mind.
32 **sort** rank
35 **pleasant** full of good humour
37 **bills** advertisements
39-40 **challenged ... bird-bolt** Presumably Benedick claims to be better at
archery (i.e. wounding hearts) than
Cupid himself. As challenger on
Cupid's behalf, Leonato's fool chooses
as his weapon a bird-bolt, whose relatively safe blunt wooden-headed arrow
for stunning birds made it favoured by
children and fools.
41 **killed and eaten** a common send-up of
affected ferocity, as in *Henry V* 3.7.91-
2, where the Dauphin is spoken of as
longing to eat all the English he kills.
44 **tax** criticize

much. But he'll be meet with you, I doubt it not.   45
MESSENGER He hath done good service, lady, in these
wars.
BEATRICE You had musty victual, and he hath holp to
eat it. He is a very valiant trencherman; he hath an
excellent stomach.   50
MESSENGER And a good soldier too, lady.
BEATRICE And a good soldier to a lady, but what is he
to a lord?
MESSENGER A lord to a lord, a man to a man, stuffed
with all honourable virtues.   55
BEATRICE It is so, indeed. He is no less than a stuffed
man. But for the stuffing—well, we are all mortal.
LEONATO You must not, sir, mistake my niece. There
is a kind of merry war betwixt Signor Benedick and
her. They never meet but there's a skirmish of wit   60
between them.
BEATRICE Alas, he gets nothing by that. In our last
conflict four of his five wits went halting off, and now
is the whole man governed with one; so that if he
have wit enough to keep himself warm, let him bear   65
it for a difference between himself and his horse, for
it is all the wealth that he hath left to be known a
reasonable creature. Who is his companion now? He
hath every month a new sworn brother.

57 stuffing—well] THEOBALD; stuffing wel Q

45 **be meet** get even
48 **holp** helped
49 **valiant trencherman** hearty eater;
   trencher = wooden platter, on which
   meals were commonly served.
50 **stomach** appetite, with a pun on stomach = courage
52 **to** compared to, faced with
54 **stuffed** full of. The expression was then
   less comic.
56-7 **stuffed man** scarecrow?
62-8 **In . . . creature** Beatrice wittily ignores Leonato's use of wit = repartee
   (presumably she refuses to think Benedick capable of a contest with her) and
   takes the word in its philosophical
   sense. The five wits or mental faculties—imagination, fantasy, estimation
   (i.e. judgement), memory, and the

'common sense' that mediates them—
were and are frequently confused with
the five senses, though not by Shakespeare here or in Sonnet 14. The wit
to keep warm (a proverbial minimum:
Tilley K10) seems at first referable to
the senses, but since superior reason
(estimation) was traditionally the difference between man and horse, Beatrice allows that something, but not
much, of Benedick's powers survived
his defeat by her; see Ruth Harvey,
*The Inward Wits: Psychological Theory
in the Middle Ages and the Renaissance*
(1975).
66 **difference** in heraldry the mark distinguishing the junior branch of a noble
   family; the horse here is senior.
68-9 **companion . . . sworn brother** Bea-

MESSENGER Is't possible?   70

BEATRICE Very easily possible. He wears his faith but
as the fashion of his hat; it ever changes with the
next block.

MESSENGER I see, lady, the gentleman is not in your
books.   75

BEATRICE No. An he were, I would burn my study. But
I pray you, who is his companion? Is there no young
squarer now that will make a voyage with him to
the devil?

MESSENGER He is most in the company of the right   80
noble Claudio.

BEATRICE O Lord, he will hang upon him like a disease.
He is sooner caught than the pestilence, and the
taker runs presently mad. God help the noble Claudio. If he have caught the Benedick, it will cost him   85
a thousand pound ere a be cured.

MESSENGER I will hold friends with you, lady.

BEATRICE Do, good friend.

LEONATO You will never run mad, niece.

BEATRICE No, not till a hot January.   90

MESSENGER Don Pedro is approached.

> *Enter Don Pedro, Claudio, Benedick, Balthasar, and*
> *Don John the Bastard*

DON PEDRO Good Signor Leonato, are you come to meet
your trouble? The fashion of the world is to avoid
cost, and you encounter it.

85 Benedick] F2; Benedict Q   91.1 Don] *not in* Q

trice is mocking the male 'bonding' of
the warrior code. 'Companion' is pejorative (see 67) and the whole speech
shocking to the Messenger.

71 **faith** lifelong oath of military brother-
hood
73 **next block** newest mould. Fashion in
hats changed with a notorious rapidity
useful to satirists.
74-5 **in ... books** now 'in your good
books'; Tilley B534
76 **study** library
77-8 **companion ... squarer** rogue, braw-
ler; both pejorative
84 **presently** at once
86 **thousand pound** The standard fee for

a physician's visit was one angel, a
gold coin worth 10s.
87 **hold** remain
91 **is approached** an obsolescent usage
typical of the messenger's precious
formality
91.2 *Bastard* A merely descriptive proto-
col title, yet Francis Bacon's use of
bastards in his *Essay of Envy* as examples of those who, unable to improve
their own, worsen the situations of
others stated the common belief. Don
John's illegitimacy is not revealed ex-
plicitly until 4.1.188, but the speech-
prefixes of 3.2 show how Shakespeare
conceived of him.

LEONATO Never came trouble to my house in the like-   95
ness of your grace; for trouble being gone, comfort
should remain. But when you depart from me, sorrow abides and happiness takes his leave.

DON PEDRO You embrace your charge too willingly. I
think this is your daughter.   100

LEONATO Her mother hath many times told me so.

BENEDICK Were you in doubt, sir, that you asked her?

LEONATO Signor Benedick, no, for then were you a
child.

DON PEDRO You have it full, Benedick. We may guess   105
by this what you are, being a man. Truly, the lady
fathers herself. Be happy, lady, for you are like an
honourable father.
(Speaks privately with Leonato)

BENEDICK If Signor Leonato be her father, she would
not have his head on her shoulders for all Messina,   110
as like him as she is.

BEATRICE I wonder that you will still be talking, Signor
Benedick; nobody marks you.

BENEDICK What, my dear Lady Disdain! Are you yet
living?   115

BEATRICE Is it possible disdain should die while she
hath such meet food to feed it as Signor Benedick?
Courtesy itself must convert to disdain if you come
in her presence.

BENEDICK Then is courtesy a turncoat. But it is certain   120
I am loved of all ladies, only you excepted. And I
would I could find in my heart that I had not a hard
heart, for truly I love none.

BEATRICE A dear happiness to women. They would else
have been troubled with a pernicious suitor. I thank   125

108.1 *Speaks . . . Leonato*] This edition; *not in* Q, F

106 **what you are** i.e. a womanizer, but
'being a man' seems both to legitimize
and indict all men
fathers herself by her resemblance to
Leonato
110 **head** Apparently this refers to Leonato's grey hair, but there is also a covert
reference to the cuckold's proverbial
horns and thus to Hero's possible ob-

jections. This provokes Beatrice's
reply, which may have been Benedick's aim.
117 **meet** appropriate
120–8 **But . . . loves me** Beatrice and
Benedick both protest their indifference, but make it clear that they are
unattached.
124 **dear happiness** precious good fortune

God and my cold blood I am of your humour for
that. I had rather hear my dog bark at a crow than
a man swear he loves me.

BENEDICK God keep your ladyship still in that mind. So
some gentleman or other shall scape a predestinate   130
scratched face.

BEATRICE Scratching could not make it worse an 'twere
such a face as yours were.

BENEDICK Well, you are a rare parrot-teacher.

BEATRICE A bird of my tongue is better than a beast of   135
yours.

BENEDICK I would my horse had the speed of your
tongue, and so good a continuer. But keep your way,
o' God's name. I have done.

BEATRICE You always end with a jade's trick. I know   140
you of old.

DON PEDRO (*ending his talk with Leonato*) That is the sum
of all, Leonato.—Signor Claudio and Signor Benedick,
my dear friend Leonato hath invited you all. I tell
him we shall stay here at the least a month, and he   145
heartily prays some occasion may detain us longer.
I dare swear he is no hypocrite, but prays from his
heart.

LEONATO If you swear, my lord, you shall not be forsworn. (*To Don John*) Let me bid you welcome, my   150
lord. Being reconciled to the Prince your brother, I
owe you all duty.

DON JOHN I thank you. I am not of many words, but I
thank you.

LEONATO (*to Don Pedro*) Please it your grace lead on?   155

DON PEDRO Your hand, Leonato. We will go together.
                    Exeunt all but Benedick and Claudio

CLAUDIO Benedick, didst thou note the daughter of
Signor Leonato?

142 *ending . . . Leonato*] This edition; *not in* Q   143 all, Leonato.] COLLIER 1876; all:
Leonato, Q   151 lord. Being . . . brother,] HANMER (*subs.*); lord, being brother: Q   156.1
Exeunt all but] Q (*Exeunt. Manent*)

134 **rare parrot-teacher** hence very good   140 **jade's trick** like a recalcitrant horse,
  at repetition   refusing to go on
135–6 **A bird . . . yours** At least birds can   149–50 **forsworn** proved false
  speak; beasts are dumb.   151 **Being** since you are
138 **so good a continuer** had such endur-
  ance

BENEDICK I noted her not, but I looked on her.

CLAUDIO Is she not a modest young lady?   160

BENEDICK Do you question me as an honest man should
  do, for my simple true judgement, or would you have
  me speak after my custom, as being a professed
  tyrant to their sex?

CLAUDIO No, I pray thee speak in sober judgement.   165

BENEDICK Why, i' faith, methinks she's too low for a
  high praise, too brown for a fair praise, and too little
  for a great praise. Only this commendation I can
  afford her, that were she other than she is she were
  unhandsome, and being no other but as she is, I do   170
  not like her.

CLAUDIO Thou thinkest I am in sport. I pray thee tell
  me truly how thou likest her.

BENEDICK Would you buy her, that you enquire after
  her?   175

CLAUDIO Can the world buy such a jewel?

BENEDICK Yea, and a case to put it into. But speak you
  this with a sad brow, or do you play the flouting
  Jack, to tell us Cupid is a good hare-finder and
  Vulcan a rare carpenter? Come, in what key shall a   180
  man take you to go in the song?

CLAUDIO In mine eye she is the sweetest lady that ever
  I looked on.

BENEDICK I can see yet without spectacles, and I see no
  such matter. There's her cousin, an she were not   185
  possessed with a fury, exceeds her as much in beauty

---

159 **noted her not** paid her no special
  attention, perhaps with the specific
  sense of sexual attention, as in *Troilus*
  5.2.11, when Ulysses says of Cressida,
  'She's noted.'

163 **my custom** Apparently Benedick's
  'custom' is witty misogyny, which, he
  recognizes, differs from 'simple true
  judgement'.
  tyrant verbally only, but the idea of
  domination is revealing

166 **low** short

176 **can the world buy** i.e. is all the
  world's wealth enough to pay for?

178 **sad** serious
  flouting Jack know-all, trouble-maker

179–80 **Cupid . . . carpenter** Spotting
  hares in the field is difficult at best, but
  Cupid was blind, and Vulcan a smith.
  Such deliberate inappropriateness is labelled '*Antiphrasis* or the Broad Flout'
  in Puttenham's *Arte of English Poesie*
  (1589).

181 **go** harmonize

185 **cousin** The term was then much less
  specific and was applied to even
  remote familial connections, as at
  5.4.110–11. Beatrice's precise place in
  Leonato's family is not fully clarified;
  hence his authority over her can seem
  loose and ambiguous.

as the first of May doth the last of December. But I
hope you have no intent to turn husband, have you?
CLAUDIO I would scarce trust myself though I had
    sworn the contrary, if Hero would be my wife.   190
BENEDICK Is't come to this? In faith, hath not the world
    one man but he will wear his cap with suspicion?
    Shall I never see a bachelor of three-score again? Go
    to, i' faith, an thou wilt needs thrust thy neck into
    a yoke, wear the print of it, and sigh away Sundays.   195
    Look, Don Pedro is returned to seek you.
        Enter Don Pedro
DON PEDRO What secret hath held you here that you
    followed not to Leonato's?
BENEDICK I would your grace would constrain me to
    tell.   200
DON PEDRO I charge thee on thy allegiance.
BENEDICK You hear, Count Claudio? I can be secret as
    a dumb man; I would have you think so. But on my
    allegiance, mark you this—on my allegiance—he is
    in love! With who? Now that is your grace's part.   205
    Mark how short his answer is—with Hero, Leonato's
    short daughter.
CLAUDIO If this were so, so were it uttered.
BENEDICK Like the old tale, my lord: 'It is not so, nor
    'twas not so, but indeed, God forbid it should be so.'   210
CLAUDIO If my passion change not shortly, God forbid
    it should be otherwise.

196.1] HANMER (*subs.*); *Enter don Pedro, Iohn the bastard.* Q

187 **first of May ... last of December** In
addition to the obvious reference, it is
likely that the boy playing Beatrice
was tall and blond (to match the large
Benedick), in contrast to the short,
dark Hero.
192 **with suspicion** (that it conceals a
cuckold's horns)
195 **sigh away Sundays** (which are no
longer available for bachelor amuse-
ments)
196.1 **Enter Don Pedro** Since Don John
first hears of the intended marriage in
1.3, Q's direction for him to enter here
(see collation) would hardly have reflected performance.

201 **charge** i.e. not merely constraint but
command
allegiance (to Don Pedro, whose command would override Benedick's 'discretion')
205 **who** On Elizabethan uses of 'who'
and 'whom' see Abbott 274.
207 **If ... uttered** An evasion: if this were
true, this is how one might tell it.
208 **old tale** The refrain is spoken by a
robber-bridegroom after his crimes are
discovered by his fiancée. A supposedly
true version of the tale, which has
many folklore analogues, is printed in
the Boswell–Malone Variorum (1821),
vii. 164–5.

DON PEDRO Amen, if you love her, for the lady is very
well worthy.

CLAUDIO You speak this to fetch me in, my lord.   215

DON PEDRO By my troth, I speak my thought.

CLAUDIO And in faith, my lord, I spoke mine.

BENEDICK And by my two faiths and troths, my lord, I
spoke mine.

CLAUDIO That I love her, I feel.   220

DON PEDRO That she is worthy, I know.

BENEDICK That I neither feel how she should be loved
nor know how she should be worthy is the opinion
that fire cannot melt out of me. I will die in it at the
stake.   225

DON PEDRO Thou wast ever an obstinate heretic in the
despite of beauty.

CLAUDIO And never could maintain his part but in the
force of his will.

BENEDICK That a woman conceived me, I thank her.   230
That she brought me up, I likewise give her most
humble thanks. But that I will have a *recheat* winded
in my forehead, or hang my bugle in an invisible
baldric, all women shall pardon me. Because I will
not do them the wrong to mistrust any, I will do   235
myself the right to trust none. And the fine is—for
the which I may go the finer—I will live a bachelor.

DON PEDRO I shall see thee ere I die look pale with love.

BENEDICK With anger, with sickness, or with hunger,
my lord; not with love. Prove that ever I lose more   240
blood with love than I will get again with drinking,
pick out mine eyes with a ballad-maker's pen and

215 **fetch me in** trick me (to confess)
218 **two faiths and troths** Benedick jokes
about his dual but not, he hopes, duplicitous loyalty to both Don Pedro and
to his sworn brother-in-arms Claudio.
226–7 **heretic . . . beauty** Chivalric 'ortho-
doxy' required gentlemen to respect
and serve beauty in women. The heresy that exposes Benedick to a figurative
burning at the stake is his scorn of this
idea.
228–9 **in . . . will** through a stubborn rejection of the gentleman's true faith

232–4 **recheat . . . baldric** Benedick has
no intention of being cuckolded or of
having to conceal it; that is, of wearing on his forehead a horn to call
hounds (*recheat*) or concealing it in an
invisible shoulder-belt (*baldric*).
236 **fine** conclusion
241 **love . . . drinking** Sighing was
thought to deplete the blood, as in
Dream 3.2.79, and drinking, especially
red wine, to increase it: Tilley W461.
242 **ballad-maker's pen** Most ballads, as
now, were about love.

hang me up at the door of a brothel house for the
sign of blind Cupid.

DON PEDRO Well, if ever thou dost fall from this faith   245
thou wilt prove a notable argument.

BENEDICK If I do, hang me in a bottle like a cat, and
shoot at me, and he that hits me, let him be clapped
on the shoulder and called Adam.

DON PEDRO Well, as time shall try. 'In time the savage   250
bull doth bear the yoke.'

BENEDICK The savage bull may, but if ever the sensible
Benedick bear it, pluck off the bull's horns and set
them in my forehead, and let me be vilely painted,
and in such great letters as they write 'Here is good   255
horse to hire', let them signify under my sign 'Here
you may see Benedick, the married man.'

CLAUDIO If this should ever happen thou wouldst be
horn-mad.

DON PEDRO Nay, if Cupid have not spent all his quiver   260
in Venice, thou wilt quake for this shortly.

BENEDICK I look for an earthquake too, then.

DON PEDRO Well, you will temporize with the hours. In
the meantime, good Signor Benedick, repair to Leonato's. Commend me to him, and tell him I will not   265
fail him at supper, for indeed he hath made great
preparation.

BENEDICK I have almost matter enough in me for such
an embassage. And so I commit you—

---

244 **blind Cupid** Edward Coke's *Third Part
of the Institutes of the Laws of England*
(1644), ch. 97, states that brothels
had signs painted on their outside
walls, but his examples are all conventional, e.g. a boar's head, a cardinal's
hat. Benedick is repeating a common
witticism, not providing evidence of
suggestive advertising.
246 **argument** instance for discussion
247 **like a cat** Cats suspended in wicker
'bottles' were used as targets by ar-
chers.
249 **Adam** Adam Bell, a famous archer
250-1 **In time ... yoke** proverbial (Tilley
T303), but popularized by Thomas
Kyd in *The Spanish Tragedy* (c. 1587)
2.1.3, who may have borrowed it from

Sonnet 47 of Thomas Watson's *Heca-
tompathia* (1582)
252 **sensible** sensitive
259 **horn-mad** enraged as a bull charg-
ing, horns down. Cuckolding was
supposed to lead the 'dishonoured'
husband to implacable fury.
261 **Venice** famous in England for its supposed sexual freedom
262 **earthquake** a disaster thought to
mark great temporal changes, such as
the death of Caesar. Note the word-
play on 'quiver' and 'quake'.
263 **temporize with the hours** unclear:
'You *will* waste time' (likely); 'become
in time more temperate in your outlook' (possible)
268 **matter** understanding (an irony)

CLAUDIO To the tuition of God. From my house, if I had   270
it—

DON PEDRO The sixth of July, your loving friend, Benedick.

BENEDICK Nay, mock not, mock not. The body of your
discourse is sometime guarded with fragments, and   275
the guards are but slightly basted on neither. Ere you
flout old ends any further, examine your conscience.
And so I leave you.   *Exit*

CLAUDIO
My liege, your highness now may do me good.

DON PEDRO
My love is thine to teach. Teach it but how   280
And thou shalt see how apt it is to learn
Any hard lesson that may do thee good.

CLAUDIO
Hath Leonato any son, my lord?

DON PEDRO
No child but Hero. She's his only heir.
Dost thou affect her, Claudio?

CLAUDIO   O my lord,   285
When you went onward on this ended action
I looked upon her with a soldier's eye,
That liked, but had a rougher task in hand
Than to drive liking to the name of love.
But now I am returned, and that war-thoughts   290
Have left their places vacant, in their rooms
Come thronging soft and delicate desires,
All prompting me how fair young Hero is,
Saying I liked her ere I went to wars.

270 **tuition** safe-keeping; ll. 270–3 parody the conclusion of a formal letter.

272 **The sixth of July** the old Midsummer
Day, a proper occasion for odd behaviour. P. H. Ditchfield, *Old English Customs* (1896), 207 places it on 5 July.

274–7 **body ... ends** The metaphor is
drawn from tailoring: the basic fabric
('body') of your chatter is embellished
with scraps ('guarded with fragments')
only loosely tacked in place.

276 **flout ... ends** mock me not only with
tailor's scraps, but with the conventional, hence dull, ends of letters

279 **do me good** help me. Note the propitiatory formality of 'liege' and 'highness', and the appropriately generous
language of Don Pedro's reply. Both
this formality and the theme of the
exchange justify the shift to blank
verse.

283 **any son** i.e. an heir. Claudio is prudent about finances, but so are Beatrice and Benedick.

285 **affect** love, from the Latin *affectio*,
stronger than the modern 'affection'

290 **now I** now that I

DON PEDRO

   Thou wilt be like a lover presently,   295
   And tire the hearer with a book of words.
   If thou dost love fair Hero, cherish it,
   And I will break with her and with her father,
   And thou shalt have her. Was't not to this end
   That thou began'st to twist so fine a story?   300

CLAUDIO

   How sweetly you do minister to love
   That know love's grief by his complexion.
   But lest my liking might too sudden seem,
   I would have salved it with a longer treatise.

DON PEDRO

   What need the bridge much broader than the flood?   305
   The fairest grant is the necessity.
   Look what will serve is fit. 'Tis once. Thou lovest,
   And I will fit thee with the remedy.
   I know we shall have revelling tonight.
   I will assume thy part in some disguise,   310
   And tell fair Hero I am Claudio.
   And in her bosom I'll unclasp my heart
   And take her hearing prisoner with the force
   And strong encounter of my amorous tale.
   Then after to her father will I break,   315
   And the conclusion is, she shall be thine.
   In practice let us put it presently.   *Exeunt*

296 **book of words** Gentlemen-lovers were expected to unburden themselves at great length, and in verse.
298 **break with** raise the question with
300 **twist** like yarn
302 **complexion** appearance, here the pallor reflecting a lover's inner state
304 **salved** accounted for (*OED v.*[2] 2) from the Latin *salvire* = save as in the phrase 'to save (account for) the appearances'
   treatise narrative. The term was then applied to literary works in general.
305–7 **What . . . fit** 'The bridge need be only a little longer than the width of the stream'; 'the gift required is the best gift'; 'whatever works is appropriate'.
307 **Look what** whatever
   'Tis once once and for all
308–14 **And . . . tale** Don Pedro's tone seems too enthusiastic, but matches arranged by superiors were not infrequent at Count Claudio's level of society. Note, however, that Hero is merely a 'prize' to the Prince; her attention is to be his 'prisoner'; 'force' and 'encounter' are also military terms he uses here.
312 **in her bosom** privately
   unclasp open (as if a book fastened with clasps)

I.2 *Enter Leonato, meeting old Antonio, his brother*

LEONATO How now, brother, where is my cousin, your
son? Hath he provided this music?

ANTONIO He is very busy about it. But brother, I can
tell you strange news that you yet dreamt not of.

LEONATO Are·they good? 5

ANTONIO As the event stamps them. But they have a
good cover; they show well outward. The Prince and
Count Claudio, walking in a thick-pleached alley in
mine orchard, were thus much overheard by a man
of mine: the Prince discovered to Claudio that he 10
loved my niece, your daughter, and meant to acknowledge it this night in a dance and, if he found
her accordant, he meant to take the present time by
the top and instantly break with you of it.

LEONATO Hath the fellow any wit that told you this? 15

ANTONIO A good sharp fellow. I will send for him, and
question him yourself.

LEONATO No, no. We will hold it as a dream till it
appear itself. But I will acquaint my daughter withal,
that she may be the better prepared for an answer if 20
peradventure this be true. Go you and tell her of it.

⌈*Enter attendants*⌉

Cousins, you know what you have to do.—O, I cry
you mercy, friend. Go you with me and I will use
your skill.—Good cousin, have a care this busy time.

Exeunt

1.2.0] Q (*Enter Leonato and an old man brother to Leonato*); ~ *meeting* CAMBRIDGE 3
ANTONIO (*and throughout the scene*)] ROWE; *Old* Q   6 *event*] F2; *euents* Q   21.1] OXFORD;
not in Q; *Exit Antonio,* | *Enter Antonio's Son, with a* Musician BOAS (subs.); ~ *and Others*
KITTREDGE; THEOBALD *places* SD *after 'to do' below*

1.2.1 **my cousin, your son?** This cousin
is not mentioned again (see Introd.,
p. 82).

5 **they** refers to 'news', a plural noun

6–7 **As the event ... outward** As the
outcome determines; yet the news
seems auspicious. 'Stamp' and 'cover'
continue the book metaphor of
1.1.296.

8 **thick-pleached alley** a path overarched
by closely interwoven branches
mine orchard Had Don Pedro and
Claudio discussed the proxy wooing a
second time?

10 **discovered** revealed

13 **accordant** willing

13–14 **present ... top** Seizing opportunity
by the forelock was a proverbial
expression (Tilley T311) arising from
emblematic representations of the goddess Fortuna as bald at the back of her
head.

18–19 **till it appear** until such an interview takes place. Leonato would
approve of such an advantageous
match.

22, 24 **Cousins ... cousin** see 1.1.185.
Some editions have Antonio exit after

I.3   *Enter Don John the Bastard and Conrad, his*
          companion

CONRAD What the goodyear, my lord. Why are you
thus out of measure sad?

DON JOHN There is no measure in the occasion that
breeds it; therefore the sadness is without limit.

CONRAD You should hear reason.   5

DON JOHN And when I have heard it, what blessing
brings it?

CONRAD If not a present remedy, at least a patient
sufferance.

DON JOHN I wonder that thou, being—as thou say'st   10
thou art—born under Saturn, goest about to apply
a moral medicine to a mortifying mischief. I cannot
hide what I am. I must be sad when I have cause,
and smile at no man's jests; eat when I have stomach, and wait for no man's leisure; sleep when I am   15
drowsy, and tend on no man's business; laugh when
I am merry, and claw no man in his humour.

CONRAD Yea, but you must not make the full show of
this till you may do it without controlment. You have
of late stood out against your brother, and he hath   20
ta'en you newly into his grace, where it is impossible
you should take true root but by the fair weather
that you make yourself. It is needful that you frame
the season for your own harvest.

DON JOHN I had rather be a canker in a hedge than a   25

1.3.0.1 *Don*] ROWE; *Sir* Q   4 it] THEOBALD; *not in* Q

21 and specify the entrance of Antonio's son, of Balthasar, or of a musician. The text requires only bustle
here, and such directions seem both
literal-minded and pre-emptive of di-
rectorial decisions.

1.3.1 **What the goodyear** A euphemistic
oath (like 'what the heck', 'heck' =
hell), which in our frank-speaking day
has no widely used equivalent. The
principle underlying the euphemism is
not modesty, but avoiding trouble by
not uttering a powerful name.
2 **measure** moderation
9 **sufferance** endurance

11 **born under Saturn** saturnine or melancholy because of planetary influence.
The planet was thought to be evil-
willed.
12 **moral medicine ... mischief** the con-
solation of proverbial advice to a
mortal disease, i.e. Don John's military
defeat and consequent dependency on
Don Pedro
17 **claw ... humour** humour no one:
claw, stroke, or soothe
22 **fair weather** opportunities for ingra-
tiating yourself
25 **canker** the wild rose or dog-rose, an
inferior, intrusive growth (analogous
to Don John's bastardy), with over-

rose in his grace. And it better fits my blood to be disdained of all than to fashion a carriage to rob love from any. In this, though I cannot be said to be a flattering honest man, it must not be denied but I am a plain-dealing villain. I am trusted with a muzzle, and enfranchised with a clog. Therefore I have decreed not to sing in my cage. If I had my mouth I would bite. If I had my liberty I would do my liking. In the meantime, let me be that I am, and seek not to alter me. 35

CONRAD Can you make no use of your discontent?

DON JOHN I make all use of it, for I use it only. Who comes here?

Enter Borachio

What news, Borachio?

BORACHIO I came yonder from a great supper. The 40 Prince your brother is royally entertained by Leonato, and I can give you intelligence of an intended marriage.

DON JOHN Will it serve for any model to build mischief on? What is he for a fool that betroths himself to 45 unquietness?

BORACHIO Marry, it is your brother's right hand.

DON JOHN Who, the most exquisite Claudio?

BORACHIO Even he.

DON JOHN A proper squire. And who, and who? Which 50 way looks he?

BORACHIO Marry, on Hero, the daughter and heir of Leonato.

36–9] *as prose,* POPE; Q *breaks at* 'discontent', 'only', *and* 'Borachio'   38.1 Q *(after* 'Borachio')   47 brother's] F; bothers Q   52 on] F; one Q

tones of disease and deformity, as in its cognates, 'chancre' and 'cancer'.

26 **blood** temperament, and here illegitimacy and high rank

27 **fashion a carriage** pretend an attitude. Characteristically, Shakespeare has his 'villains' reveal themselves clearly and early.

31 **enfranchised with a clog** let loose, but with a weight tied to my leg. The animal image serves both Don John's

sense of grievance and the author's characterization of him.

37 **use it only** am discontented *all* the time.

39 **Borachio** after the Spanish for 'winebottle'

42 **intelligence** news

44 **model** basis, here an architect's plan

45–6 **What . . . unquietness** Who is the fool who's about to marry trouble?

50 **proper squire** contemptuous: a pretty young suitor

DON JOHN A very forward March chick. How came you
to this?   55
BORACHIO Being entertained for a perfumer, as I was
smoking a musty room, comes me the Prince and
Claudio, hand in hand, in sad conference. I whipped
me behind the arras, and there heard it agreed upon
that the Prince should woo Hero for himself and,   60
having obtained her, give her to Count Claudio.
DON JOHN Come, come, let us thither. This may prove
food to my displeasure. That young start-up hath all
the glory of my overthrow. If I can cross him any
way, I bless myself every way. You are both sure,   65
and will assist me?
CONRAD To the death, my lord.
DON JOHN Let us to the great supper. Their cheer is the
greater that I am subdued. Would the cook were o'
my mind. Shall we go prove what's to be done?   70
BORACHIO We'll wait upon your lordship.   *Exeunt*

2.1   *Enter Leonato, Antonio his brother, Hero his
daughter, and Beatrice his niece*
LEONATO Was not Count John here at supper?
ANTONIO I saw him not.
BEATRICE How tartly that gentleman looks. I never can
see him but I am heartburned an hour after.

66 me?] F; me. Q   71 *Exeunt*] Q (*exit.*)
   2.1] *Actus Secundus* F; *not in* Q   0.1–2] This edition; *Enter Leonato, his brother, his
wife, Hero his daughter, and Beatrice his neece, and a kinsman* Q; ROWE, OXFORD *add* Margaret
and Ursula   2, 19, 49 ANTONIO] ROWE; *brother* Q

54 **forward March chick** a bird hatched
very early, hence 'forward', with overtones of both 'precocious' and 'upstart'.
The phrase can apply to either Hero
or Claudio, but probably applies to
Hero, in spite of its inappropriateness.
56 **entertained for a perfumer** hired to
sweeten the air by burning aromatic
herbs. Despite their draughtiness (see
59), Renaissance mansions could have
unpleasant   odours,   which   were
masked rather than eliminated.
57–9 **me . . . me** The ethical dative is colloquial here; its effect is slightly condescending.
59 **arras** a large decorative tapestry hung

before walls to deflect draughts; its
insulating distance from the wall made
it a good hiding-place.
63 **start-up** upstart
64 **cross** frustrate, in ironic contrast to
'bless'
65 **sure** loyal
69 **subdued** an ironic pun on both
'reserved' and 'conquered'
Would . . . mind Don John has poison
in mind.
70 **prove** find out
2.1.1 **I saw him not** Did Don John (or
Shakespeare) change his mind about
going? Or was Don John at the supper
but lurking in a corner?

HERO He is of a very melancholy disposition. 5

BEATRICE He were an excellent man that were made just in the midway between him and Benedick. The one is too like an image and says nothing, and the other too like my lady's eldest son, evermore tattling.

LEONATO Then half Signor Benedick's tongue in Count 10 John's mouth, and half Count John's melancholy in Signor Benedick's face—

BEATRICE With a good leg and a good foot, uncle, and money enough in his purse, such a man would win any woman in the world, if a could get her good 15 will.

LEONATO By my troth, niece, thou wilt never get thee a husband if thou be so shrewd of thy tongue.

ANTONIO In faith, she's too curst.

BEATRICE Too curst is more than curst. I shall lessen 20 God's sending that way, for it is said God sends a curst cow short horns, but to a cow too curst he sends none.

LEONATO So, by being too curst, God will send you no horns. 25

BEATRICE Just, if he send me no husband; for the which blessing I am at him upon my knees every morning and evening. Lord, I could not endure a husband with a beard on his face. I had rather lie in the woollen. 30

LEONATO You may light on a husband that hath no beard.

BEATRICE What should I do with him? Dress him in my apparel and make him my waiting gentlewoman?

7 **Benedick** Again, as in 1.1, Benedick comes suddenly to her mind.

8 **image** statue

9 **my lady's eldest son** a spoiled child, as the oldest son of a widow was supposed to be and, as the ranking family male, was encouraged to be; see e.g. Bertram in *All's Well*.

14 **money ... purse** Beatrice too is prudent about money.

18 **shrewd** sharp

19 **curst** caustic

21-2 **God ... horns** God curbs the destructiveness of the aggressive; prover-bial, Tilley G217. Beatrice carries the idea to the point of absurdity: she will be denied any horns at all, even those that come with being cuckolded in marriage. Beatrice too seems to share with men the assumption that infidelity in marriage is inevitable.

30 **in the woollen** between blankets, i.e. without linen sheets. Beatrice's fastidiousness has class overtones, woollen homespun being the cloth of the lower orders; see 'woollen vassals' in *Coriolanus* 3.2.9.

He that hath a beard is more than a youth, and he   35
that hath no beard is less than a man; and he that
is more than a youth is not for me, and he that is
less than a man, I am not for him. Therefore I will
even take sixpence in earnest of the bearherd and
lead his apes into hell.   40

LEONATO Well then, go you into hell?

BEATRICE No, but to the gate, and there will the devil
meet me like an old cuckold with horns on his head,
and say, 'Get you to heaven, Beatrice, get you to
heaven. Here's no place for you maids.' So deliver I   45
up my apes, and away to Saint Peter fore the heavens. He shows me where the bachelors sit, and there
live we as merry as the day is long.

ANTONIO (*to Hero*) Well, niece, I trust you will be ruled
by your father.   50

BEATRICE Yes, faith, it is my cousin's duty to make
curtsy and say, 'Father, as it please you.' But yet for
all that, cousin, let him be a handsome fellow, or
else make another curtsy and say, 'Father, as it
please me.'   55

LEONATO Well, niece, I hope to see you one day fitted
with a husband.

BEATRICE Not till God make men of some other mettle
than earth. Would it not grieve a woman to be

39 bearherd] F3, Q (Berrord); bearward KNIGHT   41 hell?] HANMER; hell. Q   46–7 Peter
fore the heavens. He] OXFORD; Peter: for the heauens, he Q; Peter, for the heavens; he
POPE

39 **in earnest** as down payment to seal a
  contract
  the bearherd Bear-keepers not only ex-
  hibited bears, who were attacked by
  mastiffs as a popular spectator sport,
  but they also kept other animals, presumably apes among them.
40 **lead . . . hell** Leading apes to hell was
  the proverbial fate of elderly unmar-
  ried women: Tilley M37. No explanation has been found for this odd
  commonplace.
46–7 **fore the heavens** Q's spelling and
  punctuation leave open several acceptable alternatives: 'For the heavens!'
  (a mild oath), 'For the heavens, he'
  (As my share of heaven, he), or as
  here, 'Fore' (in front of).

47 **bachelors** applied then to both sexes.
  C. T. Neely points out that Shakespeare uses the term for male bachelors, and hence that Beatrice may be
  looking forward to joining the circle of
  male comradeship—or simply to male
  company (*Broken Nuptials in Shakespeare's Plays*, New Haven, Conn.,
  1985, 46 n).
48 **merry . . . long** proverbial: Tilley D57
58 **mettle** material, with a pun on mettle
  = spirit
59–63 **Would it not . . . kindred** Beatrice
  overturns the patriarchal implications
  of Gen. 2: 7 by arguing for the superiority of creatures (women) made of a
  human rib over those (men) made of
  clay ('marl'). Moreover, the obviously

overmastered with a piece of valiant dust, to make 60
an account of her life to a clod of wayward marl?
No, uncle, I'll none. Adam's sons are my brethren,
and truly I hold it a sin to match in my kindred.

LEONATO (*to Hero*) Daughter, remember what I told
you. If the Prince do solicit you in that kind, you 65
know your answer.

BEATRICE The fault will be in the music, cousin, if you
be not wooed in good time. If the Prince be too
important, tell him there is measure in everything,
and so dance out the answer. For hear me, Hero, 70
wooing, wedding, and repenting is as a Scotch jig, a
measure, and a cinquepace. The first suit is hot and
hasty, like a Scotch jig and full as fantastical; the
wedding mannerly modest, as a measure, full of state
and ancientry. And then comes repentance, and with 75
his bad legs falls into the cinquepace faster and faster
till he sink into his grave.

LEONATO Cousin, you apprehend passing shrewdly.

BEATRICE I have a good eye, uncle; I can see a church
by daylight. 80

LEONATO (*to Antonio*) The revellers are entering,
brother.

⌈*He signals to the others to disperse and don masks*⌉
Make good room.

Enter Don Pedro, Claudio, Benedick, Balthasar,
⌈*Margaret and Ursula*⌉, *all masked; Don John*

82.1 SD] This edition; *not in* Q; *Leonato and his Company mask* CAPELL   83.1–4] This
edition; *Enter prince, Pedro, Claudio, and Benedicke, and Balthaser, or dumb Iohn* Q; ~
Maskers with a drum F; *Enter . . . Margaret and Ursula conj.* Wells

close blood relationship of men and
women through Adam and Eve seems
to Beatrice to violate the 'Table of Kindred and Affinity' in the Book of Common Prayer, and so preclude marriage.
Bemused or impatient, Leonato abrupt-
ly changes the subject.
65 **solicit you in that kind** ask you about
marriage, propose
68 **in good time** word-play on 'good musical tempo' and 'at the appropriate
moment'
important importuning

69 **measure** both (*a*) moderation and (*b*)
a dance step
71–2 **a Scotch jig . . . cinquepace** These
are popular dances: the jig lively, the
measure 'full of state and ancientry',
and the third (pronounced 'sink
apace', hence the pun on 'sink' at 77)
comprising five steps and a great leap.
See A. Brissenden, *Shakespeare and the
Dance* (1981), 49–50.
76 **bad legs** (due to old age)
78 **passing** (sur) passing, very

and Borachio, ⌈*unmasked*⌉; *and attendants and
musicians, among them a drummer*

DON PEDRO *(to Hero)* Lady, will you walk a bout with
your friend?   85

HERO So you walk softly, and look sweetly, and say
nothing, I am yours for the walk; and especially
when I walk away.

DON PEDRO With me in your company?

HERO I may say so when I please.   90

DON PEDRO And when please you to say so?

HERO When I like your favour; for God defend the lute
should be like the case.

DON PEDRO   My visor is Philemon's roof.
              Within the house is Jove.   95

HERO
Why, then, your visor should be thatched.

DON PEDRO
Speak low if you speak love.

     They move aside

⌈BALTHASAR⌉ *(to Margaret)* Well, I would you did like
me.

MARGARET So would not I for your own sake, for I have   100
many ill qualities.

⌈BALTHASAR⌉ Which is one?

MARGARET I say my prayers aloud.

---

84 a bout] WILSON; about Q   94–5, 96–7] *as here*; This edition; Q *prints each pair as
one line*   97.1, 110.1, 123.1] *not in* Q   98, 102, 104 BALTHASAR] THEOBALD; *Bene.* Q

84 **a bout** Q's 'about' probably misreads
the MS; a 'bout' is a turn around the
dance floor, a distinction unheard in
the theatre, but significant for the construction and staging of the scene.

85 **friend** Though the word was then ambiguous (close friend, lover), the context makes its use a curious misstep on
Don Pedro's part.

92 **favour** face

92–3 **God defend . . . case** God forbid that
your face should resemble your mask.
Mares suggests that as Philemon Don
Pedro wore a grotesque rustic mask.

94–7 Don Pedro and Hero speak in the
rhymed 'fourteeners' (lines of 14 syllables, or two lines alternating 6 and
8 syllables) of Arthur Golding's translation of Ovid's *Metamorphoses*. Ovid

tells the story of the old peasant couple
Philemon and Baucis, who shared
their meagre meal with the disguised
Jupiter and Mercury and became by-
words for humble virtue. The Prince's
words are clear enough, but Hero's
comment and his response are not.
Newcomer thought Hero joking at Don
Pedro's baldness, his lack of 'thatch'.
But if his visor (mask) is a roof, she
may be observing only that it lacks a
thatch. His request that she lower her
voice if she is speaking of love is inappropriate in either case. The words
have inspired the lyrics of a popular
song.

103 **prayers aloud** Margaret was unlikely
to have practised anything so un-
fashionable, indeed so puritanical.

⌈BALTHASAR⌉ I love you the better; the hearers may
cry amen.   105
MARGARET God match me with a good dancer.
BALTHASAR Amen.
MARGARET And God keep him out of my sight when
the dance is done. Answer, clerk.
BALTHASAR No more words. The clerk is answered.   110
         They move aside
URSULA (*to Antonio*) I know you well enough, you are
Signor Antonio.
ANTONIO At a word, I am not.
URSULA I know you by the waggling of your head.
ANTONIO To tell you true, I counterfeit him.   115
URSULA You could never do him so ill-well unless you
were the very man. Here's his dry hand up and
down. You are he, you are he.
ANTONIO At a word, I am not.
URSULA Come, come, do you think I do not know you   120
by your excellent wit? Can virtue hide itself? Go to,
mum, you are he. Graces will appear, and there's an
end.
         They move aside
BEATRICE (*to Benedick*) Will you not tell me who told
you so?   125
BENEDICK No, you shall pardon me.
BEATRICE Nor will you not tell me who you are?
BENEDICK Not now.
BEATRICE That I was disdainful, and that I had my good
wit out of the 'Hundred Merry Tales'—well, this was   130
Signor Benedick that said so.
BENEDICK What's he?
BEATRICE I am sure you know him well enough.

---

110 **The clerk is answered** Parish clerks led the responses during the church service. Balthasar understands that he has been rejected.
113 **At a word** in short
114 **waggling** the tremor of old age (Parkinsonism?)
117 **dry hand** Loss of moisture was thought correctly to be part of the ageing process; the dryness is due to low oil production in ageing skin.

up and down exactly
120–3 **Come . . . end** At last sensing Antonio's annoyance, Ursula turns to prudent flattery.
122 **mum** no more talk
130 **'Hundred Merry Tales'** a collection of crude anecdotes, first printed in 1526 but perennially popular. Beatrice would have been outraged by the suggestion that it was the source of her wit.

BENEDICK Not I, believe me.

BEATRICE Did he never make you laugh?   135

BENEDICK I pray you, what is he?

BEATRICE Why, he is the Prince's jester, a very dull fool. Only his gift is in devising impossible slanders. None but libertines delight in him, and the commendation is not in his wit but in his villainy, for he both   140 pleases men and angers them, and then they laugh at him and beat him. I am sure he is in the fleet. I would he had boarded me.

BENEDICK When I know the gentleman, I'll tell him what you say.   145

BEATRICE Do, do. He'll but break a comparison or two on me, which peradventure not marked, or not laughed at, strikes him into melancholy, and then there's a partridge wing saved, for the fool will eat no supper that night.   150

⌈*Music*⌉

We must follow the leaders.

BENEDICK In every good thing.

BEATRICE Nay, if they lead to any ill I will leave them at the next turning.

They dance off. Exeunt all but Don John, Borachio, and Claudio

DON JOHN (*aside to Borachio*) Sure my brother is amor-   155 ous on Hero, and hath withdrawn her father to break

---

150.1] F ('*Musike for the dance*' after 154); *not in* Q; *Music within* THEOBALD   154.1–2] THEOBALD (*subs.*); *Dance exeunt* Q

---

138 **Only his** his only; a common transposition, on which see Abbott 420, 421
   impossible unbelievable

141–9 **pleases . . . and angers** He angers those he slanders, and entertains those who listen to him.

142 **fleet** assembly of dancers
   boarded me tried to get 'fresh' with me, but 'boarded' could have deeper implications. At its least suggestive it was defined by Sir Toby Belch in *Twelfth Night* 1.3.52–4 as a synonym for 'wooing'.

146 **break** as a lance in a tournament
   comparison According to Hero (3.1.59–67), Beatrice herself had a talent for invidious comparison.

149 **partridge wing** almost meatless but delicious, according to Francis Willoughby's *Ornithology* (1678), ii. 168. Beatrice's delight in the ludicrous reference is probably more important to her than whether her wit strikes Benedick the valiant trencherman or Benedick the fastidious gourmet.

151 **the leaders** The first couple in the dance—the Prince and Hero. Evidently Beatrice and Benedick have fallen behind.

155–6 **amorous on Hero** courting Hero; yet the phrase is slightly ambiguous. Don John learned of the proxy wooing at 1.3.52, but may, like Iago, attribute illicit motives to everyone.

with him about it. The ladies follow her, and but one
visor remains.
BORACHIO (*aside to Don John*) And that is Claudio. I
know him by his bearing.   160
DON JOHN (*approaching Claudio*) Are not you Signor
Benedick?
CLAUDIO You know me well. I am he.
DON JOHN Signor, you are very near my brother in his
love. He is enamoured on Hero. I pray you dissuade   165
him from her. She is no equal for his birth. You may
do the part of an honest man in it.
CLAUDIO How know you he loves her?
DON JOHN I heard him swear his affection.
BORACHIO So did I, too, and he swore he would marry   170
her tonight.
DON JOHN Come, let us to the banquet.
                                    Exeunt all but Claudio
CLAUDIO
Thus answer I in name of Benedick,
But hear these ill news with the ears of Claudio.
'Tis certain so; the Prince woos for himself.   175
Friendship is constant in all other things
Save in the office and affairs of love.
Therefore all hearts in love use their own tongues.
Let every eye negotiate for itself,
And trust no agent; for beauty is a witch   180
Against whose charms faith melteth into blood.
This is an accident of hourly proof,
Which I mistrusted not. Farewell, therefore, Hero.
     Enter Benedick
BENEDICK Count Claudio?
CLAUDIO Yea, the same.   185
BENEDICK Come, will you go with me?

---

161 *approaching Claudio*] This edition; *not in* Q   172.1 *Exeunt . . . Claudio*] Q (*exeunt:
manet Clau.*)

164–5 **near . . . love** my brother's close
 friend
172 **banquet** a showy collation of wine,
 fruit, and sweets served after the dance
178 **Therefore all hearts** therefore let all
 hearts

181 **faith** the loyalty of friends
 blood desire
182 **This is . . . proof** This happens all the
 time.
183 **mistrusted not** did not suspect

CLAUDIO Whither?

BENEDICK Even to the next willow, about your own
business, County. What fashion will you wear the
garland of? About your neck, like an usurer's chain?   190
Or under your arm, like a lieutenant's scarf? You
must wear it one way, for the Prince hath got your
Hero.

CLAUDIO I wish him joy of her.

BENEDICK Why, that's spoken like an honest drover; so   195
they sell bullocks. But did you think the Prince would
have served you thus?

CLAUDIO I pray you leave me.

BENEDICK Ho, now you strike like the blind man. 'Twas
the boy that stole your meat, and you'll beat the   200
post.

CLAUDIO If it will not be, I'll leave you.   *Exit*

BENEDICK Alas, poor hurt fowl, now will he creep into
sedges.—But that my Lady Beatrice should know me,
and not know me! The Prince's fool! Ha, it may be   205
I go under that title because I am merry. Yea, but
so I am apt to do myself wrong. I am not so reputed!
It is the base and bitter disposition of Beatrice that
puts the world into her person, and so gives me out.

195 drover] Q (Drouier)   208 the base and bitter] This edition, *after* Craven *conj.*; the
base, the bitter JOHNSON; the base (though bitter) Q

188 **willow** an emblem of unrequited love.
    Evidently Benedick has noted Claudio's
    unhappy expression.
189 **County** Count (indifferent variants)
190 **usurer's chain** ostentatious gold
    chains often worn by rich bourgeois
191 **lieutenant's scarf** a sash worn diagon-
    ally from the left shoulder as a mark
    of rank. Foakes suggests that Claudio
    must wear a willow wreath (bear his
    sorrow) like a usurer (in exacting cash
    compensation from the Prince), or like
    a soldier (in demanding satisfaction in
    combat).
195 **honest drover** a cattle-dealer amiably
    encouraging trade; 'honest' is no
    doubt ironic.
200–1 **beat the post** This caveat against
    striking out in blind anger may have
    been drawn from Hurtado de Mendo-
    za's picaresque romance *Lazarillo de*

Tormes, widely read in England after
its 1586 translation, but the example
was a commonplace.
202 **If it will not be** if you do not leave
    me
204–5 **know me, and not know me** be
    acquainted with me but have no idea
    of my true qualities
206 **so** by being merry
208 **base and bitter** Q's 'base (though bit-
    ter)' may be explained as an extenua-
    tion of baseness by citing the supposed
    bitterness of spinsterhood or the bitter-
    ness resulting from Benedick's earlier
    behaviour, but the phrase is still cryp-
    tic. The intensity of Benedick's con-
    demnation remains; these two amusing
    lovers have seriously hurt each other.
209 **puts . . . person** assumes the world
    thinks as she does
    gives me out reports me

Well, I'll be revenged as I may.   210
    Enter Don Pedro
DON PEDRO Now, signor, where's the Count? Did you
see him?
BENEDICK Troth, my lord, I have played the part of Lady
Fame. I found him here as melancholy as a lodge in
a warren. I told him—and I think I told him true—   215
that your grace had got the good will of this young
lady, and I offéred him my company to a willow tree,
either to make him a garland, as being forsaken, or
to bind him up a rod, as being worthy to be whipped.
DON PEDRO To be whipped? What's his fault?   220
BENEDICK The flat transgression of a schoolboy who,
being overjoyed with finding a bird's nest, shows it
his companion, and he steals it.
DON PEDRO Wilt thou make a trust a transgression?
The transgression is in the stealer.   225
BENEDICK Yet it had not been amiss the rod had been
made, and the garland too, for the garland he might
have worn himself, and the rod he might have bestowed on you, who, as I take it, have stolen his
bird's nest.   230
DON PEDRO I will but teach them to sing, and restore
them to the owner.
BENEDICK If their singing answer your saying, by my
faith you say honestly.
DON PEDRO The Lady Beatrice hath a quarrel to you.   235
The gentleman that danced with her told her she is
much wronged by you.

210.1] F (*subs.*); *Enter the Prince, Hero, Leonato, Iohn and Borachio, and Conrade* Q   216
good will] Q (goodwill); will F

213–14 **the part of Lady Fame** by spread-
   ing gossip. Here fame = rumour from
   the Latin *fama*.
214–15 **lodge in a warren** a crude dwell-
   ing in an area for breeding small
   game; therefore doubly a cause of melancholy because of its rough isolation
   and the supposed effects of eating
   hare's meat
216–17 **this young lady** The phrase does
   not require Hero's actual presence on
   stage. She can enter later with Leonato, rather than as in Q. The earlier

entrance would give Hero and Leonato
nothing to do for about forty lines save
listen to (for them) awkward remarks
about Claudio and Beatrice.
221 **flat** undeniable. Note Benedick's
propitiatory adroitness in making what
he thinks the Prince's transgression
into Claudio's.
231 **them** the (love-) birds
233–4 **If...honestly** If they sing what
you say you have taught them to sing
(i.e. to marry Claudio), then you are
speaking honourably.

BENEDICK O, she misused me past the endurance of a
block. An oak but with one green leaf on it would
have answered her. My very visor began to assume   240
life and scold with her. She told me, not thinking I
had been myself, that I was the Prince's jester, that
I was duller than a great thaw, huddling jest upon
jest with such impossible conveyance upon me that
I stood like a man at a mark, with a whole army   245
shooting at me. She speaks poniards, and every word
stabs. If her breath were as terrible as her terminations, there were no living near her; she would infect
to the North Star. I would not marry her though she
were endowed with all that Adam had left him before   250
he transgressed. She would have made Hercules have
turned spit, yea, and have cleft his club to make the
fire, too. Come, talk not of her. You shall find her
the infernal Ate in good apparel. I would to God some
scholar would conjure her, for certainly, while she   255
is here a man may live as quiet in hell as in a
sanctuary, and people sin upon purpose because they
would go thither. So indeed all disquiet, horror, and
perturbation follows her.

Enter Claudio and Beatrice

DON PEDRO Look, here she comes.   260

BENEDICK Will your grace command me any service to
the world's end? I will go on the slightest errand
now to the Antipodes that you can devise to send
me on. I will fetch you a tooth-picker now from the

259.1] Q; *Enter Claudio and Beatrice, Leonato, Hero.* F

238 **misused** abused
243 **great thaw** *dull* because it made roads
     impassable and kept everyone indoors
244 **impossible conveyance** incredible
     dexterity. Benedick's rapid wit in this
     passage shows a delight in having
     been bested by a master.
245 **at a mark** near a target (to signal the
     results)
247–8 **terminations** terms
251–3 **Hercules . . . fire** Beatrice would
     have outdone the Queen of Lydia, Om-
     phale, who made Hercules wear
     women's clothing and spin cloth. The
     story turns on Hercules' attempt to
     expiate his guilt through undergoing a
     reversal of sex roles; Omphale takes

his club and lion skin. Clearly Benedick feels his male dominance challenged by Beatrice.
254 **Ate in good apparel** Ate was the eld-
     est daughter of Zeus and goddess of
     Discord; she was traditionally well
     turned out, as in Spenser's *Faerie
     Queene* 4.1.17.
255 **scholar . . . her** Benedick wishes that
     someone who knew enough Latin
     would exorcize her.
264 **tooth-picker** Toothpicks were still a
     modish Italianate affectation; often
     made of precious metals, they were the
     ideal souvenir of travel, as in *King John*
     1.1.189–90.
264–7 The passage is a pastiche of travel-

furthest inch of Asia, bring you the length of Prester   265
John's foot, fetch you a hair off the Great Cham's
beard, do you any embassage to the pigmies, rather
than hold three words' conference with this harpy.
You have no employment for me?

DON PEDRO None but to desire your good company.   270

BENEDICK O God, sir, here's a dish I love not. I cannot
endure my Lady Tongue.   *Exit*

DON PEDRO Come, lady, come, you have lost the heart
of Signor Benedick.

BEATRICE Indeed, my lord, he lent it me a while, and   275
I gave him use for it, a double heart for his single
one. Marry, once before he won it of me with false
dice. Therefore your grace may well say I have lost
it.

DON PEDRO You have put him down, lady, you have   280
put him down.

BEATRICE So I would not he should do me, my lord,
lest I should prove the mother of fools. I have
brought Count Claudio, whom you sent me to seek.

DON PEDRO Why, how now, Count, wherefore are you   285
sad?

CLAUDIO Not sad, my lord.

lers' fantasies and of traditional love tests: the legendary Prester John ruled a wealthy Christian nation thought to be Ethiopia, also the home of the Antipodes. The Grand Cham was Kubla Khan, who ruled China. Pygmies, not actually encountered in Africa by Europeans until the 19th century, were legendary dwarfs, variously placed in Ethiopia and the Far East. These and similar wonders, circulated by Marco Polo's accounts and by Sir John Mandeville's *Voyages and Travels* (1583?), provided Elizabethan writers with romantic exotica.

268 **harpy** in classical myth a malevolent bird with the face of a beautiful woman. Originally the harpies were storm-goddesses, symbolic of the destructive power of nature.

275–9 **Indeed ... lost it** Beatrice and Benedick had once been close, but evidently she was more committed to the relationship than he. Hence the reference to 'false dice' which she allows herself as an explanation for 'losing' her heart. The phrase 'once before' looks both ways, implying several earlier 'bouts' with Benedick as well as something going on at present.

276 **use** interest, i.e. another heart (her own)

double heart 'double' is more likely to mean 'deeply affectionate' rather than 'duplicitous' since it is contrasted with Benedick's 'single' heart. More attractive than either is the idea that in giving Benedick her heart Beatrice also returned his, in the sense that she rejected possessiveness in love. Much of their relationship turns on the issues of mutuality and control.

281 **put him down** bested him in wit, with the obvious sexual import at 283. The 'superior position' punningly alludes to the issue of sexual domination.

DON PEDRO How then? Sick?

CLAUDIO Neither, my lord.

BEATRICE The Count is neither sad, nor sick, nor merry,   290
nor well, but civil Count, civil as an orange, and
something of that jealous complexion.

DON PEDRO I' faith, lady, I think your blazon to be true,
though I'll be sworn, if he be so, his conceit is false.
Here, Claudio, I have wooed in thy name, and fair   295
Hero is won. I have broke with her father and his
good will obtained.
        ⌈*Don Pedro signals; enter Leonato with Hero*⌉
Name the day of marriage, and God give thee joy.

LEONATO Count, take of me my daughter, and with her
my fortunes. His grace hath made the match, and   300
all grace say amen to it.

BEATRICE Speak, Count, 'tis your cue.

CLAUDIO Silence is the perfectest herald of joy. I were
but little happy if I could say how much. (*To Hero*)
Lady, as you are mine, I am yours. I give away   305
myself for you, and dote upon the exchange.

BEATRICE (*to Hero*) Speak, cousin; or, if you cannot,
stop his mouth with a kiss, and let not him speak,
neither.

DON PEDRO In faith, lady, you have a merry heart.   310

BEATRICE Yea, my lord. I thank it, poor fool, it keeps
on the windy side of care.—My cousin tells him in
his ear that he is in her heart.

CLAUDIO And so she doth, cousin.

BEATRICE Good Lord, for alliance! Thus goes everyone   315

297.1] This edition, *after* Jenkins *conj.*; *not in* Q

291 **civil as an orange** The pun on Seville
follows from current spelling as well as
pronunciation. Like the marmalade
orange, Claudio is somewhat bitter.

292 **jealous complexion** yellow, the colour of jealousy, possibly related to the
idea of jaundice due to wasting melancholy.

293 **blazon** description, a heraldic term

294 **conceit** notion of things

296–7 **broke . . . obtained** spoken to her
father and got his permission

301 **all grace say** may God, the source of
all grace, say

303 **Silence** not only expressive of joy, but
a necessary step in play construction.
Had Claudio done what seems natural
here, and revealed his earlier
conversation with Don John, the play
could not have continued.

312 **windy side of care** upwind of trouble,
and so not affected by it

315 **Good Lord, for alliance!** Thank God
for the family! This is Beatrice's comic
response to being called 'cousin' by
Claudio, by whom she is obviously un-
impressed.

315–16 **goes . . . to the world** gets mar-

to the world but I, and I am sunburnt. I may sit in
a corner and cry 'Heigh-ho for a husband.'

DON PEDRO Lady Beatrice, I will get you one.

BEATRICE I would rather have one of your father's
getting. Hath your grace ne'er a brother like you? 320
Your father got excellent husbands if a maid could
come by them.

DON PEDRO Will you have me, lady?

BEATRICE No, my lord, unless I might have another for
working days. Your grace is too costly to wear every 325
day. But I beseech your grace, pardon me; I was
born to speak all mirth and no matter.

DON PEDRO Your silence most offends me, and to be
merry best becomes you; for out o' question, you
were born in a merry hour. 330

BEATRICE No, sure, my lord, my mother cried. But then
there was a star danced, and under that was I born.
(*To Hero and Claudio*) Cousins, God give you joy.

LEONATO Niece, will you look to those things I told you
of? 335

BEATRICE I cry you mercy, uncle. (*To Don Pedro*) By
your grace's pardon. *Exit Beatrice*

DON PEDRO By my troth, a pleasant-spirited lady.

LEONATO There's little of the melancholy element in

ried, possibly from Luke 20: 34,
where marriage is the fate of 'the
children of this world', but here with
amused intimations of something barely preferable to Flesh and the Devil.
  sunburnt according to English taste
and prejudice, ugly. See Claudio on
'Ethiope' at 5.4.38.

317 **'Heigh-ho for a husband'** go whistle
for one; proverbial, Tilley H833, but
also the title of a ballad asserting that
the 'worst [husband] that ever was, is
better than none'; see H. E. Rollins,
'An Analytical Index to the Ballad-
Entries... in the Registers of the
Company of Stationers', *Studies in
Philology*, 21 (1924), 98.

320 **getting** begetting, with a play on
'get' at 318

325 **working days... every day** Beatrice
gracefully turns aside an offer (perhaps
just as lightly meant) that is socially

inappropriate ('too costly') as well as
contrary to her affection for Benedick.
In its self-deprecation the last clause of
the speech defers to Don Pedro's rank.

328 **Your silence most offends** *not* your
speech; Don Pedro accepts Beatrice's
implied apologies with good grace.

331 **cried** in labour; Beatrice is never far
from the actualities of women's lives.

339 **melancholy element** Black bile
(thought to cause melancholy), was
one of the four bodily 'humours' or
fluids, the others being blood, phlegm,
and choler. The dominance of one humour in the mixture determined temperament. Perfectly balanced mixtures
were impossible after the Fall. Aquinas
(*Summa* 1a. 75.6) states that only
heavenly bodies are made of com-
pounds between whose elements there
is no contrariety.

her, my lord. She is never sad but when she sleeps,   340
and not ever sad then; for I have heard my daughter
say she hath often dreamt of unhappiness and waked
herself with laughing.

DON PEDRO She cannot endure to hear tell of a husband.   345

LEONATO O, by no means. She mocks all her wooers
out of suit.

DON PEDRO She were an excellent wife for Benedick.

LEONATO O Lord! My lord, if they were but a week
married they would talk themselves mad.   350

DON PEDRO County Claudio, when mean you to go to
church?

CLAUDIO Tomorrow, my lord. Time goes on crutches till
love have all his rites.

LEONATO Not till Monday, my dear son, which is hence   355
a just sevennight; and a time too brief, too, to have
all things answer my mind.

DON PEDRO Come, you shake the head at so long a
breathing, but I warrant thee, Claudio, the time shall
not go dully by us. I will in the interim undertake   360
one of Hercules' labours, which is to bring Signor
Benedick and the Lady Beatrice into a mountain of
affection th'one with th'other. I would fain have it a
match, and I doubt not but to fashion it, if you three
will but minister such assistance as I shall give you   365
direction.

LEONATO My lord, I am for you, though it cost me ten
nights' watchings.

CLAUDIO And I, my lord.

DON PEDRO And you too, gentle Hero?   370

HERO I will do any modest office, my lord, to help my
cousin to a good husband.

DON PEDRO And Benedick is not the unhopefullest husband that I know. Thus far can I praise him: he is

340 **sad** serious
341 **not ever** not always
347–16 **out of suit** out of attendance,
here out of courtship rather than out
of court
356 **just** exact

357 **answer my mind** just as I want them
359 **breathing** pause
367–8 **ten nights' watchings** ten sleepless
nights
373 **unhopefullest** least promising

of a noble strain, of approved valour and confirmed   375
honesty. I will teach you how to humour your cousin
that she shall fall in love with Benedick; and I, with
your two helps, will so practise on Benedick that, in
despite of his quick wit and his queasy stomach, he
shall fall in love with Beatrice. If we can do this,   380
Cupid is no longer an archer; his glory shall be ours,
for we are the only love-gods. Go in with me, and I
will tell you my drift.   *Exeunt*

2.2   *Enter Don John and Borachio*

DON JOHN It is so. The Count Claudio shall marry the
daughter of Leonato.

BORACHIO Yea, my lord, but I can cross it.

DON JOHN Any bar, any cross, any impediment will be
medicinable to me. I am sick in displeasure to him,   5
and whatsoever comes athwart his affection ranges
evenly with mine. How canst thou cross this marriage?

BORACHIO Not honestly, my lord, but so covertly that
no dishonesty shall appear in me.   10

DON JOHN Show me briefly how.

BORACHIO I think I told your lordship a year since how
much I am in the favour of Margaret, the waiting
gentlewoman to Hero.

DON JOHN I remember.   15

BORACHIO I can at any unseasonable instant of the
night appoint her to look out at her lady's chamber
window.

DON JOHN What life is in that to be the death of this
marriage?   20

BORACHIO The poison of that lies in you to temper. Go
you to the Prince your brother. Spare not to tell him

383 *Exeunt*] Q (*exit.*)
2.2.0.1 Don] *not in* Q

375 **strain** lineage
  approved tested (in battle)
378 **practise on** influence, with overtones
  of 'manipulate'
379 **queasy stomach** hence, small appetite
  for marriage
2.2.3 **cross** thwart

6 **affection** desire
6–7 **ranges evenly** parallels
12 **since** ago
16 **unseasonable instant** unusual or inappropriate time
17 **appoint** make an appointment with
21 **temper** concoct

that he hath wronged his honour in marrying the
renowned Claudio—whose estimation do you mightily hold up—to a contaminated stale, such a one as   25
Hero.

DON JOHN What proof shall I make of that?

BORACHIO Proof enough to misuse the Prince, to vex
Claudio, to undo Hero and kill Leonato. Look you for
any other issue?   30

DON JOHN Only to despite them I will endeavour anything.

BORACHIO Go then. Find me a meet hour to draw Don
Pedro and the Count Claudio alone. Tell them that
you know that Hero loves me. Intend a kind of zeal   35
both to the Prince and Claudio—as in love of your
brother's honour who hath made this match, and
his friend's reputation who is thus like to be cozened
with the semblance of a maid—that you have discovered thus. They will scarcely believe this without   40
trial. Offer them instances, which shall bear no less
likelihood than to see me at her chamber window,
hear me call Margaret Hero, hear Margaret term me
Claudio. And bring them to see this the very night
before the intended wedding, for in the meantime I   45
will so fashion the matter that Hero shall be absent,
and there shall appear such seeming truth of Hero's
disloyalty that jealousy shall be called assurance, and
all the preparation overthrown.

DON JOHN Grow this to what adverse issue it can, I will   50
put it in practice. Be cunning in the working this,
and thy fee is a thousand ducats.

44 Claudio] Q; Borachio THEOBALD

24 **estimation** worth
25 **stale** prostitute
28 **misuse** abuse
    vex torture. The modern 'vex' is much
    weaker and slightly precious.
33 **meet** suitable
35 **Intend** pretend
38 **cozened** cheated
41 **instances** evidence
44 **Claudio** Theobald emends Q's Claudio
    to Borachio. But Margaret, suspecting
    no harm, has been persuaded to play
    at life upstairs. Her calling Borachio

Claudio follows from her allowing herself to be called Hero. The exchange
would be doubly offensive to Claudio,
who would think himself both be-
trayed and mocked.

46 **so fashion the matter** We never learn
    how this is done; its improbability
    seems good reason.
48 **jealousy** suspicion
    assurance certainty
50 **Grow . . . can** no matter how bad the
    outcome
51 **working this** working of this; on this

BORACHIO Be you constant in the accusation, and my
cunning shall not shame me.

DON JOHN I will presently go learn their day of mar-   55
riage.   *Exeunt*

2.3   *Enter Benedick*

BENEDICK Boy!
⌈*Enter Boy*⌉

BOY Signor?

BENEDICK In my chamber window lies a book. Bring it
hither to me in the orchard.

BOY I am here already, sir.   5

BENEDICK I know that, but I would have thee hence
and here again.   ⌈*Exit Boy*⌉
I do much wonder that one man, seeing how much
another man is a fool when he dedicates his behaviours to love, will, after he hath laughed at such   10
shallow follies in others, become the argument of his
own scorn by falling in love. And such a man is
Claudio. I have known when there was no music
with him but the drum and the fife, and now had
he rather hear the tabor and the pipe. I have known   15
when he would have walked ten mile afoot to see a
good armour, and now will he lie ten nights awake
carving the fashion of a new doublet. He was wont
to speak plain and to the purpose, like an honest
man and a soldier, and now is he turned ortho-   20
graphy. His words are a very fantastical banquet, just

56 *Exeunt*] Q (*exit.*)
    2.3.0.1] Q (*Enter Benedicke alone.*); ~ and a Boy ROWE   I.I] COLLIER; *not in* Q   7 SD]
JOHNSON; exit. Q (*after* 5)

usage, see Abbott 93

2.4 The orchard (4) and arbour (37) of
Leonato's house were conventionally
suggested by property trees and a trellis.

  5 **I am here already, sir** The Boy's pert
answer (a nice line for a new boy) is
capped by Benedick's taking it literally.
Deliberately mistaking the figurative
for the literal and the other way round
is a strategy of wit demanding the high
cultivation that Beatrice and Benedick
share. The Boy does not return. In

some productions he produces the
book on the spot—to great laughter.

11 **argument** subject

14 **the drum . . . the pipe** military as contrasted with festive music; the tabor
was a small drum

18 **carving** designing
doublet a close-fitting upper-body garment with detachable sleeves. Doublets
were so varied in design and so elabor-
ately ornamented that one might well
have to stay awake to design one that
was distinctive.

20–1 **orthography** rhetorician

so many strange dishes. May I be so converted and
see with these eyes? I cannot tell; I think not. I will
not be sworn but love may transform me to an
oyster. But I'll take my oath on it: till he have made   25
an oyster of me he shall never make me such a fool.
One woman is fair, yet I am well. Another is wise,
yet I am well. Another virtuous, yet I am well. But
till all graces be in one woman, one woman shall
not come in my grace. Rich she shall be, that's   30
certain. Wise, or I'll none. Virtuous, or I'll never
cheapen her. Fair, or I'll never look on her. Mild, or
come not near me. Noble, or not I for an angel. Of
good discourse, an excellent musician, and her hair
shall be of what colour it please God.—Ha! The   35
Prince and Monsieur Love. I will hide me in the
arbour.

    He hides.
    Enter Don Pedro, Leonato, and Claudio

DON PEDRO
Come, shall we hear this music?

CLAUDIO
Yea, my good lord. How still the evening is,
As hushed on purpose to grace harmony.   40

DON PEDRO (*aside*)
See you where Benedick hath hid himself?

CLAUDIO (*aside*)
O, very well, my lord. The music ended,
We'll fit the hid fox with a pennyworth.

26 an] F; and Q   37.2] OXFORD; *Enter prince, Leonato, Claudio, Musicke* Q; F *substitutes*
Jack Wilson *for* Musicke; *most eds. substitute* Balthasar *for* Musicke; RIVERSIDE *specifies*
'*music within*'   43 hid fox] WARBURTON; kid-foxe Q; cade fox HANMER   43.1] Q; *not in* F

22 **converted** altered by love. The contrasts Benedick describes were a comic
set topic (before love and after) that
Shakespeare used in *Two Gentlemen*
2.1, the opening of *Richard III*, and
elsewhere.

25 **oyster** thought to be at the bottom of
the hierarchical chain of animal life.
Such a transformation would have
been especially daunting to the articulate Benedick.

29 **all graces** He finds beauty, wisdom,
and virtue in Beatrice at 228-30.
Benedick (see 30) is as prudent about

money as Claudio and Beatrice.

32 **cheapen** bargain for; an awkward
note here, especially given the puns at
33 on 'noble' and 'angel', coins worth
33p and 50p respectively

34 **her hair** Benedick shares Beatrice's
taste for authenticity.

43 **fit . . . pennyworth** give Benedick more
than he bargained for. 'Pennyworth'
is used as in the modern 'give him his
money's worth'.

hid fox Warburton emended Q's 'kid-
fox' (which is hard to justify as kid =
cub), to hid-fox, as in the child's hid-

Enter Balthasar with music

DON PEDRO

Come, Balthasar, we'll hear that song again.

BALTHASAR

O good my lord, tax not so bad a voice   45
To slander music any more than once.

DON PEDRO

It is the witness still of excellency
To put a strange face on his own perfection.
I pray thee sing, and let me woo no more.

BALTHASAR

Because you talk of wooing I will sing,   50
Since many a wooer doth commence his suit
To her he thinks not worthy, yet he woos.
Yet will he swear he loves.

DON PEDRO   Nay, pray thee, come;
Or if thou wilt hold longer argument,
Do it in notes.

BALTHASAR   Note this before my notes: 55
There's not a note of mine that's worth the noting.

DON PEDRO

Why, these are very crotchets that he speaks.
Note notes, forsooth, and nothing!

58 nothing] Q; noting THEOBALD   58.1] CAPELL (*Air*); *not in* Q

ing game alluded to by Hamlet in
4.2.30. The emendation is strength-
ened by 'hid' two lines earlier, which
justifies the slightly awkward compound. Also, a script *h* is easily misread as *k*.

43.1 Q's 'Enter Balthasar with Music' is
infrequently retained by editors, who
often add Balthasar to the Q entrance
of the Prince and others after 36. The
repeated direction for Music (an ac-
companist? the singer alone?) suggests Shakespeare's awareness of the
need for it but his prudent postponement of greater precision until the play
was in rehearsal. For 'Music' F gives
the name of Jack Wilson; most recent
editions substitute Balthasar or call
for music within. Placing the stage
direction here has the advantage of
somewhat isolating the Benedick-plot
conversation and the aristocratic plot-
ters. Jack Wilson has been inconclu-

sively identified as an actor, an Oxford
professor, a singer and songwriter who
dined with the actor Edward Alleyn,
and a John Wilson who resided in the
parish of St Bartholomew the Less; see
Variorum 109–10.

45 **tax** command
   so bad a voice How bad is it? See
   Introd., pp. 44–5.
47 **the witness still** always proof
48 **put a strange face** pretend not to recognize
   his its
49 **pray thee, come** By this time Don
   Pedro finds Balthasar a bit tedious, and
   by 57–8 completely so.
56 **noting** taking notice of, and setting
   down in musical notation
57 **crotchets** both quarter notes and trivial eccentricities
58 **nothing** nothing else. Don Pedro
   commands Balthasar to get on with

The accompaniment begins

BENEDICK Now, divine air! Now is his soul ravished. Is
it not strange that sheep's guts should hale souls out   60
of men's bodies? Well, a horn for my money, when
all's done.

BALTHASAR (*sings*)
        Sigh no more, ladies, sigh no more.
          Men were deceivers ever,
        One foot in sea, and one on shore,   65
          To one thing constant never.
        Then sigh not so, but let them go,
          And be you blithe and bonny,
        Converting all your sounds of woe
          Into hey nonny, nonny.   70

        Sing no more ditties, sing no more
          Of dumps so dull and heavy.
        The fraud of men was ever so
          Since summer first was leafy.
        Then sigh not so, but let them go,
          And be you blithe and bonny,   75
        Converting all your sounds of woe
          Into hey nonny, nonny.

DON PEDRO By my troth, a good song.
BALTHASAR And an ill singer, my lord.   80
DON PEDRO Ha, no, no, faith. Thou sing'st well enough
for a shift.
BENEDICK (*aside*) An he had been a dog that should

---

63 BALTHASAR (*Sings*.)] CAPELL (*subs.*); *The Song.* Q   71 more] OXFORD; moe Q   75–8]
Q *prints only* 'Then sigh not so, &c.'

the song. The word-play on noting–
nothing was encouraged by their apparent similarity in Elizabethan pronunciation because of the long *o* sounded in
'nothing' and the current acceptability
of the *t–th* exchange.

60 **sheep's guts** The accompaniment is a
stringed instrument, most likely a lute.
61 **a horn for my money** Benedick, unlike
the lover he has described, prefers the
'music' of the hunt or battle. Possibly
an unwitting evocation of the idea of
cuckoldry, which Benedick will later

accept as one of life's possibilities.
63–78 On the song see Appendix.
64 **Men were deceivers ever** This line, like
'The fraud of men was ever so' (73),
attributes to men the sexual unreliability attributed to women in the play's
pervasive allusions to cuckoldry.
71 **more** Q's 'moe' is retained by some
editors as the old comparative of
'many' (*OED* s. v. *adj.* 2).
71–2 **ditties . . . dumps** Both words had
more dignity than now.
83 **An** If

have howled thus, they would have hanged him.
And I pray God his bad voice bode no mischief. I had   85
as lief have heard the night-raven, come what plague
could have come after it.

DON PEDRO Yea, marry, dost thou hear, Balthasar? I
pray thee get us some excellent music, for tomorrow
night we would have it at the Lady Hero's chamber   90
window.

BALTHASAR The best I can, my lord.

DON PEDRO Do so. Farewell.   *Exit Balthasar*
Come hither, Leonato. What was it you told me of
today, that your niece Beatrice was in love with   95
Signor Benedick?

CLAUDIO (*aside*) O, ay, stalk on, stalk on; the fowl sits.
⌈*Raising his voice*⌉ I did never think that lady would
have loved any man.

LEONATO No, nor I neither. But most wonderful that   100
she should so dote on Signor Benedick, whom she
hath in all outward behaviours seemed ever to abhor.

BENEDICK (*aside*) Is't possible? Sits the wind in that
corner?

LEONATO By my troth, my lord, I cannot tell what to   105
think of it. But that she loves him with an enraged
affection, it is past the infinite of thought.

DON PEDRO Maybe she doth but counterfeit.

CLAUDIO Faith, like enough.

LEONATO O God! Counterfeit? There was never   110
counterfeit of passion came so near the life of passion
as she discovers it.

93 SD] Q (*at 85*); *Exeunt Bal⟨thasar⟩ and Music* CAPELL   98 SD] *This edition; not in* Q
106–7 it. But . . . affection,] *This edition, after* POPE (it; but . . . affection;) it, but . . .
affection, Q; it, but . . . affection; STEEVENS 1778

86 **night-raven** Its croaking proverbially
   (Tilley R33) portended disaster.
97 **stalk on** like a stalking horse that advances slowly on the game, concealing
   the hunter behind it
103–4 **Sits . . . corner** Is that how things
   are? Proverbial: Tilley W419.
106 **enraged** most intense
106–7 Q's light punctuation makes the
   speech difficult. Since 'past the infinite
   of thought' means something like 'it's
   incredible', Steevens's substitution of a

semi-colon for Q's comma after 'affection' seems inferior to Pope's period
after 'it'. In addition, Steevens's punctuation gives 'but' the force of 'save'
or 'except'—which it can hardly have
if it begins the sentence as Pope proposes—and Steevens permits the final
clause to have the rhetorical force of
rhythmic isolation and too general and
vague a reference.
112 **discovers** reveals

DON PEDRO Why, what effects of passion shows she?

CLAUDIO (*aside*) Bait the hook well. This fish will bite.

LEONATO What effects, my lord? She will sit you—you   115
heard my daughter tell you how.

CLAUDIO She did indeed.

DON PEDRO How, how, I pray you? You amaze me. I
would have thought her spirit had been invincible
against all assaults of affection.   120

LEONATO I would have sworn it had, my lord, especially
against Benedick.

BENEDICK (*aside*) I should think this a gull, but that the
white-bearded fellow speaks it. Knavery cannot, sure,
hide himself in such reverence.   125

CLAUDIO (*aside*) He hath ta'en th'infection. Hold it up.

DON PEDRO Hath she made her affection known to
Benedick?

LEONATO No, and swears she never will. That's her
torment.   130

CLAUDIO 'Tis true, indeed, so your daughter says. 'Shall
I,' says she, 'that have so oft encountered him with
scorn, write to him that I love him?'

LEONATO This says she now when she is beginning to
write to him; for she'll be up twenty times a night,   135
and there will she sit in her smock till she have writ
a sheet of paper. My daughter tells us all.

CLAUDIO Now you talk of a sheet of paper, I remember
a pretty jest your daughter told us of.

LEONATO O, when she had writ it and was reading it   140
over, she found 'Benedick' and 'Beatrice' between the
sheet.

CLAUDIO That.

LEONATO O, she tore the letter into a thousand halfpence, railed at herself that she should be so immod-   145

139 us of] F; of us Q

115 **sit you** the ethical dative used to arouse interest. Words fail Leonato, probably because of his literal-mindedness. He covers by calling on Claudio for help. Don Pedro mischievously pursues the question at 118, but prudently does not wait for an answer.

123 **gull** trick
126 **Hold it up** keep on going
136 **smock** slip.
143 **That** Claudio's laconic expression of disappointment at having told the oldest joke since the use of bedclothes; even Leonato knows it.

est to write to one that she knew would flout her. 'I
measure him,' says she, 'by my own spirit, for I
should flout him if he writ to me. Yea, though I loved
him I should.'

CLAUDIO Then down upon her knees she falls, weeps,   150
sobs, beats her heart, tears her hair, prays, curses.
'O sweet Benedick! God give me patience.'

LEONATO She doth indeed; my daughter says so. And
the ecstasy hath so much overborne her that my
daughter is sometime afeard she will do a desperate   155
outrage to herself. It is very true.

DON PEDRO It were good that Benedick knew of it by
some other, if she will not discover it.

CLAUDIO To what end? He would make but a sport of
it and torment the poor lady worse.   160

DON PEDRO An he should, it were an alms to hang him.
She's an excellent sweet lady and, out of all suspicion, she is virtuous.

CLAUDIO And she is exceeding wise.

DON PEDRO In everything but in loving Benedick.   165

LEONATO O my lord, wisdom and blood combating in
so tender a body, we have ten proofs to one that
blood hath the victory. I am sorry for her, as I have
just cause, being her uncle and her guardian.

DON PEDRO I would she had bestowed this dotage on   170
me. I would have doffed all other respects and made
her half myself. I pray you tell Benedick of it, and
hear what a will say.

LEONATO Were it good, think you?

---

148 loved] This edition, *after* Wells *conj.*; loue Q   171 doffed] Q (daft), OXFORD, daffed
most eds.

144–5 **halfpence** bits; the coin was very
small

148 Stanley Wells suggests that Q's 'loue'
might have been a misprint for 'lou'd'
(loved), certainly more idiomatic here.

154 **ecstasy** colloquially a fit; an ecstasy
was literally an intense state in which
the soul left the body.

161 **alms** act of charity

166–6 **blood** passion

169 **guardian** Evidently Beatrice is an orphan.

171 **doffed** put off. For Q's 'daft' most
editors print 'daffed', an awkward ar-
chaic variant.
other respects Among them are the
lack of rank and possibly a large
enough dowry; one cannot tell how
serious the Prince is here.

173 **a** he

CLAUDIO Hero thinks surely she will die; for she says   175
she will die if he love her not, and she will die ere
she make her love known, and she will die if he woo
her, rather than she will bate one breath of her
accustomed crossness.

DON PEDRO She doth well. If she should make tender of   180
her love 'tis very possible he'll scorn it, for the man,
as you know all, hath a contemptible spirit.

CLAUDIO He is a very proper man.

DON PEDRO He hath indeed a good outward happiness.

CLAUDIO Before God, and in my mind, very wise.   185

DON PEDRO He doth indeed show some sparks that are
like wit.

CLAUDIO And I take him to be valiant.

DON PEDRO As Hector, I assure you. And in the mana-
ging of quarrels you may say he is wise, for either   190
he avoids them with great discretion or undertakes
them with a most Christianlike fear.

LEONATO If he do fear God, a must necessarily keep
peace. If he break the peace, he ought to enter into
a quarrel with fear and trembling.   195

DON PEDRO And so will he do, for the man doth fear
God, howsoever it seems not in him by some large
jests he will make. Well, I am sorry for your niece.
Shall we go seek Benedick and tell him of her love?

CLAUDIO Never tell him, my lord. Let her wear it out   200
with good counsel.

LEONATO Nay, that's impossible. She may wear her
heart out first.

DON PEDRO Well, we will hear further of it by your
daughter. Let it cool the while. I love Benedick well,   205
and I could wish he would modestly examine himself

188 CLAUDIO] Q; *Leon.* F

178 **bate** abate
180 **make tender of** offer
182 **contemptible** contemptuous
183 **proper** good-looking
184 **good outward happiness** pleasant ap-
      pearance
187 **wit** intelligence
190 **you . . . wise** This praise of Benedick's
      virtues (which parallel those attributed

to Beatrice) is slyly undercut by the
emphasis on his great discretion and
'Christian-like fear' in quarrels, and
here by 'You may say', implying the
scepticism of 'That's one way to look
at it.'
197 **large** broad, inappropriate
200–1 **wear . . . counsel** survive it with
      the help of intelligent self-examination

to see how much he is unworthy so good a lady.
LEONATO My lord, will you walk? Dinner is ready.
CLAUDIO (*aside*) If he do not dote on her upon this, I
will never trust my expectation.   210
DON PEDRO (*aside*) Let there be the same net spread for
her, and that must your daughter and her
gentlewomen carry. The sport will be when they hold
one opinion of the other's dotage, and no such
matter. That's the scene that I would see, which will   215
be merely a dumb show. Let us send her to call him
in to dinner.
                    Exeunt Don Pedro, Claudio, and Leonato
BENEDICK (*coming forward*) This can be no trick. The
conference was sadly borne. They have the truth of
this from Hero. They seem to pity the lady; it seems   220
her affections have their full bent. Love me? Why,
it must be requited. I hear how I am censured. They
say I will bear myself proudly if I perceive the love
come from her. They say too that she will rather die
than give any sign of affection. I did never think to   225
marry. I must not seem proud. Happy are they that
hear their detractions and can put them to mending.
They say the lady is fair; 'tis a truth, I can bear
them witness. And virtuous; 'tis so, I cannot reprove
it. And wise, but for loving me. By my troth, it is no   230
addition to her wit nor no great argument of her
folly, for I will be horribly in love with her. I may
chance have some odd quirks and remnants of wit
broken on me because I have railed so long against
marriage, but doth not the appetite alter? A man   235

---

214 one opinion of the other's] This edition, *after* Craven *conj.* (one opinion of another's);
one an opinion of an others Q   216.1] F (*Exeunt.*); *not in* Q

209 **upon** after
214–15 **and no such matter** and they will
  be wrong. But *Don Pedro* is wrong.
216 **be . . . dumb show** they will be
  speechless; also it will be an entertainment
219 **sadly borne** carried on seriously
221 **full bent** like a bow, stretched to the
  limit
222 **requited** a cardinal rule of romantic
love, as in Dante, *Inferno* 5.103,
  'Amor, ch'a nullo amato amar perdo-
  na': Love which frees no one loved
  from the obligation of loving in return.
  censured judged, but without the modern sense of condemnation
229 **reprove** disprove
231 **argument** evidence
232 **horribly** exceedingly
233 **odd quirks** old jokes

loves the meat in his youth that he cannot endure
in his age. Shall quips and sentences and these paper
bullets of the brain awe a man from the career of
his humour? No. The world must be peopled. When
I said I would die a bachelor, I did not think I should   240
live till I were married. Here comes Beatrice.

     Enter Beatrice

By this day, she's a fair lady. I do spy some marks
of love in her.

BEATRICE Against my will I am sent to bid you come
in to dinner.   245

BENEDICK
Fair Beatrice, I thank you for your pains.

BEATRICE I took no more pains for those thanks than
you take pains to thank me. If it had been painful I
would not have come.

BENEDICK You take pleasure, then, in the message?   250

BEATRICE Yea, just so much as you may take upon a
knife's point and not choke a daw withal.—You have
no stomach, signor? Fare you well.   *Exit*

BENEDICK Ha! 'Against my will I am sent to bid you
come in to dinner.' There's a double meaning in that.   255
'I took no more pains for those thanks than you took
pains to thank me.' That's as much as to say 'Any
pains that I take for you is as easy as thanks.' If I
do not take pity of her I am a villain. If I do not love
her I am a Jew. I will go get her picture.   *Exit*   260

241.1] Q (*after 226*)   252 and not choke] This edition, *after* COLLIER 1853 MS; and
choake Q

236 **meat** food
237 **sentences** maxims
238 **career of his humour** pursuit of his
     inclination. 'Career', as at 5.1.133,
     refers to the galloping charge of a
     horse, especially in a tournament.
246 Appropriately, Benedick greets his
     beloved in blank verse.
252 **not choke** This emends Q's 'and
     choake'. Without the easily overlooked
     'not' the comparison, though plaus-
     ible, loses force.
     withal an emphatic form of 'with',
     compensating for the weakness of a

prepositional ending to a clause
253 **no stomach** no appetite. Apparently
     Benedick has not moved.
260 **a Jew** therefore, from an Elizabethan
     viewpoint, faithless
     get her picture Benedick means to
     commission an ornamental miniature,
     a small portrait as a keepsake or to be
     worn on his person in a locket. This
     was the great moment of English por-
     trait miniaturists, the greatest of
     whom, Nicholas Hilliard, was commis-
     sioned in 1600 to write a treatise on
     his art.

3.1   *Enter Hero and two gentlewomen, Margaret and*
        Ursula

HERO

Good Margaret, run thee to the parlour.
There shalt thou find my cousin Beatrice
Proposing with the Prince and Claudio.
Whisper her ear, and tell her I and Ursula
Walk in the orchard, and our whole discourse   5
Is all of her. Say that thou overheard'st us,
And bid her steal into the pleachèd bower
Where honeysuckles, ripened by the sun,
Forbid the sun to enter, like favourites
Made proud by princes, that advance their pride   10
Against that power that bred it. There will she hide
    her
To listen our propose. This is thy office.
Bear thee well in it, and leave us alone.

MARGARET

I'll make her come, I warrant you, presently.   *Exit*

HERO

Now, Ursula, when Beatrice doth come,   15
As we do trace this alley up and down
Our talk must only be of Benedick.
When I do name him, let it be thy part
To praise him more than ever man did merit.
My talk to thee must be how Benedick   20
Is sick in love with Beatrice. Of this matter
Is little Cupid's crafty arrow made,
That only wounds by hearsay.

3.1] *Actus Tertius* F; *not in* Q   12 propose] Q; purpose F   14 SD] F2; *not in* Q   23
SD] Q (*'Enter Beatrice' after* 25); F (*'Enter Beatrice' after* 'begin'); ~ *who hides* This edition

3.1.1 **parlour** In a great house like Leonato's the parlour was reserved for
private family use.
3 **Proposing** conversing
4 **Whisper her ear** See Abbott 200 on
omitted prepositions.
  Ursula Q's 'Ursley', a familiar pronunciation, suggests the intimacy of Hero
and her gentlewomen. That honorific
term reflects their sometimes ambiguous social position.
7 **pleachèd** See 1.2.8. Beatrice hides behind the prop that hid Benedick, en-

forcing visually the parallel in their
situations.
8–11 **Where honeysuckles . . . bred it**
not a topical allusion, but one of the
conventional moral lessons of natural
history taught to persons of good family; Nature was God's other Book.
12 **listen our propose** See 3 and 4 above.
   office task
14 **presently** at once
21 **this matter** i.e. praise, gossip
23 **only wounds** wounds only

Enter Beatrice, who hides

                  Now begin,
For look where Beatrice like a lapwing runs
Close by the ground to hear our conference.   25
URSULA *(aside to Hero)*
  The pleasant'st angling is to see the fish
  Cut with her golden oars the silver stream
  And greedily devour the treacherous bait.
  So angle we for Beatrice, who even now
  Is couchèd in the woodbine coverture.   30
  Fear you not my part of the dialogue.
HERO *(aside to Ursula)*
  Then go we near her, that her ear lose nothing
  Of the false-sweet bait that we lay for it.
    (Approaching Beatrice's hiding-place)
  No, truly, Ursula, she is too disdainful.
  I know her spirits are as coy and wild   35
  As haggards of the rock.
URSULA   But are you sure
  That Benedick loves Beatrice so entirely?
HERO
  So says the Prince and my new-trothèd lord.
URSULA
  And did they bid you tell her of it, madam?
HERO
  They did entreat me to acquaint her of it,   40
  But I persuaded them, if they loved Benedick,
  To wish him wrestle with affection
  And never to let Beatrice know of it.
URSULA
  Why did you so? Doth not the gentleman
  Deserve as full as fortunate a bed   45
  As ever Beatrice shall couch upon?

33.1] OXFORD (*subs.*); *not in* Q; *They advance to the bower* STEEVENS 1778

24–5 **lapwing . . . ground** The plover, or lapwing, protects itself and its nest by moving through the grass in this fashion.
25 **conference** conversation
30 **woodbine coverture** shelter made by thickly grown honeysuckle
35 **coy** disdainful
36 **haggards** mature wild female hawks.

The term's probable relation with 'hag' through the Old High German for 'grove' suggests the social penalty for a woman's remaining 'untamed' and hunting for herself rather than for a master (i.e. resisting marriage).
44–6 **Doth not . . . upon** Doesn't Benedick deserve a wife as good as Beatrice?

HERO

O god of love! I know he doth deserve
As much as may be yielded to a man,
But nature never framed a woman's heart
Of prouder stuff than that of Beatrice.   50
Disdain and scorn ride sparkling in her eyes,
Misprising what they look on, and her wit
Values itself so highly that to her
All matter else seems weak. She cannot love,
Nor take no shape nor project of affection,   55
She is so self-endeared.

URSULA   Sure, I think so,
And therefore certainly it were not good
She knew his love, lest she'll make sport at it.

HERO

Why, you speak truth. I never yet saw man,
How wise, how noble, young, how rarely featured,   60
But she would spell him backward. If fair-faced,
She would swear the gentleman should be her sister;
If black, why nature, drawing of an antic,
Made a foul blot; if tall, a lance ill-headed;
If low, an agate very vilely cut;   65
If speaking, why, a vane blown with all winds;
If silent, why, a block movèd with none.
So turns she every man the wrong side out,
And never gives to truth and virtue that
Which simpleness and merit purchaseth.   70

URSULA

Sure, sure, such carping is not commendable.

HERO

No, not to be so odd and from all fashions
As Beatrice is cannot be commendable.
But who dare tell her so? If I should speak,

---

52 **Misprising** underestimating
55 **project** idea
60 **How** however
   rarely splendidly
61 **spell him backward** see 68
63 **black** swarthy
   antic grotesque
65 **agate** Small human figures were com-

monly cut in the agates on seal-rings.
In *2 Henry IV* 1.2.16 Falstaff refers to
his diminutive page as an agate.
70 **simpleness** integrity
   purchaseth earns
71, 73 **commendable** The stress fell on
   the first syllable.
72 **from** contrary to

She would mock me into air; O, she would laugh me   75
Out of myself, press me to death with wit.
Therefore let Benedick, like covered fire,
Consume away in sighs, waste inwardly.
It were a better death than die with mocks,
Which is as bad as die with tickling.   80

URSULA

Yet tell her of it; hear what she will say.

HERO

No. Rather I will go to Benedick
And counsel him to fight against his passion.
And truly, I'll devise some honest slanders
To stain my cousin with. One doth not know   85
How much an ill word may empoison liking.

URSULA

O, do not do your cousin such a wrong.
She cannot be so much without true judgement,
Having so swift and excellent a wit
As she is prized to have, as to refuse   90
So rare a gentleman as Signor Benedick.

HERO

He is the only man of Italy,
Always excepted my dear Claudio.

URSULA

I pray you be not angry with me, madam;
Speaking my fancy, Signor Benedick,   95
For shape, for bearing, argument, and valour
Goes foremost in report through Italy.

HERO

Indeed, he hath an excellent good name.

91 as Signor Benedick] Q; as Benedick POPE, *conj.* Craven

76 **press me to death** Pressing was the *peine forte et dure*, the torture inflicted on those who chose to remain silent at their arraignment rather than pleading either innocent or guilty to a charge of felony. Often their motive for silence was the hope of preventing the confiscation—after their conviction—of property destined for their heirs. They were placed in solitary confinement, kept without food, and their bodies were loaded with heavy iron weights increased until they entered a plea or died.

77 **covered** banked

84 **honest slanders** well-intentioned lies that will not really harm her. The speech is an ironic anticipation of Hero's own situation.

90 **prized** esteemed

92 **only** unrivalled, as in *Hamlet* 3.2.116: 'your only jig-maker'

96 **argument** discourse

URSULA

His excellence did earn it ere he had it.
When are you married, madam? 100

HERO

Why, every day, tomorrow. Come, go in.
I'll show thee some attires and have thy counsel
Which is the best to furnish me tomorrow.

URSULA (*aside*)

She's limed, I warrant you. We have caught her,
madam.

HERO (*aside*)

If it prove so, then loving goes by haps. 105
Some Cupid kills with arrows, some with traps.

Exeunt Hero and Ursula

BEATRICE (*coming forward*)

What fire is in mine ears? Can this be true?
Stand I condemned for pride and scorn so much?
Contempt, farewell; and maiden pride, adieu.
No glory lives behind the back of such. 110
And, Benedick, love on. I will requite thee,
Taming my wild heart to thy loving hand.
If thou dost love, my kindness shall incite thee
To bind our loves up in a holy band.
For others say thou dost deserve, and I 115
Believe it better than reportingly. *Exit*

104] *as one line,* POPE; *as two lines, ending at* 'you' *and* 'madam', Q   106.1] F (*Exit.*);
not in Q; ~ *Hero and Ursula* MALONE

100 **married** to be married
101 **tomorrow** after tomorrow
102 **attires** apparel, but sometimes specifically head-dresses
103 **furnish** adorn
104 **limed** Small birds were caught in bird-lime, a sticky plant material smeared on twigs where they were likely to land.
105 **haps** accidents
107 **fire is in mine ears** Burning sensations in the ears were a proverbial sign

(Tilley E14) that one was being talked about. Beatrice, like Benedick, speaks in verse as she consciously accepts being in love, but she outdoes him, as usual, by speaking all but a quatrain of a sonnet, rather than mere blank verse as he does.
110 **behind the back** after
112 **Taming** This recalls the imagery of the haggard at 36.
116 **reportingly** mere hearsay

3.2 *Enter Don Pedro, Claudio, Benedick, and Leonato*

DON PEDRO I do but stay till your marriage be consummate, and then go I toward Aragon.

CLAUDIO I'll bring you thither, my lord, if you'll vouchsafe me.

DON PEDRO Nay, that would be as great a soil in the   5
new gloss of your marriage as to show a child his
new coat and forbid him to wear it. I will only be
bold with Benedick for his company, for from the
crown of his head to the sole of his foot he is all
mirth. He hath twice or thrice cut Cupid's bow-   10
string, and the little hangman dare not shoot at him.
He hath a heart as sound as a bell, and his tongue
is the clapper, for what his heart thinks his tongue
speaks.

BENEDICK Gallants, I am not as I have been.   15

LEONATO So say I. Methinks you are sadder.

CLAUDIO I hope he be in love.

DON PEDRO Hang him, truant! There's no true drop of
blood in him to be truly touched with love. If he be
sad, he wants money.   20

BENEDICK I have the toothache.

DON PEDRO Draw it.

BENEDICK Hang it.

CLAUDIO You must hang it first and draw it afterwards.

DON PEDRO What? Sigh for the toothache?   25

LEONATO Where is but a humour or a worm.

BENEDICK Well, everyone can master a grief but he that
has it.

CLAUDIO Yet say I he is in love.

DON PEDRO There is no appearance of fancy in him,   30

3.2.0 *Don Pedro*] Q (*Prince*)   27 can] POPE; cannot Q

3.2.1–2 **consummate** consummated, an
  acceptable past participle, according to
  Abbott 342
  3 **bring** escort
    vouchsafe permit
  7–8 **only be bold** be bold only
  11 **little hangman** little rascal
  18 **truant** the truant (from love)
  22 **Draw** extract (the tooth) with a pun
    at 24 on draw = disembowel

23 **Hang it** Hanging was the fate of teeth,
  which were hung as advertisements of
  services outside barber shops, and also
  the fate of some convicted felons, who
  also were 'drawn', i.e. disembowelled.
26 **humour or a worm** Stephen Batman,
  Upon Bartholeme (1582), states in 5.20
  that toothaches are caused by worms
  breeding in rotten humours (fluids) in
  the hollows inside teeth.

unless it be a fancy that he hath to strange disguises:
as to be a Dutchman today, a Frenchman tomorrow,
or in the shape of two countries at once, as a German
from the waist downward, all slops, and a Spaniard
from the hip upward, no doublet. Unless he have a   35
fancy to this foolery, as it appears he hath, he is no
fool for fancy, as you would have it appear he is.

CLAUDIO If he be not in love with some woman, there
is no believing old signs. A brushes his hat o' morn-
ings; what should that bode?   40

DON PEDRO Hath any man seen him at the barber's?

CLAUDIO No, but the barber's man hath been seen with
him, and the old ornament of his cheek hath already
stuffed· tennis balls.

LEONATO Indeed, he looks younger than he did by the   45
loss of a beard.

DON PEDRO Nay, a rubs himself with civet. Can you
smell him out by that?

CLAUDIO That's as much as to say the sweet youth's
in love.   50

DON PEDRO The greatest note of it is his melancholy.

CLAUDIO And when was he wont to wash his face?

33–5 or . . . doublet] Q; *not in* F   51 DON PEDRO] F (Prin⟨ce⟩); Bene⟨dick⟩ Q

30, 31 **fancy** Don Pedro puns on 'fancy'
as both 'love' and 'whim'; see also
36–7.

31 **disguises** The extravagant imitation of
European fashions by young English-
men was satirized in the theatre (e.g.
by Portia in *Merchant of Venice* 1.2.60–
1) and by traditionalists who feared for
the corruption of English wholesomeness.

33–5 **or . . . doublet** F omits this passage,
perhaps to avoid giving offence when
the play was revived in 1612–13 as
part of the entertainment during the
celebration of the wedding of Princess
Elizabeth to the Elector Palatine. King
James was sensitive to satires on for-
eigners.

34 **slops** baggy breeches

35 **no doublet** Possibly it was hidden
under a long Spanish cape.

36–7 **no fool for fancy** not playing the fool
because of love

44 **stuffed tennis balls** a popular joke

based on a common practice. Benedick
apparently knows of Beatrice's dislike
of beards.

47 **civet** a perfume affected by fashionable
gentlemen. It was extracted from the
genital glands of the civet cat.

51 **note** indication

52 **wash his face** Elizabethans were notoriously underwashed. Forks were
just coming in from Italy and so hands
were routinely washed—but see the
fuss over perfumed gloves at 3.4.59—
especially by the cultivated, among
some of whom there was a concern for
personal hygiene. At 2.3.63 of *Coriolanus* the aristocratic hero urges that
the citizens of Rome be told to 'wash
their faces | And keep their teeth
clean'. Benedick deserves the benefit
of the doubt; he probably washes his
face, though possibly more often post-
Beatrice. The phrase evidently refers to
his 'washing' it with perfume.

DON PEDRO Yea, or to paint himself? For the which I
hear what they say of him.

CLAUDIO Nay, but his jesting spirit, which is now crept   55
into a lute-string, and now governed by stops.

DON PEDRO Indeed, that tells a heavy tale for him.
Conclude, conclude, he is in love.

CLAUDIO Nay, but I know who loves him.

DON PEDRO That would I know, too. I warrant, one that   60
knows him not.

CLAUDIO Yes, and his ill conditions, and in despite of
all, dies for him.

DON PEDRO She shall be buried with her face upwards.

BENEDICK Yet is this no charm for the toothache. Old   65
signor, walk aside with me. I have studied eight or
nine wise words to speak to you which these hobby-
horses must not hear.   *Exeunt Benedick and Leonato*

DON PEDRO For my life, to break with him about Beatrice.   70

CLAUDIO 'Tis even so. Hero and Margaret have by this
played their parts with Beatrice, and then the two
bears will not bite one another when they meet.

    Enter Don John the Bastard

DON JOHN My lord, and brother, God save you.

---

55 now crept] Q; new crept WILSON   56 now governed] Q; new-governed DYCE   68
SD] THEOBALD; *not in* Q   73.1 Don] *not in* Q   74 DON JOHN] ROWE; *Bastard* Q (*subs.
throughout the scene*)

53 **paint himself** use cosmetics
53–4 **For . . . him** His use of cosmetics has
started the gossip I hear about him.
55–6 **now . . . stops** Benedick's satiric
spirit has dwindled to the string of a
lute, the instrument often accompa-
nying love songs. He is now regulated
by the denials ('stops') typically imposed on male lovers, as a lutestring
is regulated by the frets, the thin rings
of gut—now wood or metal bars—on
the fingerboard. Pressing the string
against a fret determined the string's
effective length and hence the note
played.
57 **tells . . . him** gives us *his* sad story
62 **ill conditions** miserable character
63 **dies for him** A trite pun on die = pine
away and die = have an orgasm;
hence the reference at 64 to Beatrice's

burial face upwards.
67 **words . . . to you** A loose end; at
5.4.21–2 Benedick seems to be raising
the question of marriage as if for the
first time with Leonato.
67–8 **hobby-horses** buffoons, after the
stylized horse of wood frame and cloth
worn during the morris (Moorish)
dance.
71 **Margaret** Ursula played a much larger
part than Margaret.
72–3 **two bears will not bite** That bears
(and wolves) would not bite one another was proverbial (Tilley W606),
but hardly appropriate since these two
bears habitually bit one another and
are now less bear-like because of love.
Aphorism is such a universal comfort
as explanation that it is invoked even
when it makes no sense.

DON PEDRO Good-e'en, brother.   75

DON JOHN If your leisure served I would speak with you.

DON PEDRO In private?

DON JOHN If it please you. Yet Count Claudio may hear, for what I would speak of concerns him.   80

DON PEDRO What's the matter?

DON JOHN (*to Claudio*) Means your lordship to be married tomorrow?

DON PEDRO You know he does.

DON JOHN I know not that when he knows what I   85 know.

CLAUDIO If there be any impediment, I pray you discover it.

DON JOHN You may think I love you not. Let that appear hereafter, and aim better at me by that I now   90 will manifest. For my brother, I think he holds you well, and in dearness of heart hath holp to effect your ensuing marriage—surely suit ill spent, and labour ill bestowed.

DON PEDRO Why, what's the matter?   95

DON JOHN I came hither to tell you; and, circumstances shortened—for she has been too long a-talking of— the lady is disloyal.

CLAUDIO Who, Hero?

DON JOHN Even she—Leonato's Hero, your Hero, every   100 man's Hero.

CLAUDIO Disloyal?

DON JOHN The word is too good to paint out her wickedness; I could say she were worse. Think you of a worse title, and I will fit her to it. Wonder not   105 till further warrant. Go but with me tonight, you shall see her chamber window entered, even the

---

75 **Good-e'en** Many editions preserve Q's less clear 'Good den'; both are contracted forms of 'God give you a good even[ing]'.

89–90 **Let that appear hereafter** Whether I love you will be made clear after what I am about to do—a highly ironic remark.

90–1 **aim … manifest** Judge me more accurately by what I am about to reveal—another hard irony.

91–2 **holds you well** thinks highly of you

96–7 **circumstances shortened** sparing you the details

103 **paint out** describe fully

night before her wedding day. If you love her then,
tomorrow wed her. But it would better fit your
honour to change your mind.   110
CLAUDIO May this be so?
DON PEDRO I will not think it.
DON JOHN If you dare not trust that you see, confess
not that you know. If you will follow me I will show
you enough, and when you have seen more and   115
heard more, proceed accordingly.
CLAUDIO If I see anything tonight why I should not
marry her, tomorrow, in the congregation where I
should wed, there will I shame her.
DON PEDRO And as I wooed for thee to obtain her, I   120
will join with thee to disgrace her.
DON JOHN I will disparage her no farther till you are
my witnesses. Bear it coldly but till midnight, and let
the issue show itself.
DON PEDRO O day untowardly turned!   125
CLAUDIO O mischief strangely thwarting!
DON JOHN O plague right well prevented! So will you
say when you have seen the sequel.   *Exeunt*

3.3   *Enter Dogberry and his partner Verges, with the
      Watch*
DOGBERRY Are you good men and true?
VERGES Yea, or else it were pity but they should suffer
salvation, body and soul.

108 her then,] HANMER; her, then Q   118 her, tomorrow, in] CAPELL (*subs.*); her tomorrow in Q; her tomorrow, in ROWE   128 SD] *not in* Q
     3.3.0.1 *partner Verges*] Q (*compartner*); ~ *Verges* ROWE; *not in* Q

113–14 **If . . . know** Portentous but un-
     clear, as A. B. Dawson points out in
     Studies in English Literature (1982),
     214. Roughly: 'If you won't believe
     your eyes, don't think you know any-
     thing.'
     that . . . that what . . . what
123 **Bear it coldly** Take it calmly. Claudio
     hardly needs such advice, but coolness
     here is not only a character trait but
     a theatrical convenience. Passionate
     outrage might have led to a confron-
     tation of Borachio or of the imagined
     Hero, either at once or immediately

after Don John's charade. For the sake
of the plot it was best for the audience
to *be told* of Claudio's rage at 3.3.156–
61. The missing passion needed to end
the scene is supplied in the triad of
operatic interjections beginning with
'O'.
3.3.0 The Watch was a group of citizens
chosen for police duty. Their reputation for incompetence was proverbial,
Tilley C616 ('You might be a constable
for your wit'), and made them a reliable butt for comedy. It also reflected
the fact that Watch duty was unpaid

DOGBERRY Nay, that were a punishment too good for
them if they should have any allegiance in them,   5
being chosen for the Prince's watch.
VERGES Well, give them their charge, neighbour Dogberry.
DOGBERRY First, who think you the most desertless man
to be constable?   10
⌈A WATCHMAN⌉ Hugh Oatcake, sir, or George Seacoal,
for they can write and read.
DOGBERRY Come hither, neighbour Seacoal, God hath
blessed you with a good name. To be a well-favoured
man is the gift of fortune, but to write and read   15
comes by nature.
⌈A WATCHMAN⌉ Both which, Master Constable—
DOGBERRY You have. I knew it would be your answer.
Well, for your favour, sir, why, give God thanks, and
make no boast of it. And for your writing and read-   20
ing, let that appear when there is no need of such
vanity. You are thought here to be the most senseless
and fit man for the constable of the watch; therefore,
bear you the lantern. This is your charge: you shall
comprehend all vagrom men. You are to bid any man   25
stand, in the Prince's name.
⌈A WATCHMAN⌉ How if a will not stand?
DOGBERRY Why then take no note of him, but let him

---

11 A WATCHMAN] This edition (*see Introd., Speech-Prefixes*); *Watch* 1 Q; SECOND WATCH-
MAN OXFORD   17 A WATCHMAN] This edition; *Watch* 2 Q; SEACOAL MARES; FIRST
WATCHMAN OXFORD   27 A WATCHMAN] This edition; *Watch* 2 Q; SEACOAL MARES;
FIRST WATCHMAN OXFORD

and avoidable upon payment for a de-
puty; see *Measure* 2.1.257–73. Dogberry is the Head Constable and
Verges, though his 'partner', is a
Headborough, and thus a petty constable of lower rank.
3 **salvation** for 'damnation'. This is the
first of many peculiar verbal impro-
visations whose energy and assurance
are a 'downstairs' version of the
word-play and happy perversions of
meaning typical of Beatrice and
Benedick.

7 **charge** duties

9 **desertless** without merit, for 'deserving'
11 On Watch speech-prefixes, see Introd.,
pp. 82–3.
14 **well-favoured** good-looking
15–16 **fortune … nature** On close con-
sideration Dogberry's apparent misuse
of these polar terms takes on some
plausibility. Certainly 'fortune' as
either status or genetic portion leads
to good looks, and any good Chomsky-
an could make out a case for 'nature'
as the source of reading and writing.
25 **vagrom** vagrant, an apparently common mispronunciation
26 **stand** halt

go, and presently call the rest of the watch together, and thank God you are rid of a knave.   30

VERGES If he will not stand when he is bidden, he is none of the Prince's subjects.

DOGBERRY True, and they are to meddle with none but the Prince's subjects. You shall also make no noise in the streets, for for the watch to babble and to talk   35
is most tolerable and not to be endured.

A WATCHMAN We will rather sleep than talk. We know what belongs to a watch.

DOGBERRY Why, you speak like an ancient and most quiet watchman, for I cannot see how sleeping   40
should offend. Only have a care that your bills be not stolen. Well, you are to call at all the alehouses and bid those that are drunk get them to bed.

A WATCHMAN How if they will not?

DOGBERRY Why then, let them alone till they are sober.   45
If they make you not then the better answer, you may say they are not the men you took them for.

A WATCHMAN Well, sir.

DOGBERRY If you meet a thief you may suspect him, by virtue of your office, to be no true man; and for such   50
kind of men, the less you meddle or make with them, why, the more is for your honesty.

A WATCHMAN If we know him to be a thief, shall we not lay hands on him?

DOGBERRY Truly, by your office you may, but I think   55
they that touch pitch will be defiled. The most peaceable way for you if you do take a thief is to let him show himself what he is, and steal out of your company.

VERGES You have been always called a merciful man,   60
partner.

DOGBERRY Truly, I would not hang a dog by my will, much more a man who hath any honesty in him.

---

39 **ancient** experienced
41 **bills** halberds, basic infantry weapons with a combined spear- and axe-head
50 **true** honest, reliable
51 **make with** have to do with
56 **they ... defiled** a portentous tag from

Eccles. 13: 1, which Shakespeare thought appropriate for Falstaff's mockery of paternal wisdom in *1 Henry IV* 2.4.398–9. Turning logic, received opinion, or sound doctrine upside down in order to moralize their oppo

VERGES If you hear a child cry in the night, you must
call to the nurse and bid her still it. 65
A WATCHMAN How if the nurse be asleep and will not
hear us?
DOGBERRY Why then, depart in peace and let the child
wake her with crying, for the ewe that will not hear
her lamb when it baas will never answer a calf when 70
he bleats.
VERGES 'Tis very true.
DOGBERRY This is the end of the charge. You, constable,
are to present the Prince's own person. If you meet
the Prince in the night you may stay him. 75
VERGES Nay, by'r Lady, that I think a cannot.
DOGBERRY Five shillings to one on't with any man that
knows the statutes he may stay him. Marry, not
without the Prince be willing, for indeed the watch
ought to offend no man, and it is an offence to stay 80
a man against his will.
VERGES By'r Lady, I think it be so.
DOGBERRY Ha ha ha! Well, masters, good night. An
there be any matter of weight chances, call up me.
Keep your fellows' counsels, and your own, and good 85
night. (*To Verges*) Come, neighbour.
A WATCHMAN Well, masters, we hear our charge. Let
us go sit here upon the church bench till two, and
then all to bed.
DOGBERRY One word more, honest neighbours. I pray 90
you watch about Signor Leonato's door, for the
wedding being there tomorrow, there is a great coil
tonight. Adieu. Be vigitant, I beseech you.

                Exeunt Dogberry and Verges

93.1 SD] *Dogberry and Verges* POPE; Q (*exeunt.*)

sites is the kind of wit displayed by
Beatrice.
62 **by my will** if I had a choice

69–71 **ewe ... bleats** This sounds like
proverbial 'wisdom' but it is a parodic
invention.
74 **present** represent
78 **statutes** A Dogberryism? This is a case
of reader's or actor's choice: F prints

'statues', Q 'statutes': either may be
a printer's error. Editors must choose Q.
80–1 **it is ... will** Dogberry has discovered
a principle to end all law enforcement.
83 **Ha ha ha** Having wrung agreement
from Verges, Dogberry allows himself
an expression of triumph.
92 **coil** bustle
93 **vigitant** (for 'vigilant')

Enter Borachio and Conrad

BORACHIO What, Conrad!

A WATCHMAN (*aside*) Peace, stir not.   95

BORACHIO Conrad, I say.

CONRAD Here, man, I am at thy elbow.

BORACHIO Mass, an my elbow itched, I thought there
would a scab follow.

CONRAD I will owe thee an answer for that. And now,   100
forward with thy tale.

BORACHIO Stand thee close then under this penthouse,
for it drizzles rain; and I will, like a true drunkard,
utter all to thee.

A WATCHMAN (*aside*) Some treason, masters. Yet stand   105
close.

BORACHIO Therefore, know I have earned of Don John
a thousand ducats.

CONRAD Is it possible that any villainy should be so
dear?   110

BORACHIO Thou shouldst rather ask if it were possible
any villainy should be so rich. For when rich villains
have need of poor ones, poor ones may make what
price they will.

CONRAD I wonder at it.   115

BORACHIO That shows thou art unconfirmed. Thou
knowest that the fashion of a doublet, or a hat, or
a cloak is nothing to a man.

98 **Mass** by the mass; a mild oath

98–9 **elbow . . . scab** An itchy elbow
proverbially (Tilley E98) warned of the
need to change bedfellows or companions. A scab would follow from
scratching the itch, and a scab = rascal
would be the object of the warning.

102 **penthouse** overhang. Probably the
projection over part of the stage was
used here.

103 **like a true drunkard** i.e. truthfully (*in
vino veritas*) and indiscreetly.

108 **thousand ducats** a considerable, but
not an immense, sum. The ducat was
a coin of varying value issued in several countries and metals at various
times; its worth in today's purchasing
power cannot be estimated accurately.
Yet in *Merchant* Graziano was willing
to bet that sum on his being first to

father a male heir; Shylock had to
turn to Tubal to raise 3,000 ducats,
which he did not have on hand; and
the rich and generous Portia was willing to pay Shylock 6,000 ducats (twice
the sum owed) to discharge Antonio's
obligation.

116 **unconfirmed** inexperienced

118 **nothing to a man** no clue to character. Conrad misunderstands, and so objects that doublets *are* something to a
man, namely apparel. Borachio's argument is that fashions rob their wearers
of their true character. The idea links
Hero's character, stolen by Margaret's
disguise, with the characters of 'hot
bloods', outlandishly transformed by the
fashions they wear. There is an intelligence and a moral attitude underneath Borachio's alcoholic obscurity.

CONRAD Yes, it is apparel.

BORACHIO I mean the fashion.   120

CONRAD Yes, the fashion is the fashion.

BORACHIO Tush, I may as well say the fool's the fool.
But seest thou not what a deformed thief this fashion
is?

A WATCHMAN (*aside*) I know that Deformed. A has been   125
a vile thief this seven year. A goes up and down like
a gentleman. I remember his name.

BORACHIO Didst thou not hear somebody?

CONRAD No, 'twas the vane on the house.

BORACHIO Seest thou not, I say, what a deformed thief   130
this fashion is, how giddily a turns about all the
hot-bloods between fourteen and five-and-thirty,
sometimes fashioning them like Pharaoh's soldiers in
the reechy painting, sometime like god Bel's priests
in the old church window, sometime like the shaven   135
Hercules in the smirched, worm-eaten tapestry,
where his codpiece seems as massy as his club?

CONRAD All this I see, and I see that the fashion wears
out more apparel than the man. But art not thou
thyself giddy with the fashion, too, that thou hast   140
shifted out of thy tale into telling me of the fashion?

BORACHIO Not so, neither. But know that I have tonight
wooed Margaret, the Lady Hero's gentlewoman, by
the name of Hero. She leans me out at her mistress'
chamber window, bids me a thousand times good   145
night.—I tell this tale vilely. I should first tell thee
how the Prince, Claudio, and my master, planted and

105, 125 A WATCHMAN] Q; *Sec. Watch* HUMPHREYS; SEACOAL MARES

123 **deformed** possibly a linking of the
physically grotesque with perverse behaviour
134 **reechy** grimy, from the smoking fire-
place, perhaps in a tavern, where biblical themes seemed appropriate, at
least to Falstaff in *2 Henry IV* 2.1.135.
Bel's priests In the Apocrypha they
were slain by the King of Persia when
Daniel proved that they worshipped a
false god.
137 **codpiece** a conspicuous, sometimes
ornamented, pouch at the front of

men's breeches; by 1600 something
of a joke. The contrast with an unpre-
cedentedly shaven Hercules is particularly ludicrous. Has Borachio confused
Hercules with Sampson? Is he merely
wild and eccentric here (Foakes) or is
he only a little tipsy (see repetitions at
147–8) and aware of it (146)?
141 **shifted** changed, with a pun on shift
= to change one's clothes
145–6 **thousand times good night** So says
Juliet at *Romeo* 2.2.154 during a quite
different balcony scene.

placed and possessed by my master Don John, saw
afar off in the orchard this amiable encounter.

CONRAD And thought they Margaret was Hero?   150

BORACHIO Two of them did, the Prince and Claudio. But
the devil my master knew she was Margaret. And
partly by his oaths, which first possessed them, partly
by the dark night, which did deceive them, but
chiefly by my villainy, which did confirm any slander   155
that Don John had made—away went Claudio en-
raged, swore he would meet her as he was appointed
next morning at the temple, and there, before the
whole congregation, shame her with what he saw
o'ernight, and send her home again without a hus-   160
band.

⌈A WATCHMAN⌉ (*coming forward*) We charge you in the
Prince's name. Stand!

⌈A WATCHMAN⌉ Call up the right Master Constable. We
have here recovered the most dangerous piece of   165
lechery that ever was known in the commonwealth.

⌈A WATCHMAN⌉ And one Deformed is one of them. I
know him; a wears a lock.

CONRAD Masters, masters—

⌈A WATCHMAN⌉ You'll be made bring Deformed forth,   170
I warrant you.

⌈CONRAD⌉ Masters—

⌈A WATCHMAN⌉ Never speak, we charge you. Let us
obey you to go with us.

BORACHIO (*to Conrad*) We are like to prove a goodly   175
commodity, being taken up of these men's bills.

CONRAD A commodity in question, I warrant you. (*To
the Watch*) Come, we'll obey you.   *Exeunt*

162 A WATCHMAN] This edition; *Watch* 1 Q, OXFORD; *Sec. Watch* HUMPHREYS; SEACOAL
MARES   164 A WATCHMAN] This edition, OXFORD (*subs.*); *Watch* 2 Q, MARES   167 A
WATCHMAN] This edition; *Watch* 1 Q, MARES, OXFORD (*subs.*); *Sec. Watch* HUMPHREYS
170 A WATCHMAN] This edition, OXFORD (*subs.*); *Watch* 2 Q; *First Watch* HUMPHREYS,
MARES   172-4 CONRAD Masters— | A WATCHMAN Never speak . . . us] THEOBALD (*subs.*),
and most eds.; CONRAD Masters, neuer speake . . . vs Q, STEVENSON, MARES (*subs.*)

148 **possessed them** convinced them, but
  with stronger implications of the de-
  monic than at 152.
155 **my villainy** Obviously Borachio lied
  to Claudio and the Prince after the
  charade.

156-7 **enraged** See note at 3.2.123.
158 **temple** church
166 **lechery** for 'treachery'
168 **lock** lovelock, a fashionable affectation
176 **commodity . . . bills** A nest of puns:

3.4   *Enter Hero, Margaret, and Ursula*

HERO Good Ursula, wake my cousin Beatrice, and
desire her to rise.

URSULA I will, lady.

HERO And bid her come hither.

URSULA Well.   *Exit*   5

MARGARET Troth, I think your other rebato were better.

HERO No, pray thee, good Meg, I'll wear this.

MARGARET By my troth, 's not so good, and I warrant
your cousin will say so.

HERO My cousin's a fool, and thou art another; I'll   10
wear none but this.

MARGARET I like the new tire within excellently, if the
hair were a thought browner. And your gown's a
most rare fashion, i' faith. I saw the Duchess of
Milan's gown that they praise so.   15

HERO O, that exceeds, they say.

MARGARET By my troth, 's but a night-gown in respect
of yours—cloth o' gold, and cuts, and laced with
silver, set with pearls, down sleeves, side sleeves, and

3.4.0 *Margaret*] Q (*and Margaret*)   5 *Exit*] HANMER; *not in* Q   8, 17 troth 's] CAPELL;
troth's Q   17 in] F; it Q

commodity = useful article = goods
gotten on credit; taken up = arrested
= received (sometimes from a usurer)
on credit; bills = halberds = bonds
given as security. For much the same
reasons, the word 'commodity' came
to have the same noxious ubiquity as
the word 'product' today; 'This bawd,
this broker, this all-changing word',
Philip the Bastard called it in *King John*
2.1.582. Shakespeare calls attention to
the word in several plays, here with
virtuoso punning.

177 **commodity in question** a multiple
pun: a commodity subject to legal pro-
ceedings, sought after, or of doubtful
value.

3.4.6 **rebato** a stiff ornamented collar of
linen stretched over a wire frame
pinned to the neck of the gown and
bent back to set off the face

8 **troth, 's** troth it's

10 **My cousin's a fool** Both Margaret and
Hero are excited. After her patience

with 'good Meg' three lines earlier,
Hero's assertion of will here is a warning not to dismiss her submissiveness
without question; this firmness can be
played as Hero's chafing at her own
conformity and resentment of Beatrice's freedom, or as merely an assertion of annoyance and status.

12 **tire** an elaborate head-dress much
mocked, as were all women's fashions.
It was made up of false hair and orna-
ments built up on a frame.
within in another room

16 **exceeds** excels, beats all

17 **night-gown** dressing-gown, denigrated
by Margaret but often an elegant garment of silk with fur facings; not to
be confused with modern lingerie

18 **cuts** slashes in the main fabric of a
garment, placed to reveal the rich
cloth beneath

19 **down sleeves, side sleeves** sleeves
close-fitted down to the wrists, and
loose, open sleeves draped becomingly
from the shoulders

skirts round underborne with a bluish tinsel. But for   20
a fine, quaint, graceful, and excellent fashion, yours
is worth ten on't.

HERO God give me joy to wear it, for my heart is
exceeding heavy.

MARGARET 'Twill be heavier soon by the weight of a   25
man.

HERO Fie upon thee, art not ashamed?

MARGARET Of what, lady? Of speaking honourably? Is
not marriage honourable in a beggar? Is not your
lord honourable without marriage? I think you   30
would have me say 'saving your reverence, a husband'. An bad thinking do not wrest true speaking,
I'll offend nobody. Is there any harm in 'the heavier
for a husband'? None, I think, an it be the right
husband and the right wife; otherwise 'tis light and   35
not heavy. Ask my Lady Beatrice else. Here she
comes.

Enter Beatrice

HERO Good morrow, coz.

BEATRICE Good morrow, sweet Hero.

HERO Why, how now? Do you speak in the sick tune?   40

BEATRICE I am out of all other tune, methinks.

MARGARET Clap 's into 'Light o' love'; that goes without a burden. Do you sing it, and I'll dance it.

42 Clap 's] ROWE 1714 *(subs.)*; Clap's Q

20 **underborne** trimmed at the skirt hem
as ornament and stiffener, or hemmed
to a petticoat worn beneath the skirt
bluish tinsel a light-blue silk cloth shot
through with threads of either gold or
silver

21 **quaint** complex and elegant. Gowns
like the Duchess of Milan's, some of
which Shakespeare might have seen at
court performances, were political as
well as fashion 'statements'.

29 **marriage honourable** proverbial: Tilley M863, scriptural: Heb. 13: 4, and
doctrinal as in 'The Form of the Solem-
nisation of Matrimony' in the Book of
Common Prayer. But the issue is not
only Hero's supposed prudishness as
against Margaret's plain-speaking, but
also one of taste; there is a touch of

vulgarity in Margaret.

35 **light** as contrasted with *heavy*, but also
a pun: *light*, wanton, as in 42

40 **sick tune** sad manner

42 **Clap 's into 'Light o' love'** start singing
'Light o' love': clapping hands to es-
tablish rhythm is a natural way for
informal unaccompanied singing in
unison to begin. The song was long a
popular dance tune and is mentioned
in *Two Gentlemen* 1.2.83 and *Two
Noble Kinsmen* 5.2.55. The words have
not been found, but a 'light o' love'
was someone careless or promiscuous
in love.

42-3 **without a burden** The burden was
a bass part for male voice; Beatrice
notes the sexual innuendo.

BEATRICE Ye light o' love with your heels! Then if your
husband have stables enough, you'll see he shall lack   45
no barns.

MARGARET O illegitimate construction! I scorn that
with my heels.

BEATRICE (*to Hero*) 'Tis almost five o'clock, cousin. 'Tis
time you were ready. By my troth, I am exceeding   50
ill. Heigh-ho!

MARGARET For a hawk, a horse, or a husband?

BEATRICE For the letter that begins them all—h.

MARGARET Well, an you be not turned Turk, there's no
more sailing by the star.   55

BEATRICE What means the fool, trow?

MARGARET Nothing, I. But God send everyone their
heart's desire.

HERO These gloves the Count sent me, they are an
excellent perfume.   60

BEATRICE I am stuffed, cousin; I cannot smell.

MARGARET A maid, and stuffed! There's goodly catching of cold.

BEATRICE O, God help me, God help me. How long have
you professed apprehension?   65

MARGARET Ever since you left it. Doth not my wit
become me rarely?

---

44 **with your heels** To be *light-*, short-, or
in recent slang round-heeled is to be
promiscuous. Beatrice's exclamation is
clearly meant as a rebuke to Margaret.

45–6 **stables . . . barns** This continues
Beatrice's punning rebuke of Margaret.
Barns puns on bairns = babies: 'If
your husband has enough stables,
you'll give him many children.'
Enough stables may refer either to the
wealth of the husband—permitting a
large family—or to the number of his
tenants and farmhands—permitting,
though illicitly, the same result.

47 **illegitimate construction** false interpretation. But Margaret persists in erotic
allusion.

47–8 **scorn . . . heels** spurn it with a rearward kick as would a horse

51 **Heigh-ho** As Margaret's response to it
shows, the phrase could be a call to a

hawk or a horse; as a sigh, which is
how it is intended here, it could 'call'
a husband; cf. 2.1.317.

53 **h** punning on 'ache', then pronounced
like the letter, with a backward glance
at Beatrice's feeling ill

54 **turned Turk** become an apostate by
abandoning mockery for love; the
phrase was proverbial, Tilley T609

55 **the star** the Pole Star, now possibly
unreliable, if even a Beatrice can
change

56 **trow** I wonder

59 **are** have

62 **stuffed** with a head cold; Margaret
interprets it as 'pregnant'.

65 **professed apprehension** set yourself up
as a wit

67 **rarely** marvellously well. Beatrice
takes it to mean 'infrequently'.

BEATRICE It is not seen enough. You should wear it in your cap. By my troth, I am sick.

MARGARET Get you some of this distilled *carduus bene-* 70 *dictus*, and lay it to your heart. It is the only thing for a qualm.

HERO There thou prick'st her with a thistle.

BEATRICE *Benedictus*—why *benedictus*? You have some moral in this *benedictus*. 75

MARGARET Moral? No, by my troth, I have no moral meaning. I meant plain holy-thistle. You may think perchance that I think you are in love. Nay, by'r Lady, I am not such a fool to think what I list. Nor I list not to think what I can, nor indeed I cannot 80 think—if I would think my heart out of thinking— that you are in love, or that you will be in love, or that you can be in love. Yet Benedick was such another, and now is he become a man. He swore he would never marry, and yet now in despite of his 85 heart he eats his meat without grudging. And how you may be converted I know not, but methinks you look with your eyes, as other women do.

BEATRICE What pace is this that thy tongue keeps?

MARGARET Not a false gallop. 90

Enter Ursula

URSULA (*to Hero*) Madam, withdraw. The Prince, the Count, Signor Benedick, Don John, and all the gallants of the town are come to fetch you to church.

HERO Help to dress me, good coz, good Meg, good Ursula. *Exeunt* 95

95 SD] ROWE; *not in* Q

69 **in your cap** as a fool does a coxcomb
70–1 *carduus benedictus* The 'holy thistle' was a 'preservative against all diseases' according to Thomas Brasbridge, *The Poor Man's Jewel* (1578), D2ᵛ.
72 **qualm** sudden faintness or nausea
73 **prick'st** give her a light hit, as in fencing—a verbal form of which this exchange is. The erotic allusion seems out of character for Hero, but possible.

77 **plain** literally
79 **list** please
85–6 **in despite . . . grudging** in spite of being in love, Benedick does not make such a fuss about it
89 **what . . . keeps?** What are you trying to say?
90 **Not a false gallop** not anything untrue. A false gallop was a rapid canter, called false because of its artificiality.

3.5   *Enter Leonato, Dogberry the constable, and*
        Verges the Headborough

LEONATO What would you with me, honest neighbour?
DOGBERRY Marry, sir, I would have some confidence
    with you that decerns you nearly.
LEONATO Brief, I pray you, for you see it is a busy time
    with me.   5
DOGBERRY Marry, this it is, sir.
VERGES Yes, in truth it is, sir.
LEONATO What is it, my good friends?
DOGBERRY Goodman Verges, sir, speaks a little off the
    matter—an old man, sir, and his wits are not so   10
    blunt as, God help, I would desire they were. But in
    faith, honest as the skin between his brows.
VERGES Yes, I thank God, I am as honest as any man
    living that is an old man and no honester than I.
DOGBERRY Comparisons arc odorous. '*Palabras*', neigh-   15
    bour Verges.
LEONATO Neighbours, you are tedious.
DOGBERRY It pleases your worship to say so, but we are
    the poor Duke's officers. But truly, for mine own part,
    if I were as tedious as a king I could find in my heart   20
    to bestow it all of your worship.
LEONATO All thy tediousness on me, ah?
DOGBERRY Yea, an 'twere a thousand pound more than
    'tis, for I hear as good exclamation on your worship
    as of any man in the city, and though I be but a   25
    poor man, I am glad to hear it.

3.5.0.1–2] Q (*Enter Leonato, and the Constable, and the Headborough*)   7 VERGES] ROWE;
Headb. (*throughout the scene*) Q   9 off] REED–STEEVENS; of Q

3.5.2 **confidence** conference, with the
    idea of confidentiality. The word is
    used in this way in *Merry Wives*
    1.4.172 and in *Romeo* 2.4.141, so it
    is probably not a Dogberryism here.
3 **decerns you nearly** closely concerns
    you
12 **skin . . . brows** proverbial, Tilley S506.
    I have found no convincing explana-
    tion for this odd expression.
15 **odorous** for 'odious'. Both the idea and
    the word-play were common; that
    comparisons were generally thought to

be offensive is clear from 2.1.145.
    '*Palabras*' for '*pocas palabras*' = few
    words. The popularity of the saying
    can be traced to Kyd's *Spanish Tragedy*
    3.14.118.
19 **poor Duke's** Duke's poor; *Measure*
    2.1.47 has a similar phrasing.
20 **tedious** Dogberry mistakes the word
    for a compliment.
21 **of** on
24 **exclamation** for 'acclamation', but liter-
    ally here an outcry against

VERGES And so am I.

LEONATO I would fain know what you have to say.

VERGES Marry, sir, our watch tonight, excepting your
worship's presence, ha' ta'en a couple of as arrant   30
knaves as any in Messina.

DOGBERRY A good old man, sir. He will be talking. As
they say, when the age is in, the wit is out. God help
us, it is a world to see. Well said, i' faith, neighbour
Verges. Well, God's a good man. An two men ride   35
of a horse, one must ride behind. An honest soul, i'
faith, sir, by my troth he is, as ever broke bread. But
God is to be worshipped; all men are not alike, alas,
good neighbour.

LEONATO Indeed, neighbour, he comes too short of you.   40

DOGBERRY Gifts that God gives!

LEONATO I must leave you.

DOGBERRY One word, sir. Our watch, sir, have indeed
comprehended two auspicious persons, and we would
have them this morning examined before your wor-   45
ship.

LEONATO Take their examination yourself, and bring it
me. I am now in great haste, as it may appear unto
you.

DOGBERRY It shall be suffigance.   50

LEONATO Drink some wine ere you go. Fare you well.
          Enter a Messenger

MESSENGER My lord, they stay for you to give your
daughter to her husband.

LEONATO I'll wait upon them, I am ready.
                          Exeunt Leonato and Messenger

---

32 talking. As] CAPELL (*subs.*); talking as Q   51.1] ROWE; *not in* Q   54.1] ROWE (*Ex⟨it⟩*
Leon⟨ato⟩); Q ('*exit*' *after* 50)

29–30 **excepting . . . presence** respecting
your presence. The deference is
double-edged: 'We've taken two of the
worst knaves in Messina, your worship
excepted.'

33 **age** In the proverb (Tilley W471) it is
ale not age that drives out wit. The
rest of Dogberry's speech is a pastiche
of proverbs and pieties: Tilley W878,

T638, and M68.

40 **too short** not only in wisdom but, as
Foakes points out, in size as well.

44 **comprehended . . . persons** apprehended
two suspicious persons; but Dogberry
did *understand* what Borachio and Conrad were up to, and they *were* auspicious for the outcome of the play.

50 **suffigance** sufficient

DOGBERRY Go, good partner, go get you to Francis   55
   Seacoal. Bid him bring his pen and inkhorn to the
   jail. We are now to examination these men.
VERGES And we must do it wisely.
DOGBERRY We will spare for no wit, I warrant you.
   Here's that shall drive some of them to a non-com.   60
   Only get the learned writer to set down our excom-
   munication, and meet me at the jail.   *Exeunt*

4.1   *Enter Don Pedro the Prince, Don John the*
      Bastard, Leonato, Friar Francis, Claudio,
      Benedick, Hero, and Beatrice, with Guests and
      Attendants

LEONATO Come, Friar Francis, be brief. Only to the
   plain form of marriage, and you shall recount their
   particular duties afterwards.
FRIAR (*to Claudio*) You come hither, my lord, to marry
   this lady?   5
CLAUDIO No.
LEONATO To be married to her. Friar, you come to
   marry her.
FRIAR (*to Hero*) Lady, you come hither to be married
   to this count?   10
HERO I do.
FRIAR If either of you know any inward impediment
   why you should not be conjoined, I charge you on
   your souls to utter it.
CLAUDIO Know you any, Hero?   15
HERO None, my lord.
FRIAR Know you any, Count?
LEONATO I dare make his answer—none.

---

62 SD] *not in* Q
   4.1] *Actus Quartus* F; *not in* Q   0.1 *Enter . . . Beatrice*] Q (*Enter Prince, Bastard, Leonato,*
Frier, Claudio, Benedicke, Hero and Beatrice); ~ *Guests and Attendants* DYCE (*subs.*)

55–6 **Francis Seacoal** Most editors take
   this to be a slip for George Seacoal
   (3.3. 11), but there is no way of proving this.
60 **that** Here Dogberry points to his head.
   non-com Dogberry means *nonplus* or
   perplex, but the phrase suggests (appropriately) *non compos mentis*, i.e.
   insane.
4.1.1 **be brief** Here Leonato also speaks for
   the audience, which wants a dramatic
   confrontation rather than the conventional and interminable disquisition on
   the sacrament of marriage.

CLAUDIO O, what men dare do! What men may do!
What men daily do, not knowing what they do!   20
BENEDICK How now! Interjections? Why then, some be
of laughing, as 'ah, ha, he!'
CLAUDIO
Stand thee by, Friar. (*To Leonato*) Father, by your
            leave,
Will you with free and unconstrainèd soul
Give me this maid, your daughter?   25
LEONATO
As freely, son, as God did give her me.
CLAUDIO
And what have I to give you back whose worth
May counterpoise this rich and precious gift?
DON PEDRO
Nothing, unless you render her again.
CLAUDIO
Sweet Prince, you learn me noble thankfulness.   30
There, Leonato, take her back again.
Give not this rotten orange to your friend!
She's but the sign and semblance of her honour.
Behold how like a maid she blushes here.
O, what authority and show of truth   35
Can cunning sin cover itself withal!
Comes not that blood as modest evidence
To witness simple virtue? Would you not swear—
All you that see her—that she were a maid,
By these exterior shows? But she is none.   40
She knows the heat of a luxurious bed.
Her blush is guiltiness, not modesty.
LEONATO
What do you mean, my lord?
CLAUDIO   Not to be married,
Not to knit my soul to an approvèd wanton.

43–4] *as here* Q; DYCE, HUMPHREYS *as three lines, ending at* 'lord', 'soul', 'wanton'

21 **Interjections** Benedick echoes William
  Lyly's standard school grammar text
  (1538) sig. C. viii^v, on interjections:
  'Some are of . . . laughing: as *Ha, ha,
  he.*' Parodic references to Lyly were
  frequent since it was so well known.

23 **Father, by your leave** father, if I may
  call you so
30 **learn** teach, a correct usage
38 **To witness** to give witness to
41 **luxurious** lascivious
44 **approved** proven

LEONATO

    Dear my lord, if you in your own proof   45
    Have vanquished the resistance of her youth
    And made defeat of her virginity—

CLAUDIO

    I know what you would say. If I have known her,
    You will say she did embrace me as a husband,
    And so extenuate the forehand sin.   50
    No, Leonato,
    I never tempted her with word too large,
    But as a brother to his sister showed
    Bashful sincerity and comely love.

HERO

    And seemed I ever otherwise to you?   55

CLAUDIO

    Out on thy seeming! I will write against it.
    You seem to me as Dian in her orb,
    As chaste as is the bud ere it be blown.
    But you are more intemperate in your blood
    Than Venus or those pampered animals   60
    That rage in savage sensuality.

HERO·

    Is my lord well that he doth speak so wide?

LEONATO

    Sweet Prince, why speak not you?

DON PEDRO   What should I speak?

    I stand dishonoured, that have gone about
    To link my dear friend to a common stale.   65

LEONATO

    Are these things spoken, or do I but dream?

50–1] *as here* POPE; *as one line*, Q   56 thy] POPE; thee Q   57 seem] Q; seem'd HANMER
67, 110 DON JOHN] CAPELL (*subs.*); *Bast.* Q

45 **your own proof** a test that you have
    made
52 **large** broad, immodest
56 **Out on thy seeming** Enough of your
    pretending!
    write against it denounce it in public
57 **Dian in her orb** the moon-goddess of
    chastity in her proper sphere

58 **blown** opened.
60 **pampered animals** horses? *Winter's
    Tale* 1.2.288 uses 'horse' as a verb for
    erotic play; the association was a com-
    mon one.
62 **wide** wide of the mark, inaccurately
65 **stale** whore

DON JOHN

Sir, they are spoken, and these things are true.

BENEDICK

This looks not like a nuptial.

HERO   True? O God!

CLAUDIO

Leonato, stand I here?

Is this the Prince? Is this the Prince's brother?   70

Is this face Hero's? Are our eyes our own?

LEONATO

All this is so. But what of this, my lord?

CLAUDIO

Let me but move one question to your daughter,

And by that fatherly and kindly power

That you have in her, bid her answer truly.   75

LEONATO (*to Hero*)

I charge thee do so, as thou art my child.

HERO

O God defend me! How am I beset!

What kind of catechizing call you this?

CLAUDIO

To make you answer truly to your name.

HERO

Is it not Hero? Who can blot that name   80

With any just reproach?

CLAUDIO   Marry, that can Hero.

Hero itself can blot out Hero's virtue.

What man was he talked with you yesternight

Out at your window betwixt twelve and one?

Now, if you are a maid, answer to this.   85

HERO

I talked with no man at that hour, my lord.

DON PEDRO

Why, then are you no maiden. Leonato,

I am sorry you must hear. Upon mine honour,

Myself, my brother, and this grievèd Count

74 **kindly** natural, as a father
79 **answer...name** The Anglican ca-
   techism first asks 'What is your
   name?' Answering to the name of
   Hero meant upholding the faithfulness

attributed to the heroine of the Hero
and Leander story and thus deserving
of the name.
89 **grievèd** wronged

Did see her, hear her, at that hour last night   90
Talk with a ruffian at her chamber window,
Who hath indeed, most like a liberal villain,
Confessed the vile encounters they have had
A thousand times in secret.
DON JOHN   Fie, fie, they are
Not to be named, my lord, not to be spoke of.   95
There is not chastity enough in language
Without offence to utter them. Thus, pretty lady,
I am sorry for thy much misgovernment.
CLAUDIO
O Hero! What a Hero hadst thou been
If half thy outward graces had been placed   100
About thy thoughts and counsels of thy heart!
But fare thee well, most foul, most fair; farewell
Thou pure impiety and impious purity.
For thee I'll lock up all the gates of love,
And on my eyelids shall conjecture hang   105
To turn all beauty into thoughts of harm,
And never shall it more be gracious.
LEONATO
Hath no man's dagger here a point for me?
    Hero falls to the ground
BEATRICE
Why, how now, cousin, wherefore sink you down?
DON JOHN
Come, let us go. These things come thus to light   110
Smother her spirits up.
            Exeunt Don Pedro, Don John, and Claudio
BENEDICK
How doth the lady?
BEATRICE   Dead, I think. Help, uncle.
Hero, why Hero! Uncle, Signor Benedick, Friar—

94-5] *as here* HANMER; *breaks at* 'lord', Q   108.1] HANMER (*subs.*), *not in* Q   111.1]
ROWE; *not in* Q

92 **liberal** licentious
98 **misgovernment** misconduct
104 **the gates of love** the senses, particu-
    larly the eyes
105 **conjecture** suspicion
110 **Come, let us go** Don John wants to
    leave before second thoughts and sym-

pathy—or a quarrel—develop. Benedick makes a crucial choice in remaining, and ideally his stage business
reflects this.
111 **spirits** vital powers which control
    bodily functions

LEONATO

  O Fate, take not away thy heavy hand.
  Death is the fairest cover for her shame   115
  That may be wished for.

BEATRICE   How now, cousin Hero?

FRIAR Have comfort, lady.

LEONATO Dost thou look up?

FRIAR Yea, wherefore should she not?

LEONATO

  Wherefore? Why, doth not every earthly thing   120
  Cry shame upon her? Could she here deny
  The story that is printed in her blood?
  Do not live, Hero, do not ope thine eyes;
  For did I think thou wouldst not quickly die,
  Thought I thy spirits were stronger than thy shames,   125
  Myself would, on the rearward of reproaches,
  Strike at thy life. Grieved I, I had but one?
  Chid I for that at frugal nature's frame?
  O one too much by thee! Why had I one?
  Why ever wast thou lovely in my eyes?   130
  Why had I not with charitable hand
  Took up a beggar's issue at my gates,
  Who, smirchèd thus, and mired with infamy,
  I might have said 'No part of it is mine;
  This shame derives itself from unknown loins.'   135
  But mine, and mine I loved, and mine I praised,
  And mine that I was proud on; mine so much
  That I myself was to myself not mine,
  Valuing of her—why she, O she is fallen
  Into a pit of ink, that the wide sea   140
  Hath drops too few to wash her clean again,
  And salt too little which may season give
  To her foul, tainted flesh.

BENEDICK   Sir, sir, be patient.

120 Why, doth] THEOBALD; why doth Q   126 rearward] Q (rereward)   143 foul,
tainted] Q; soul-tainted *conj.* Collier 1853

118 **look up** to heaven, as if innocent and
    imploring aid
122 **printed in her blood** (*a*) shown in her
    blushes of shame, (*b*) an innate weak-
    ness In the sexual make-up of women
126 **on the rearward of** immediately after

128 **frugal . . . frame** a plan frugal in
    granting him only one child
136-7 **mine . . . mine** I cared so much for
    her that I cared nothing for myself
140 **that** so black that
142 **season** wholesomeness

For my part, I am so attired in wonder
I know not what to say.   145

BEATRICE
O, on my soul, my cousin is belied.

BENEDICK
Lady, were you her bedfellow last night?

BEATRICE
No, truly not, although until last night
I have this twelvemonth been her bedfellow.

LEONATO
Confirmed, confirmed. O, that is stronger made   150
Which was before barred up with ribs of iron.
Would the two princes lie? And Claudio lie,
Who loved her so that, speaking of her foulness,
Washed it with tears? Hence from her, let her die.

FRIAR Hear me a little,   155
For I have only silent been so long
And given way unto this course of fortune.
By noting of the lady, I have marked
A thousand blushing apparitions
To start into her face, a thousand innocent shames   160

143–4, 155–6] *as verse*, POPE; *as prose*, Q   156 silent been] WHITE 1858, DYCE 1714,
FOAKES; bin silent Q   155–7 fortune. | By . . . lady, I have marked] *This edition*; fortune,
by . . . lady, I haue market, Q; POPE *and most eds. end sentence at* 'lady'; F *ends it at*
'marked'; *lacuna after* 156, *conj.* Oxford

147 **bedfellow last night** We never learn
how Borachio was able to bring about
these two improbabilities: getting
Hero from her bed in the middle of the
night, and separating her from Beatrice. Sharing beds by adults of the
same sex was then unremarkable.

154 **Washed it with tears** Claudio seems
not to warrant this description nor is
it staged. At 5.1.287 he *does* cry, or
says he does, but with tears of relief
at Leonato's generosity in offering him
another wife, and so erasing the stain
of his behaviour toward Hero.

155–8 In Q this passage is set as prose at
the foot of a crowded page and is
difficult to follow despite its obvious
general import, which is not signific-
antly altered or made more idiomatic
by editors' variations in lineation or
punctuation. The crowding probably

did not result from an error in casting-
off copy. Compositorial eye-skip between the 'I have' of 156 and that of
158 was suggested by Newcomer. This
may have contributed to the omission
of material later crammed into place.
This edition alters Q only minimally:
'I have merely been quiet till now and
given way to this tragedy.' In addition
to only = merely, only = alone perhaps
glances at the fact that Leonato (at
great length) and Beatrice and Benedick have had their say while he, a
friar, has said almost nothing. The
syntactical link between 'By noting of
this lady' with 'I have marked' also
seems stronger than in the alternatives.

160 **innocent shames** feelings of un-
merited shame that have led to pale
anger

In angel whiteness beat away those blushes,
And in her eye there hath appeared a fire
To burn the errors that these princes hold
Against her maiden truth. Call me a fool,
Trust not my reading nor my observations,   165
Which with experimental seal doth warrant
The tenor of my book. Trust not my age,
My reverence, calling, nor divinity,
If this sweet lady lie not guiltless here
Under some biting error.
LEONATO   Friar, it cannot be.   170
Thou seest that all the grace that she hath left
Is that she will not add to her damnation
A sin of perjury. She not denies it.
Why seek'st thou then to cover with excuse
That which appears in proper nakedness?   175
FRIAR
Lady, what man is he you are accused of?
HERO
They know that do accuse me; I know none.
If I know more of any man alive
Than that which maiden modesty doth warrant,
Let all my sins lack mercy. O my father,   180
Prove you that any man with me conversed
At hours unmeet, or that I yesternight
Maintained the change of words with any creature,
Refuse me, hate me, torture me to death.
FRIAR
There is some strange misprision in the princes.   185
BENEDICK
Two of them have the very bent of honour,
And if their wisdoms be misled in this

162–3 **a fire | To burn** Religious heretics were 'purified' of error by burning at the stake.
164 **her maiden truth** the truth of her virginity, with an overtone of the idea that truth came more easily to the sexually pure
166 **experimental seal** the confirmation of experience
warrant validate

167 **tenor of my book** teachings of my reading in moral philosophy
173 **not denies** does not deny. See Abbott 305 on this construction.
175 **proper** authentic
182 **unmeet** inappropriate
184 **Refuse** disown
185 **misprision** mistake
186 **the very bent** a true inclination to

The practice of it lives in John the Bastard,
Whose spirits toil in frame of villainies.

LEONATO

I know not. If they speak but truth of her,   190
These hands shall tear her. If they wrong her honour,
The proudest of them shall well hear of it.
Time hath not yet so dried this blood of mine,
Nor age so eat up my invention,
Nor fortune made such havoc of my means,   195
Nor my bad life reft me so much of friends,
But they shall find awaked in such a kind
Both strength of limb and policy of mind,
Ability in means, and choice of friends,
To quit me of them throughly.

FRIAR   Pause a while,   200
And let my counsel sway you in this case.
Your daughter here the princes left for dead.
Let her a while be secretly kept in,
And publish it that she is dead indeed.
Maintain a mourning ostentation,   205
And on your family's old monument
Hang mournful epitaphs, and do all rites
That appertain unto a burial.

LEONATO

What shall become of this? What will this do?

FRIAR

Marry, this, well carried, shall on her behalf   210
Change slander to remorse. That is some good.

202 princes . . . dead.] THEOBALD (*subs.*); princesse (left for dead,) Q

188 **practice** trickery
   Bastard called so in the text for the first time
189 **frame** devising
193 **dried** Ageing resulted in a loss of all types of bodily moisture.
194 **invention** inventiveness, here strategic resourcefulness
195 **Nor . . . of friends** nor has my life been so bad as to cost me so many friends
198 **policy of mind** practicality
200 **quit . . . throughly** avenge myself on them completely
202 **princes** Q's 'princess (left for dead)' is

not incoherent, but Hero is not a princess. Most editors follow Theobald's emendation to 'princes'. Possibly a careless second *s* in the copy led Compositor A to make sense of it by putting the phrase 'left for dead', as explanatory, in parentheses.
205 **mourning ostentation** show, pretence, of mourning
206 **monument** burial vault
207 **Hang . . . epitaphs** (commonly done for illustrious persons)
209 **shall . . . will** Elizabethan usage is treated by Abbott 321.

But not for that dream I on this strange course,
But on this travail look for greater birth.
She dying—as it must be so maintained—
Upon the instant that she was accused,   215
Shall be lamented, pitied, and excused
Of every hearer. For it so falls out
That what we have we prize not to the worth
Whiles we enjoy it, but being lacked and lost,
Why, then we rack the value, then we find   220
The virtue that possession would not show us
Whiles it was ours. So will it fare with Claudio.
When he shall hear she died upon his words,
Th'idea of her life shall sweetly creep
Into his study of imagination,   225
And every lovely organ of her life
Shall come apparelled in more precious habit,
More moving, delicate, and full of life,
Into the eye and prospect of his soul
Than when she lived indeed. Then shall he mourn,   230
If ever love had interest in his liver,
And wish he had not so accusèd her—
No, though he thought his accusation true.
Let this be so, and doubt not but success
Will fashion the event in better shape   235
Than I can lay it down in likelihood.
But if all aim but this be levelled false,
The supposition of the lady's death
Will quench the wonder of her infamy.

213 **on this travail** from this labour, with a pun on travail = labour pains, and a glance at 'course' in 212 for travail = travel
218 **not to the worth** below its value
218–22 **what we have ... was ours** proverbial, Tilley W934
225 **study of imagination** the review of events as he recreates their images. See 'eye and prospect of his soul' at 229.
226 **organ** work (from the Greek *ergon*), and instrument (from the Latin *organum*). The phrase refers to Hero's behaviour and to her physical and spiritual faculties: 'every lovely aspect of her life'.
227 **habit** dress
231 **had interest in** had the right or title to share in
   liver thought to be the seat of love and violent passion; see F. D. Hoeniger, *Medicine and Shakespeare in the English Renaissance* (Newark, Del., 1992), 173–4.
234 **success** succeeding events, not necessarily good or bad
235 **event** outcome
237 **if ... false** if all our other wishes are frustrated
239 **wonder** speculation about, gossip

And if it sort not well, you may conceal her,   240
As best befits her wounded reputation,
In some reclusive and religious life,
Out of all eyes, tongues, minds, and injuries.
BENEDICK
Signor Leonato, let the Friar advise you;
And though you know my inwardness and love   245
Is very much unto the Prince and Claudio,
Yet, by mine honour, I will deal in this
As secretly and justly as your soul
Should with your body.
LEONATO   Being that I flow in grief,
The smallest twine may lead me.   250
FRIAR
'Tis well consented. Presently away,
For to strange sores strangely they strain the cure.
(*To Hero*) Come, lady, die to live. This wedding day
Perhaps is but prolonged. Have patience and endure.
                    Exeunt all but Beatrice and Benedick
BENEDICK Lady Beatrice, have you wept all this while?   255
BEATRICE Yea, and I will weep a while longer.
BENEDICK I will not desire that.
BEATRICE You have no reason; I do it freely.
BENEDICK Surely I do believe your fair cousin is
    wronged.   260
BEATRICE Ah, how much might the man deserve of me
    that would right her!
BENEDICK Is there any way to show such friendship?
BEATRICE A very even way, but no such friend.
BENEDICK May a man do it?   265
BEATRICE It is a man's office, but not yours.

240 **sort** turn out
245 **inwardness** intimate friendship
246 **Is** a correct usage, according to Ab-
    bott 336
249 **flow in grief** am overcome by tears
250 **twine** weak thread
252 **to . . . cure** proverbial, Tilley D357:
    'A desperate disease must have a des-
    perate remedy'; essentially Hippo-
    crates' sixth aphorism
254 **perhaps . . . endure** The 12-syllable
    alexandrine is used here and elsewhere

with blank verse (as in the *Faerie
Queene* stanza) for an effect of emphatic
closure. The medium changes at once
to prose.
258 **no reason** no need (to desire it)
262 **right** avenge (her honour)
264 **even** direct
    friend Beatrice seems to be testing the
    word, whose outer limit is 'lover'; see
    'how much might the man deserve of
    me' at 261.
266 **office, but not yours** task, but not for

BENEDICK I do love nothing in the world so well as you.
Is not that strange?

BEATRICE As strange as the thing I know not. It were
as possible for me to say I loved nothing so well as   270
you. But believe me not, and yet I lie not. I confess
nothing nor I deny nothing; I am sorry for my
cousin.

BENEDICK By my sword, Beatrice, thou lovest me.

BEATRICE Do not swear and eat it.   275

BENEDICK I will swear by it that you love me, and I
will make him eat it that says I love not you.

BEATRICE Will you not eat your word?

BENEDICK With no sauce that can be devised to it. I
protest I love thee.   280

BEATRICE Why then, God forgive me.

BENEDICK What offence, sweet Beatrice?

BEATRICE You have stayed me in a happy hour. I was
about to protest I loved you.

BENEDICK And do it with all thy heart.   285

BEATRICE I love you with so much of my heart that
none is left to protest.

BENEDICK Come, bid me do anything for thee.

BEATRICE Kill Claudio.

BENEDICK Ha! Not for the wide world.   290

BEATRICE You kill me to deny it. Farewell.

BENEDICK ⌈*barring her way*⌉ Tarry, sweet Beatrice.

254.1] ROWE (*subs.*); *exit.* Q   292 SD] This edition; *not in* Q

you since (*a*) you are too close to Claudio; (*b*) you are not a family member
whose honour is involved; and (*c*) I
have not earned the right to ask you
to do it. Benedick responds to (*c*).

269 **the thing I know not** This equivocation takes off from Benedick's 'nothing' at 267. Is love the thing Beatrice
does not know, or only what she hesi-
tates to acknowledge? Such verbal
concealments only reveal what is in
plain view: she loves him.

274 **by my sword** the oath of a gentleman
ready to defend his honour with a
weapon whose hilt conveniently
formed a cross

275 **eat it** eat the sword, as having to eat
his words; proverbial, Tilley W825

280 **protest** insist

281 **God forgive me** for nearly breaching
the convention that deters the woman
from being the first to declare herself
in love. *Much Ado* carefully reflects the
social codification of gender differences, which Beatrice is tenderly mocking here. Beatrice, like Helen in *All's
Well*, feels capable of choosing a lover
for herself and of conducting the
wooing too.

283 **stayed** forestalled

289 **Kill Claudio** i.e. challenge him to a
duel

BEATRICE I am gone though I am here. There is no love
in you.—Nay, I pray you, let me go.
BENEDICK Beatrice—   295
BEATRICE In faith, I will go.
BENEDICK We'll be friends first.
BEATRICE You dare easier be friends with me than fight
with mine enemy.
BENEDICK Is Claudio thine enemy?   300
BEATRICE Is a not approved in the height a villain, that
hath slandered, scorned, dishonoured my kinswo-
man? O that I were a man! What, bear her in hand
until they come to take hands, and then with public
accusation, uncovered slander, unmitigated ran-   305
cour—O God that I were a man! I would eat his
heart in the market place.
BENEDICK Hear me, Beatrice—
BEATRICE Talk with a man out at a window—a proper
saying!   310
BENEDICK Nay, but Beatrice—
BEATRICE Sweet Hero! She is wronged, she is slandered, she is undone.
BENEDICK Beat—
BEATRICE Princes and counties! Surely a princely testi-   315
mony, a goodly count; Count Comfit, a sweet gallant,
surely. O that I were a man for his sake! Or that I
had any friend would be a man for my sake! But
manhood is melted into curtsies, valour into compliment, and men are only turned into tongue, and trim   320

305–6 rancour—] ROWE; rancour? Q   316 Comfit] Q (Comfect)   319 curtsies] Q
(cursies); courtesies F3

301 **approved in the height** confirmed
  thoroughly
303 **bear her in hand** mislead her (with
  false hopes)
304–1 **take hands** The 'handfast' or formal joining of hands as in the older
  forms of betrothal unconsecrated by
  the church was incorporated in the
  conventional ceremony.
305 **uncovered** bare-faced
306–7 **eat . . . market place** Beatrice now
  seems to accept the male violence she
  rejected in 1.1 when she offered to eat
  whatever Benedick killed in battle.

309–10 **a proper saying** a likely story
316 **count** puns on count = account
  (story) and count = specific charge in
  an indictment
  Count Comfit Count Candy
319 **curtsies** Many editors modernize and
  emend Q's 'cursies' to 'courtesies', a
  more general meaning than Beatrice
  seems to intend. But curtsies, obeisan-
  ces by both sexes, makes sense and
  seems more incongruous, hence more
  likely, here.
320 **only turned into tongue** become all
  talk

ones, too. He is now as valiant as Hercules that only
tells a lie and swears it. I cannot be a man with
wishing; therefore I will die a woman with grieving.

BENEDICK Tarry, good Beatrice. By this hand, I love
thee.   325

BEATRICE Use it for my love some other way than
swearing by it.

BENEDICK Think you in your soul the Count Claudio
hath wronged Hero?

BEATRICE Yea, as sure as I have a thought or a soul.   330

BENEDICK Enough, I am engaged; I will challenge him.
I will kiss your hand, and so I leave you. By this
hand, Claudio shall render me a dear account. As
you hear of me, so think of me. Go comfort your
cousin. I must say she is dead. And so, farewell.   335

Exeunt

4.2   *Enter Dogberry, Verges and the Sexton in gowns;*
        and the Watch, with Conrad and Borachio

DOGBERRY Is our whole dissembly appeared?

VERGES O, a stool and a cushion for the Sexton.

SEXTON ⌈*sits*⌉ Which be the malefactors?

DOGBERRY Marry, that am I, and my partner.

335.1 SD] *not in* Q
   4.2.0.1–2] CAPELL; *Enter the Constables, Borachio, and the Towne clarke in gownes.* Q
1 DOGBERRY] CAPELL; *Keeper* Q (*see* 9 *below*)   2, 5, 67 VERGES] CAPELL; *Cowley* (2, 5),
Couley (63) Q   3 (*sits*)] OXFORD; *not in* Q   4 DOGBERRY] CAPELL; *Andrew* Q; VERGES ROWE

320 **trim** smooth

4.2.0 **gowns** Black gowns were the official
   dress of both constable and sexton,
   and thus appropriate for taking testimony.
   1 DOGBERRY Q's speech-prefixes in 4.2 are
   inconsistent; see Introd., p. 5. Dogberry was played by the great low-
   comedy actor Will Kemp, best known
   for a morris dance from London to
   Norwich, a feat suggestive of his
   barrel-chested physique and bluff manner, an excellent contrast to the actor
   playing Verges. Q's speech-prefix here
   for the Dogberry role is '*Keeper*', probably a mistaken expansion of '*Ke*' (for

Kemp). The next prefix is '*Andrew*' (for
Merry Andrew), a generic term of unknown origin for the buffoon-role;
thereafter the prefixes are variously
abbreviated (see collation).
   2 VERGES Q uses Sexton rather than Verges as a speech-prefix in this scene;
the name Verges, like Dogberry, came
after the generic conception. Q's first
speech-prefix for the role is '*Cowley*',
later '*Couley*'. Considerable confusion
in the Q text of this scene resulted from
the compositor's evident difficulty with
Cowley speech-prefixes. Richard Cowley was also a comic actor: his spindly
frame and pale complexion were in
fine contrast to Kemp.

VERGES Nay, that's certain; we have the exhibition to   5
examine.

SEXTON But which are the offenders that are to be
examined? Let them come before Master Constable.

DOGBERRY Yea, marry, let them come before me. What
is your name, friend?   10

BORACHIO Borachio.

DOGBERRY (*to the Sexton*) Pray write down 'Borachio'.
(*To Conrad*) Yours, sirrah?

CONRAD I am a gentleman, sir, and my name is Conrad.

DOGBERRY Write down 'Master Gentleman Conrad'.   15
Masters, do you serve God?

CONRAD *and* BORACHIO Yea, sir, we hope.

DOGBERRY Write down that they hope they serve God.
And write 'God' first, for God defend but God should
go before such villains. Masters, it is proved already   20
that you are little better than false knaves, and it
will go near to be thought so shortly. How answer
you for yourselves?

CONRAD Marry, sir, we say we are none.

DOGBERRY A marvellous witty fellow, I assure you, but   25
I will go about with him.—Come you hither, sirrah.
A word in your ear, sir. I say to you it is thought
you are false knaves.

BORACHIO Sir, I say to you we are none.

DOGBERRY Well, stand aside. Fore God, they are both   30
in a tale. Have you writ down that they are none?

SEXTON Master Constable, you go not the way to
examine. You must call forth the watch that are their
accusers.

DOGBERRY Yea, marry, that's the eftest way. Let the   35

9 DOGBERRY] CAPELL; *Kemp* Q (*also as Kemp, Kem, Kee, Ke, and at 66 as Constable*)   17
CONRAD *and* BORACHIO] Q (*Both*)   35 eftest] Q; deftest. *conj.* Theobald

5–6 **exhibition to examine** commission
   (authority) to conduct an examination
13 **sirrah** a contemptuous form of address
   to social inferiors, hence Conrad's tart
   reply
17–20 **Yea ... villains** F omits this passage, probably because of the 1606
   statute against profanity (3 Jac. 1 C.
   21).
19 **defend** forbid

26 **go about with** handle
30–1 **in a tale** telling the same lie
32 **the way** the proper way
35 **eftest** shortest; Dogberry's coinage for
   'aptest' or 'deftest'. But in *Lewis Theobald and the Editing of Shakespeare*
   ([Oxford, 1990], 157–9) Peter Seary,
   noting the unusually large spaces on
   either side of the comma after 'marry'
   in Capell's copy of the Quarto, defends

watch come forth.—Masters, I charge you in the
Prince's name accuse these men.
⌈A WATCHMAN⌉ This man said, sir, that Don John, the
Prince's brother, was a villain.
DOGBERRY Write down Prince John a villain. Why, this   40
is flat perjury, to call a prince's brother villain.
BORACHIO Master Constable—
DOGBERRY Pray thee, fellow, peace. I do not like thy
look, I promise thee.
SEXTON What heard you him say else?   45
⌈A WATCHMAN⌉ Marry, that he had received a thousand
ducats of Don John for accusing the Lady Hero
wrongfully.
DOGBERRY Flat burglary, as ever was committed.
VERGES Yea, by th'mass, that it is.   50
SEXTON What else, fellow?
⌈A WATCHMAN⌉ And that Count Claudio did mean upon
his words to disgrace Hero before the whole assem-
bly, and not marry her.
DOGBERRY O villain! Thou wilt be condemned into ever-   55
lasting redemption for this.
SEXTON What else?
A WATCHMAN This is all.
SEXTON And this is more, masters, than you can deny.
Prince John is this morning secretly stolen away.   60
Hero was in this manner accused, in this very man-
ner refused, and upon the grief of this suddenly died.
Master Constable, let these men be bound and
brought to Leonato's. I will go before and show him
their examination.   *Exit*   65
DOGBERRY Come, let them be opinioned.
VERGES Let them be in the hands—
⌈*Watchmen seize Conrad and Borachio*⌉
⌈CONRAD⌉ Off, coxcomb!

38, 52 A WATCHMAN] This edition; *Watch.* 1 Q; SEACOAL MARES   46 A WATCHMAN] *This
edition; Watch* 2 Q   50 th'mass] F; mass Q   58 A WATCHMAN] Q (*Watch.*); 2 Watch.
ROWE; SEACOAL MARES   65 SD] THEOBALD; *not in* Q   67–8] MALONE; *as one line* ('Let

Theobald's conjecture that a 'd' had   ward 'by mass'
fallen out of the line of type.   66 **opinioned** for 'pinioned'
                                         67–8 ll. 67–8 were run together in Q and
50 **by th'mass** F's correction of Q's awk-   attributed to Cowley; l. 66 was at-

DOGBERRY God s' my life, where's the Sexton? Let him
write down the Prince's officer coxcomb. Come, bind   70
them. ⌈*To Conrad, who resists*⌉—Thou naughty varlet!
CONRAD Away, you are an ass; you are an ass.
DOGBERRY Dost thou not suspect my place? Dost thou
not suspect my years? O that he were here to write
me down an ass! But masters, remember that I am   75
an ass. Though it be not written down, yet forget
not that I am an ass. No, thou villain, thou art full
of piety, as shall be proved upon thee by good
witness. I am a wise fellow, and which is more, an
officer; and which is more, a householder; and   80
which is more, as pretty a piece of flesh as any is in
Messina; and one that knows the law, go to; and a
rich fellow enough, go to; and a fellow that hath
had losses; and one that hath two gowns, and
everything handsome about him.—Bring him away.   85
O that I had been writ down an ass!   *Exeunt*

5.1   *Enter Leonato and Antonio his brother*
ANTONIO
If you go on thus, you will kill yourself,
And 'tis not wisdom thus to second grief
Against yourself.
LEONATO   I pray thee cease thy counsel,
Which falls into mine ears as profitless

them be in the handes of Coxcombe') *spoken by Verges* ⟨*Couley*⟩ Q; in the hands of |
CONRAD Coxcomb! STAUNTION; *as one line spoken by Conrad* THEOBALD, MARES   67 in the
hands] Q; in bands *conj.* Capell   67.1] This edition; *not in* Q   71 them. Thou] F3
(*subs.*); them, thou Q   71 SD] This edition; *not in* Q   86 Exeunt] Q (*exit.*)
   5.1] *Actus Quintus* F; *not in* Q   0.1 Antonio] ROWE; *not in* Q   1 ANTONIO] ROWE;
Brother Q (*throughout the scene save at 100: Ant.*)

tributed to Constable. The telescoping
may have resulted from the compositor's trouble with easily confused abbreviations: 'Con' for Constable and
Conrad, and 'Cou' for Cowley; and
easily confused letters: 'n' and 'u'.

69 **God s' my life** God save my life
71 **naughty** The word had the force of
'wicked'.
73 **suspect** for 'respect'
81 **pretty a piece of flesh** Evidently Dogberry fancies himself an object of sexual interest.

82, 83 **go to** an intensifier like 'You had
better believe it.'
84 **losses** Evidently even losses are an
occasion for Dogberry's self-satisfac-
tion; they are, after all, a measure of
(former) wealth.
   two gowns quite enough to indicate
Dogberry's comfortable circumstances,
especially if the gowns were cloaks of
fine, richly trimmed materials.
5.1.2. **second grief** augment the destructive effects of grief by turning it against
yourself; proverbial advice, Tilley
D126

As water in a sieve. Give not me counsel,   5
Nor let no comforter delight mine ear
But such a one whose wrongs do suit with mine.
Bring me a father that so loved his child,
Whose joy of her is overwhelmed like mine,
And bid him speak of patience.   10
Measure his woe the length and breadth of mine,
And let it answer every strain for strain,
As thus for thus, and such a grief for such,
In every lineament, branch, shape, and form.
If such a one will smile and stroke his beard,   15
Bid sorrow wag, cry 'hem' when he should groan,
Patch grief with proverbs, make misfortune drunk
With candle-wasters, bring him yet to me,
And I of him will gather patience.
But there is no such man. For, brother, men   20
Can counsel and speak comfort to that grief
Which they themselves not feel. But tasting it,
Their counsel turns to passion, which before
Would give preceptial medicine to rage,
Fetter strong madness in a silken thread,   25
Charm ache with air and agony with words.
No, no, 'tis all men's office to speak patience
To those that wring under the load of sorrow,
But no man's virtue nor sufficiency
To be so moral when he shall endure   30

---

16 Bid sorrow wag,] CAPELL; And sorrow, wagge Q; And, sorry wag STEEVENS, FOAKES; And sorrow; wag MARES; Bid sorrow raze, *conj.* Craven

7 **suit with** resemble
12 **strain for strain** emotion for emotion, with the suggestion of musical antiphony in 'answer'
16–18 **Bid ... candle-wasters** This passage, defective in Q, has prompted many emendations (see collation), none altering the general meaning. 'And' at 16 demands Capell's emendation since the idea of 'such a one' sorrowing would undermine his smiling, crying hem, and so on. This piece on the futility of comfort is a setspeech in the Kyd manner, but undermines the genre by conveying ostentatious self-pity rather than authentic sorrow.
16 **wag** be off; *OED v.* 7
     cry 'hem' clear his throat
17 **Patch grief** console himself
18 **candle-wasters** stay-up-lates, either scholars or carousers
22 **not feel** do not feel; see Abbott 305 on the omission of the auxiliary.
24 **give ... rage** try to cure rage with maxims
27 **office** business
28 **wring** writhe
29 **virtue nor sufficiency** power or capacity
30 **moral** glib

The like himself. Therefore give me no counsel.
My griefs cry louder than advertisement.

ANTONIO
Therein do men from children nothing differ.

LEONATO
I pray thee peace. I will be flesh and blood,
For there was never yet philosopher   35
That could endure the toothache patiently,
However they have writ the style of gods,
And made a pish at chance and sufferance.

ANTONIO
Yet bend not all the harm upon yourself.
Make those that do offend you suffer too.   40

LEONATO
There thou speak'st reason; nay, I will do so.
My soul doth tell me Hero is belied,
And that shall Claudio know; so shall the Prince,
And all of them that thus dishonour her.
            Enter Don Pedro the Prince and Claudio

ANTONIO
Here comes the Prince and Claudio hastily.   45

DON PEDRO
Good e'en, good e'en.

CLAUDIO   Good day to both of you.

LEONATO
Hear you, my lords!

DON PEDRO   We have some haste, Leonato.

LEONATO
Some haste, my lord! Well, fare you well, my lord.
Are you so hasty now? Well, all is one.

DON PEDRO
Nay, do not quarrel with us, good old man.   50

---

38 pish] OXFORD, after Q (push);   44.1 *Don Pedro*] *not in* Q   47 lords!] ROWE; lords?
Q   52–3] MALONE; ~ him? | Mary Q *and most eds.*

32 **advertisement** advice
33 **Therein ... differ** This is a polite way
   of saying that Leonato is being child-
   ish.
37 **writ the style** signed themselves with
   the titles

38 **pish** an indifferent variant of 'push',
   which is less expressive of the contempt intended
   sufferance suffering
49 **all is one** never mind that

ANTONIO

 If he could right himself with quarrelling,
 Some of us would lie low.

CLAUDIO   Who wrongs him?

LEONATO   Marry,

 Thou dost wrong me, thou dissembler, thou.
 Nay, never lay thy hand upon thy sword;
 I fear thee not.

CLAUDIO   Marry, beshrew my hand   55

 If it should give your age such cause of fear.
 In faith, my hand meant nothing to my sword.

LEONATO

 Tush, tush, man, never fleer and jest at me.
 I speak not like a dotard nor a fool,
 As under privilege of age to brag   60
 What I have done being young, or what would do
 Were I not old. Know Claudio, to thy head,
 Thou hast so wronged mine innocent child and me
 That I am forced to lay my reverence by,
 And with grey hairs and bruise of many days   65
 Do challenge thee to trial of a man.
 I say thou hast belied mine innocent child.
 Thy slander hath gone through and through her
   heart,
 And she lies buried with her ancestors—
 O, in a tomb where never scandal slept   70
 Save this of hers, framed by thy villainy.

CLAUDIO

 My villainy?

LEONATO   Thine, Claudio, thine I say.

DON PEDRO

 You say not right, old man.

LEONATO   My lord, my lord,

 I'll prove it on his body if he dare,

---

53 **Thou** To Claudio Leonato uses the intimate, condescending 'thou'; to Don Pedro at 49 the polite 'you'.
55 **beshrew** a curse on
57 **meant nothing to** intended nothing in moving toward (my sword)
58 **fleer** grin in an evil manner
62 **head** face

66 **trial of a man** single combat
71 **framed** contrived
72 **My villainy** His honour alone, rather than the death of Hero, occupies Claudio's mind. Leonato's 'thine', the intimate form used in speaking with children, makes the point.

Despite his nice fence and his active practice,   75
His May of youth and bloom of lustihood.
CLAUDIO
Away, I will not have to do with you.
LEONATO
Canst thou so doff me? Thou hast killed my child.
If thou kill'st me, boy, thou shalt kill a man.
ANTONIO
He shall kill two of us, and men indeed.   80
But that's no matter, let him kill one first.
Win me and wear me. Let him answer me.
Come follow me, boy; come, sir boy, come follow me.
Sir boy, I'll whip you from your foining fence.
Nay, as I am a gentleman, I will.   85
LEONATO Brother—
ANTONIO
Content yourself. God knows, I loved my niece,
And she is dead, slandered to death by villains
That dare as well answer a man in deed
As I dare take a serpent by the tongue.   90
Boys, apes, braggarts, jacks, milksops!
LEONATO   Brother Antony—
ANTONIO
Hold you content. What, man, I know them, yea,
And what they weigh, even to the utmost scruple:
Scambling, outfacing, fashion-monging boys,
That lie and cog and flout, deprave and slander,   95

78 doff] Q (daffe)

75 **nice fence** over-refined swordplay.
Leonato's generation scorned the new
'scientific' fencing techniques being
taught in England by such Italian masters as Vincentio Saviolo, whose *His
Practise in Two Books* (1595) was widely known. That Shakespeare probably
had him in mind is evidenced by 'foining fence' at 84; the term 'foin' is
given by Saviolo to a thrust over an
opponent's hand and then downward.
Its obvious sexual implication is em-
ployed at 84 (contemptuously), in *2
Henry IV* 2.4 and elsewhere. Saviolo
was one of John Burbage's partners
when in 1596 he leased the fencing
school at which Saviolo taught for

use as a part of Blackfriars Theatre;
Shakespeare may have met him.
78 **doff** put me off, a variant of Q's 'daff'
82 **Win me and wear me** who can beat
me can give me orders: a proverbial
dare, Tilley W408
83 **boy ... boy** Antonio's repetition of
'boy' is particularly apt after the
epithet 'old' used slightingly by Claudio and Don Pedro.
93 **scruple** 20 grains in apothecary's
measure, a small amount
94 **Scambling, outfacing, fashion-monging boys** scuffling, bullying clothes-
horses; a perennial description
95 **cog and flout** cheat and insult
deprave vilify

Go anticly, and show an outward hideousness,
And speak off half a dozen dangerous words,
How they might hurt their enemies, if they durst,
And this is all.

LEONATO
But brother Antony—

ANTONIO   Come, 'tis no matter.   100
Do not you meddle, let me deal in this.

DON PEDRO
Gentlemen both, we will not wake your patience.
My heart is sorry for your daughter's death,
But on my honour she was charged with nothing
But what was true and very full of proof.   105

LEONATO
My lord, my lord—

DON PEDRO   I will not hear you.

LEONATO   No?
Come brother, away. I will be heard.

ANTONIO
And shall, or some of us will smart for it.

                                   Exeunt Leonato and Antonio
          Enter Benedick

DON PEDRO
See, see, here comes the man we went to seek.

CLAUDIO Now, signor, what news?   110

BENEDICK *(to Don Pedro)* Good day, my lord.

DON PEDRO Welcome, signor. You are almost come to
part almost a fray.

CLAUDIO We had liked to have had our two noses
snapped off with two old men without teeth.   115

---

96 anticly] Q (antiquely)   an] ROWE; *not in* Q   97 off] THEOBALD; of Q   106–7] COLLIER;
as three lines ending at 'Lord', 'No' *and* 'heard' Q   108.1] CAPELL (*subs.*); *Exeunt amb.* Q
(*after 107*)   108.2] Q; F (*at 106*); ROWE (*after 109*)   114 liked] Q (likt); like F2,
HUMPHREYS, MARES

96 **Go anticly ... hideousness** dress grot-
    esquely and put on a frightening ap-
    pearance
102 **wake your patience** counsel you (or
    further cause you the need) to be pa-
    tient
108 **some of us** an evasion: Leonato
    means to include the Prince as well as

Claudio, but defers to the Prince's rank.
111 **Good ... lord** Benedick ignores Claud-
    io and is merely formal with Don
    Pedro.
114 **liked** *OED* supports this reading; see
    like v.² 2.
115 **with** by

DON PEDRO Leonato and his brother. What thinkest
thou? Had we fought, I doubt we should have been
too young for them.

BENEDICK In a false quarrel there is no true valour. I
came to seek you both.   120

CLAUDIO We have been up and down to seek thee, for
we are high-proof melancholy and would fain have
it beaten away. Wilt thou use thy wit?

BENEDICK It is in my scabbard. Shall I draw it?

DON PEDRO Dost thou wear thy wit by thy side?   125

CLAUDIO Never any did so, though very many have
been beside their wit. I will bid thee draw as we do
the minstrels; draw to pleasure us.

DON PEDRO As I am an honest man, he looks pale. Art
thou sick, or angry?   130

CLAUDIO What, courage, man! What though care killed
a cat, thou hast mettle enough in thee to kill care.

BENEDICK Sir, I shall meet your wit in the career, an
you charge it against me. I pray you choose another
subject.   135

CLAUDIO Nay then, give him another staff. This last was
broke cross.

DON PEDRO By this light, he changes more and more. I
think he be angry indeed.

CLAUDIO If he be, he knows how to turn his girdle.   140

BENEDICK Shall I speak a word in your ear?

CLAUDIO God bless me from a challenge.

BENEDICK (*aside to Claudio*) You are a villain. I jest not.
I will make it good how you dare, with what you
dare, and when you dare. Do me right, or I will   145

117 **doubt** fear
122 **high-proof** in the highest degree
124 **draw** as a sword; a menacing metaphor
131–2 **care killed a cat** proverbial, Tilley
C84
133 **in the career** at a full gallop. Benedick's imagery here is taken from
jousting; earlier it was derived from
swordplay. The images suggest the soldierliness of the role.
136 **staff** lance. A lance snapped in the
middle, rather than splintering along
its length from a direct strike at an

opponent, was considered a sign of
clumsiness or fear. Claudio evidently
still has no idea that Benedick is angry.
140 **turn his girdle** The literal meaning is
unclear, but proverbially (Tilley B698)
turning one's girdle (belt) so that the
buckle was at the rear signified that
one had decided to put up with a
provocation rather than contest it.
144 **make it good** back up my statement
that you are a villain
145 **Do me right** give me satisfaction by
taking up my challenge
protest proclaim

protest your cowardice. You have killed a sweet lady,
and her death shall fall heavy on you. Let me hear
from you.

CLAUDIO (*aside to Benedick*) Well, I will meet you, so I
may have good cheer.   150

DON PEDRO What, a feast, a feast?

CLAUDIO I' faith, I thank him. He hath bid me to a
calf's head and a capon, the which if I do not carve
most curiously, say my knife's naught. Shall I not
find a woodcock too?   155

BENEDICK Sir, your wit ambles well; it goes easily.

DON PEDRO I'll tell thee how Beatrice praised thy wit
the other day. I said thou hadst a fine wit. 'True,'
said she, 'a fine little one.' 'No,' said I, 'a great wit.'
'Right,' says she, 'a great gross one.' 'Nay,' said I,   160
'a good wit.' 'Just,' said she, 'it hurts nobody.' 'Nay,'
said I, 'the gentleman is wise.' 'Certain,' said she, 'a
wise gentleman.' 'Nay,' said I, 'he hath the tongues.'
'That I believe,' said she, 'for he swore a thing to
me on Monday night which he forswore on Tuesday   165
morning. There's a double tongue; there's two tongues.' Thus did she an hour together trans-shape thy
particular virtues. Yet at last she concluded with a
sigh thou wast the properest man in Italy.

CLAUDIO For the which she wept heartily and said she   170
cared not.

DON PEDRO Yea, that she did. But yet for all that, an
if she did not hate him deadly, she would love him
dearly. The old man's daughter told us all.

149-50 **so ... cheer** only if I can be assured of entertainment. Claudio is
being thoroughly insolent.
153-5 **calf's head ... capon, woodcock** a
fool, a coward, and a simpleton. The
calf was proverbially naïve, the capon
a castrated rooster, and the woodcock
very easily caught.
154 **curiously** skilfully
156 **ambles** goes at a very slow pace
157 **wit** In an appendix to his Oxford
edition of *As You Like It* Alan Brissenden argues that 'wit' was a euphemism for 'penis'; the usage parallels
brains = testicles in US slang, *c*.1940.

Its application here transforms Don
Pedro's speech.
163 **wise gentleman** Johnson thought the
expression ironic; if so the irony must
be indicated in the actor's delivery.
the tongues several languages, sometimes specifically 'the three tongues':
Hebrew, Greek, and Latin.
169 **properest** finest. The numerous variants of 'proper', all terms of praise,
suggest the high social value of deco-
rum and the pervasiveness of beliefs in
fixed worth.
173 **hate him deadly ... love him dearly**
The stereotypical view of women's

CLAUDIO All, all. And moreover, God saw him when he   175
was hid in the garden.

DON PEDRO But when shall we set the savage bull's
horns on the sensible Benedick's head?

CLAUDIO Yea, and text underneath, 'Here dwells Benedick the married man'.   180

BENEDICK (*to Claudio*) Fare you well, boy, you know my
mind. I will leave you now to your gossip-like
humour. You break jests as braggarts do their blades
which, God be thanked, hurt not. (*To Don Pedro*) My
lord, for your many courtesies I thank you. I must   185
discontinue your company. Your brother the Bastard
is fled from Messina. You have among you killed a
sweet and innocent lady. For my Lord Lackbeard
there, he and I shall meet; and till then, peace be
with him.   *Exit*   190

DON PEDRO He is in earnest.

CLAUDIO In most profound earnest and, I'll warrant
you, for the love of Beatrice.

DON PEDRO And hath challenged thee?

CLAUDIO Most sincerely.   195

DON PEDRO What a pretty thing man is when he goes
in his doublet and hose and leaves off his wit!

Enter Dogberry and Verges, the Watch, Conrad, and
Borachio

CLAUDIO He is then a giant to an ape. But then is an
ape a doctor to such a man.

178 on] F; one Q   188 Lackbeard there,] F; Lacke- beard, there Q   190 SD] *not in* Q
197.1–2] ROWE (*subs.*), Q (*Enter Constables, Conrade, and Borachio*); HANMER, HUMPHREYS,
MARES *place SD after* 201

supposed emotional extremism was
proverbial, Tilley W651.

174 **old man's daughter** Apparently Don
Pedro (or more likely Shakespeare) has
forgotten that he has been told that
Hero is dead.

175–6 **God ... garden** This allusion to
Gen. 3:8 and Adam's vain attempt to
hide from God hints at the plot against
Benedick in 2.3; Benedick does not
understand the hint.

177–8 **savage ... head** These allusions to
cuckoldry and marriage recall Benedick's resolution to remain single in 1.1.

182 **gossip-like** chattering, generally, though
not exclusively, gender-specific, but
here an intended insult; gossip = god-
parent.

183 **braggarts do their blades** i.e. not in
combat, but pretending so, as Falstaff
was accused of doing in 1 *Henry IV*
which refers to 'jests'

196 **goes** gets dressed and goes out. The
sing-song rhythm and the rhyme
(goes–hose) add to the mockery.

198–9 **He ... man** To a fool (ape) he
seems a hero (saint), but compared to
a man who forgets his wits, a fool is
a learned scholar (doctor).

DON PEDRO But soft you, let me be. Pluck up, my heart,   200
and be sad. Did he not say my brother was fled?

DOGBERRY (*to a prisoner*) Come you, sir. If justice cannot
tame you, she shall ne'er weigh more reasons in her
balance. Nay, an you be a cursing hypocrite once,
you must be looked to.   205

DON PEDRO How now, two of my brother's men bound?
Borachio one!

CLAUDIO Hearken after their offence, my lord.

DON PEDRO Officers, what offence have these men done?

DOGBERRY Marry, sir, they have committed false report.   210
Moreover they have spoken untruths; secondarily
they are slanders; sixth and lastly they have belied
a lady; thirdly they have verified unjust things and,
to conclude, they are lying knaves.

DON PEDRO First I ask thee what they have done;   215
thirdly I ask thee what's their offence; sixth and
lastly why they are committed and, to conclude,
what you lay to their charge.

CLAUDIO Rightly reasoned and in his own division. And
by my troth there's one meaning well suited.   220

DON PEDRO (*to Conrad and Borachio*) Who have you
offended, masters, that you are thus bound to your
answer? This learned constable is too cunning to be
understood. What's your offence?

BORACHIO Sweet Prince, let me go no farther to mine   225
answer. Do you hear me, and let this Count kill me.
I have deceived even your very eyes. What your
wisdoms could not discover, these shallow fools have
brought to light, who in the night overheard me
confessing to this man how Don John your brother   230
incensed me to slander the Lady Hero, how you were
brought into the orchard and saw me court Margaret
in Hero's garments, how you disgraced her when you

---

200 **soft you** wait a minute
  Pluck up, my heart I have to pull
  myself together
203 **reasons** pronounced 'raisins'; Falstaff uses the pun in *1 Henry IV*
  2.4.232
204 **cursing** accursed
  once in a word. See Abbott 57 on this

usage.
219 **in his own division** in its proper place
  in a logical argument
220 **one meaning well suited** Between
  them Dogberry and Don Pedro have
  dressed up one idea six ways.
223 **cunning** ingenious
233 **in Hero's garments** This is mentioned

should marry her. My villainy they have upon record, which I had rather seal with my death than   235
repeat over to my shame. The lady is dead upon mine
and my master's false accusation; and, briefly, I
desire nothing but the reward of a villain.

DON PEDRO (*to Claudio*)
Runs not this speech like iron through your blood?

CLAUDIO
I have drunk poison whiles he uttered it.   240

DON PEDRO (*to Borachio*)
But did my brother set thee on to this?

BORACHIO
Yea, and paid me richly for the practice of it.

DON PEDRO
He is composed and framed of treachery,
And fled he is upon this villainy.

CLAUDIO
Sweet Hero, now thy image doth appear   245
In the rare semblance that I loved it first.

DOGBERRY Come, bring away the plaintiffs. By this time
our Sexton hath reformed Signor Leonato of the
matter. And, masters, do not forget to specify, when
time and place shall serve, that I am an ass.   250

VERGES Here, here comes Master Signor Leonato, and
the Sexton too.

Enter Leonato, Antonio his brother, and the Sexton

LEONATO
Which is the villain? Let me see his eyes,
That when I note another man like him
I may avoid him. Which of these is he?   255

BORACHIO
If you would know your wronger, look on me.

LEONATO
Art thou the slave that with thy breath hast killed
Mine innocent child?

---

251 VERGES] ROWE; *Con⟨stable⟩*. 2 Q   252.1 *Antonio*] not in Q   257–8] *as verse* Q; *as prose* F

for the first time.   tion of trickery
236 **mine and my** On Shakespeare's usage   246 **rare semblance** precious likeness
    here see Abbott 237, 238.   **that** in which
242 **practice** execution, with the implica-   248 **reformed** for 'informed'

BORACHIO   Yea, even I alone.
LEONATO
No, not so, villain, thou beliest thyself.
Here stand a pair of honourable men.   260
A third is fled that had a hand in it.
I thank you, Princes, for my daughter's death.
Record it with your high and worthy deeds.
'Twas bravely done, if you bethink you of it.
CLAUDIO
I know not how to pray your patience,   265
Yet I must speak. Choose your revenge yourself;
Impose me to what penance your invention
Can lay upon my sin. Yet sinned I not
But in mistaking.
DON PEDRO   By my soul, nor I.
And yet to satisfy this good old man   270
I would bend under any heavy weight
That he'll enjoin me to.
LEONATO
I cannot bid you bid my daughter live;
That were impossible; but, I pray you both,
Possess the people in Messina here   275
How innocent she died. And if your love
Can labour aught in sad invention,
Hang her an epitaph upon her tomb
And sing it to her bones; sing it tonight.
Tomorrow morning come you to my house,   280
And since you could not be my son-in-law,
Be yet my nephew. My brother hath a daughter,
Almost the copy of my child that's dead,
And she alone is heir to both of us.
Give her the right you should have giv'n her cousin,   285
And so dies my revenge.
CLAUDIO   O noble sir!

265 **patience** The variant trisyllabic pronunciation was useful metrically, especially for line-endings. 'Patience' could
also be disyllabic as at 5.1.102; see
Sipe 10, 11, 33 n. and Cercignani
294, 309.
266 **Impose me** impose on me
invention imagination, trisyllabic;

see 277
275 **Possess** inform
284 **heir to both** Antonio's son (see 1.2.1)
is forgotten, and so Claudio can be
reassured on the matter of inheritance.
The daughter is an invention for the
moment.
285 **right** a pun on 'rite'

Your overkindness doth wring tears from me.
I do embrace your offer, and dispose
For henceforth of poor Claudio.

LEONATO
Tomorrow then I will expect your coming;   290
Tonight I take my leave. This naughty man
Shall face to face be brought to Margaret,
Who, I believe, was packed in all this wrong,
Hired to it by your brother.

BORACHIO   No, by my soul, she was not;
Nor knew not what she did when she spoke to me,   295
But always hath been just and virtuous
In anything that I do know by her.

DOGBERRY (*to Leonato*) Moreover, sir, which indeed is
not under white and black, this plaintiff here, the
offender, did call me ass. I beseech you let it be   300
remembered in his punishment. And also the watch
heard them talk of one Deformed. They say he wears
a key in his ear and lock hanging by it, and borrows
money in God's name, the which he hath used so
long and never paid, that now men grow hard-   305
hearted and will lend nothing for God's sake. Pray
you examine him upon that point.

LEONATO
I thank thee for thy care and honest pains.

DOGBERRY Your worship speaks like a most thankful
and reverend youth, and I praise God for you.   310

LEONATO (*giving him money*) There's for thy pains.

DOGBERRY God save the foundation!

LEONATO Go, I discharge thee of thy prisoner, and I
thank thee.

DOGBERRY I leave an arrant knave with your worship,   315
which I beseech your worship to correct yourself, for

---

310 reverend] F; reuerent Q   311 *giving ... money*] OXFORD; *not in* Q

293 **packed** implicated
299 **under white and black** written down
303 **key ... lock** Dogberry misinterprets
the lovelock of 3.3.168.
303–4 **borrows ... in God's name.** Prov.
19:17 equates alms-giving with lend-
ing to God, as beggars were fond of

reminding prospective donors.
312 **God save the foundation** Dogberry
responds with a well-known catch-
phrase used by veterans of institu-
tional begging; its use here must have
greatly amused Shakespeare's audience.

the example of others. God keep your worship; I wish
your worship well. God restore you to health. I
humbly give you leave to depart, and if a merry
meeting may be wished, God prohibit it. Come, neigh-   320
bour.   *Exeunt Dogberry and Verges*

LEONATO
Until tomorrow morning, lords, farewell.

ANTONIO
Farewell, my lords. We look for you tomorrow.

DON PEDRO
We will not fail.

CLAUDIO   Tonight I'll mourn with Hero.
                    Exeunt Don Pedro and Claudio

LEONATO (*to the Watch*)
Bring you these fellows on.—We'll talk with Margaret,   325
How her acquaintance grew with this lewd fellow.
                                  Exeunt

5.2   *Enter Benedick and Margaret*

BENEDICK Pray thee, sweet Mistress Margaret, deserve
well at my hands by helping me to the speech of
Beatrice.

MARGARET Will you then write me a sonnet in praise
of my beauty?   5

BENEDICK In so high a style, Margaret, that no man
living shall come over it, for in most comely truth,
thou deservest it.   .

MARGARET To have no man come over me? Why, shall
I always keep below stairs?   10

BENEDICK Thy wit is as quick as the greyhound's
mouth; it catches.

---

321 SD] CAMBRIDGE; *Exeunt* F (*after 322*); *not in* Q   324 SD] *not in* Q   325–6] *as verse*
POPE; *as prose* Q
   5.2.0.1] Q; ~, *meeting* CAPELL

326 **lewd** base
5.2.6 high a style word-play on high =
    exalted and literally high, and on style
    as both manner and the series of steps
    or rungs enabling one to go over a fence
  7 **come over** both 'cross' and 'outdo'
    comely pleasing, becoming. The adjec-
    tive is a syntactically displaced compli-
    ment.

9 **come over** Here the phrase is an erotic
    and not wholly playful expression of
    Margaret's fear (made clear in the
    phrase 'below stairs') that no man of
    a higher social station will marry her.
10 **keep** remain
12 **catches** takes a sudden and successful
    bite (as a greyhound at its prey)

MARGARET And yours as blunt as the fencer's foils,
which hit but hurt not.

BENEDICK A most manly wit, Margaret; it will not hurt   15
a woman. And so, I pray thee, call Beatrice. I give
thee the bucklers.

MARGARET Give us the swords; we have bucklers of
our own.

BENEDICK If you use them, Margaret, you must put in   20
the pikes with a vice; and they are dangerous weapons for maids.

MARGARET Well, I will call Beatrice to you, who I think
hath legs.   *Exit*

BENEDICK And therefore will come.   25

(*Sings*)   The god of love
              That sits above,
              And knows me, and knows me,
              How pitiful I deserve—

I mean in singing. But in loving—Leander the good   30
swimmer, Troilus the first employer of panders, and
a whole book full of these quondam carpet-mongers
whose names yet run smoothly in the even road of
a blank verse—why they were never so truly turned
over and over as my poor self in love. Marry, I   35
cannot show it in rhyme. I have tried. I can find out
no rhyme to 'lady' but 'baby'—an innocent rhyme;
for 'scorn' 'horn'—a hard rhyme; for 'school'

24 SD] Q (*Exit Margarite*)   26–9] *as verse* CAPELL; *as prose* Q

16–7 I... bucklers I give you my shield,
i.e. I surrender.
18–19 swords... our own Swords = male
genitals, bucklers = female legs and
thighs; see *Troilus* 1.2.47 for Cressida's 'Upon my back to defend my
belly'.
20–1 put in ... vice Continuing the *double
entendres*, this refers to using a screw
to fix a pike in the centre of a shield.
24 hath legs will come to you; continues
the bawdy talk by picking up 'bucklers
of our own': 'Beatrice has a woman's
usual means of defending herself from
your advances.'
26–9 These lines are from a well-known

song about unrequited love written by
the actor William Elderton. The song
was published in 1562, reprinted, and
much imitated; see Appendix.
29 pitiful I deserve how much pity I
deserve. Bad singing seems to be a
continuing joke in this play.
30–1 Leander... panders   Leander
drowned in the Hellespont visiting his
faithful lover Hero. Troilus was be-
trayed by his beloved Cressida, introduced to him by her uncle Pandarus.
32 quondam carpet-mongers one-time
ladies' men, from their haunting of
carpeted boudoirs
37 innocent word-play on innocent=silly

'fool'—a babbling rhyme. Very ominous endings. No,
I was not born under a rhyming planet, nor I cannot   40
woo in festival terms.

    Enter Beatrice

Sweet Beatrice, wouldst thou come when I called
    thee?

BEATRICE Yea, signor, and depart when you bid me.

BENEDICK O, stay but till then.   45

BEATRICE 'Then' is spoken. Fare you well now. And yet,
ere I go, let me go with that I came for, which is
with knowing what hath passed between you and
Claudio.

BENEDICK Only foul words, and thereupon I will kiss   50
thee.

BEATRICE Foul words is but foul wind, and foul wind
is but foul breath, and foul breath is noisome. Therefore I will depart unkissed.

BENEDICK Thou hast frighted the word out of his right   55
sense, so forcible is thy wit. But I must tell thee
plainly, Claudio undergoes my challenge; and either
I must shortly hear from him or I will subscribe him
a coward. And I pray thee now tell me, for which of
my bad parts didst thou first fall in love with me?   60

BEATRICE For them all together, which maintained so
politic a state of evil that they will not admit any
good part to intermingle with them. But for which
of my good parts did you first suffer love for me?

BENEDICK 'Suffer love'—a good epithet. I do suffer love   65
indeed, for I love thee against my will.

BEATRICE In spite of your heart, I think. Alas, poor
heart! If you spite it for my sake I will spite it for

41.1] F; Q (*after 42*)   47 came for] ROWE 1714; came Q

42–6 **Sweet . . . now** The passage glances
ironically at *The Taming of the Shrew*,
especially at Petruccio's wager over
whose wife will come 'at first when he
do send for her'.
47 **came for** Q's omission of the preposi-
tion seems a compositor's oversight.
52–3 **Foul . . . noisome** proverbial, Tilley
W833
57 **plainly** without metaphor

58 **subscribe him** proclaim him over my
signature
64, 65 **suffer** Beatrice and Benedick play
with the limits of the meanings of
'suffer' as 'allow' and 'experience anguish'. She compliments him on his
'conversion' as an act of reason; he
jokingly refers to it as a pain that
overwhelmed him.
68–70 **If . . . hates** If you love in spite of

yours, for I will never love that which my friend
hates.   70
BENEDICK Thou and I are too wise to woo peaceably.
BEATRICE It appears not in this confession. There's not
one wise man among twenty that will praise himself.
BENEDICK An old, an old instance, Beatrice, that lived
in the time of good neighbours. If a man do not erect   75
in this age his own tomb ere he dies, he shall live
no longer in monument than the bell rings and the
widow weeps.
BEATRICE And how long is that, think you?
BENEDICK Question—why, an hour in clamour and a   80
quarter in rheum. Therefore is it most expedient for
the wise, if Don Worm his conscience find no impediment to the contrary, to be the trumpet of his own
virtues, as I am to myself. So much for praising
myself who—I myself will bear witness—is praise-   85
worthy. And now tell me, how doth your cousin?
BEATRICE Very ill.
BENEDICK And how do you?
BEATRICE Very ill too.
BENEDICK Serve God, love me, and mend. There will I   90
leave you too, for here comes one in haste.
    Enter Ursula

84 myself. So] ROWE (*subs.*); my self so Q   91.1] Q; F (*after 89*)

your heart (desires), I will reject your
heart too, since I will not love something that my lover hates. This is a
sophistic way of saying that she will
not love Benedick unless he loves her
freely, with all his heart.
71 **too wise ... peaceably** since we are
bound to plumb the depths of every
statement
72 **It ... confession** That you are wise
does not appear in this admission that
we are too wise to love peaceably.
Beatrice protests against self-compli-
ment but, less obviously, also denies
that there is any impediment to their
wooing peaceably.
74 **instance** argument
    lived was credible or applicable
75 **time of good neighbours** Tilley N117:
'He has ill neighbours that is fain to
praise himself.' Benedick rejects the

proverb since the age of neighbourli-
ness is past, and so people must now
praise themselves.
76–7 **live ... monument** be remembered
no longer
80 **Question** This is an archly formal de-
bater's phrasing: the question is put;
the answer follows.
80–1 **clamour ... rheum** the noise of the
funeral bells (about which there were
complaints and ineffectual statutes)
and tearful sobbing
82 **Don Worm his conscience** The worm
or serpent is a traditional image for the
conscience, probably from Mark 9:
44: 'Their worm dieth not, and the
fire is not quenched'—which recalls an
almost identical passage in Isa. 66:
24; on the construction of the phrase
see Abbott 217.

URSULA Madam, you must come to your uncle. Yonder's old coil at home. It is proved my Lady Hero hath been falsely accused, the Prince and Claudio mightily abused, and Don John is the author of all,   95
who is fled and gone. Will you come presently?
BEATRICE Will you go hear this news, signor?
BENEDICK I will live in thy heart, die in thy lap, and be buried in thy eyes; and, moreover, I will go with thee to thy uncle's.   *Exeunt*   100

5.3   *Enter Claudio, Don Pedro the Prince, and three*
           or four Attendants with tapers, all wearing
           mourning; Balthasar and musicians

CLAUDIO
   Is this the monument of Leonato?
A LORD
   It is, my lord.
⌈CLAUDIO⌉ (*reading from a scroll*)
           Done to death by slanderous tongues
           Was the Hero that here lies.
           Death, in guerdon of her wrongs,   5
              Gives her fame which never dies.
           So the life that died with shame
           Lives in death with glorious fame.
           He hangs the epitaph on the tomb
           Hang thou there upon the tomb,
              Praising her when I am dumb.   10
   Now music sound, and sing your solemn hymn.
           ⌈*Musicians play*⌉

100 Exeunt] Q (*exit.*)
    5.3.0.1–2] Q (*Enter Claudio, Prince, and three or foure with tapers*); ~ *all wearing mourning*
FOAKES; ~ *Balthasar and musicians* CAPELL (*subs.*)   2 A LORD] CAMBRIDGE; *Lord* Q   3
CLAUDIO . . . *scroll*] CAPELL; *not in* Q (*which has title 'Epitaph'*)   3–11] *spoken by Claudio*
CAPELL; *spoken by Lord* Q   8 SD] CAPELL (*subs.*); *not in* Q   10 dumb] F; *dead* Q   11
Now] CAPELL; *Claudio Now* Q   11.1 *Musicians play*] This edition; *not in* Q

93 **old coil** great confusion; 'old' is (as now) a common colloquial intensifier.
98–9 **die . . . eyes** Dying = orgasm was a common euphemism but, since Benedick hoped to spend the rest of his life with Beatrice, the image of burial in her eyes (his reflection there being his last sight) is not merely erotic.

5.3.3 CLAUDIO Q has no speech-heading for Claudio here, but Capell's assignment of this speech to him seems right despite the warm tone; however, epitaphs of this sort were routinely commissioned.
5 **guerdon** recompense, a slightly precious 'poetical' word

⌜BALTHASAR⌝ (*sings*)
> Pardon, goddess of the night,
> Those that slew thy virgin knight,
> For the which with songs of woe
> Round about her tomb they go.   15
>> Midnight, assist our moan,
>> Help us to sigh and groan,
>>> Heavily, heavily.
> Graves yawn, and yield your dead
> Till death be utterèd,   20
>>> Heavily, heavily.

⌜CLAUDIO⌝
> Now, unto thy bones good night.
> Yearly will I do this rite.

DON PEDRO
Good morrow, masters, put your torches out.
The wolves have preyed, and look, the gentle day   25
Before the wheels of Phoebus round about
> Dapples the drowsy east with spots of grey.
Thanks to you all, and leave us. Fare you well.

CLAUDIO
Good morrow, masters. Each his several way.

DON PEDRO
Come, let us hence, and put on other weeds,   30
And then to Leonato's we will go.

12 BALTHASAR] WILSON; *not in* Q (*which has title 'Song'*)   16–17] ROWE; *as one line* Q
22 CLAUDIO] ROWE; *Lord.* Q   22–3] ROWE 1714; *as one line* Q   23 rite] Q (*right*)   24–7]
POPE; Q (*unindented*)

12–21 No contemporary setting of the
song has been found.

12–13 night . . . knight Identical rhymes,
now in disfavour, were then acceptable.

12 Q names no singer, and most editors
follow Dover Wilson in giving the song
to Balthasar. The comic by-play with
Balthasar's singing is usually ignored
although warrant for a poor singer
augmented with one or two better singers is Q's 'our' at 16, and 'us' at 17.
goddess of the night The moon-
goddess Diana, herself chaste, was the
patron of virgins, who were her
knights.

15 **Round . . . tomb** The mourners circle
the tomb in a propitious, i.e. clockwise,

direction.

19–20 **Graves . . . utterèd** If *uttered* is
taken to mean 'fully expressed' then
the lines call on the dead as well as
midnight to 'assist our moan'. More
relevant to the ensuing action and
slightly less odd would be the uttering
as ejecting (*OED v.* 3b), of death itself,
which would occur when the graves
yielded their dead at the Day of Judgement. F's version of 21, 'Heavenly,
heavenly', might then. be a plausible
emendation. Yet exact meaning here
is less important than the sadness of
the music.

26 **wheels of Phoebus** chariot of the sun-
god

30 **weeds** clothes (from the Old English for

DIO

...d Hymen now with luckier issue speeds
...an this for whom we rendered up this woe.

       Exeunt

Enter Leonato, Antonio, Benedick, Beatrice,
Margaret, Ursula, Friar Francis, and Hero

...

I not tell you she was innocent?

...TO

...are the Prince and Claudio, who accused her
...n the error that you heard debated.
    Margaret was in some fault for this,
Although against her will, as it appears   5
In the true course of all the question.

ANTONIO

Well, I am glad that all things sorts so well.

BENEDICK

And so am I, being else by faith enforced
To call young Claudio to a reckoning for it.

LEONATO

Well, daughter, and you gentlewomen all,   10
Withdraw into a chamber by yourselves,
And when I send for you, come hither masked.
    Exeunt Beatrice, Hero, Margaret, and Ursula
The Prince and Claudio promised by this hour
To visit me. (*To Antonio*) You know your office,
    brother;
You must be father to your brother's daughter,   15
And give her to young Claudio.

32 speeds] Q; speed 's *conj. Thirlby,* THEOBALD, *and most recent eds.*
  5.4.0.1–2] Q (*Enter Leonato, Benedick, Margaret, Ursula, old man, Frier, Hero.*); ~
Beatrice ROWE (*inserted after 'Benedick'*)   7 sorts] Q; sort F   7, 17 ANTONIO] ROWE; Q

'garment'), now obsolete, but until recently a term used specifically for tokens of mourning. The mourners on stage have been wearing black cloaks, and must now change for the wedding.

32 **Hymen** god of marriage
  luckier issue happier outcome
  speeds comes towards us rapidly (since day is coming soon). Many editors emend Q to 'speed 's': May Hymen

speed us, i.e. bring us good fortune. But the emendation is not needed.

33 **this** this outcome

5.4.3 **Upon** as a result of. Abbott 191 discusses this construction.

5 **against her will** unintentionally

6 **question** inquiry

7 **sorts** turn out

8 **faith** his pledge to Beatrice and his challenge

14 **office** function

ANTONIO
Which I will do with confirmed countenance.
BENEDICK
Friar, I must entreat your pains, I think.
FRIAR To do what, signor?
BENEDICK
To bind me or undo me, one of them.   20
Signor Leonato, truth it is, good signor,
Your niece regards me with an eye of favour.
LEONATO
That eye my daughter lent her, 'tis most true.
BENEDICK
And I do with an eye of love requite her.
LEONATO
The sight whereof I think you had from me,   25
From Claudio and the Prince. But what's your will?
BENEDICK
Your answer, sir, is enigmatical.
But for my will—my will is your good will
May stand with ours this day to be conjoined
In the state of honourable marriage—   30
In which, good Friar, I shall desire your help.
LEONATO
My heart is with your liking.
FRIAR   And my help.
Here comes the Prince and Claudio.
          Enter Don Pedro and Claudio with attendants
DON PEDRO
Good morrow to this fair assembly.
LEONATO
Good morrow, Prince. Good morrow, Claudio.   35
We here attend you. Are you yet determined
Today to marry with my brother's daughter?

(*Old.*)   12.1] Q (*'Exeunt Ladies' after 16*)   33.1] F (*subs.*); Q (*Enter Prince, and Claudio,
and two or three other.*)

17 **confirmed countenance** straight face
20 **undo** This puns on 'unbind' and
    'ruin'. Yet the unbinding is not only
    word-play. It suggests the idea of free-
    dom from his present constraints as a

man of honour and a tyrant to women
has entered Benedick's thinking about
marriage.
34 **assembly** pronounced as four syllables
    because of the syllabized *l*.

CLAUDIO

I'll hold my mind, were she an Ethiope.

LEONATO

Call her forth, brother; here's the Friar ready.

Exit Antonio

DON PEDRO

Good morrow, Benedick. Why, what's the matter   40
That you have such a February face,
So full of frost, of storm and cloudiness?

CLAUDIO

I think he thinks upon the savage bull.
Tush, fear not, man, we'll tip thy horns with gold,
And all Europa shall rejoice at thee   45
As once Europa did at lusty Jove
When he would play the noble beast in love.

BENEDICK

Bull Jove, sir, had an amiable low,
And some such strange bull leapt your father's cow
And got a calf in that same noble feat   50
Much like to you, for you have just his bleat.

*Enter Antonio with Hero, Beatrice, Margaret, and
Ursula, the ladies masked*

CLAUDIO

For this I owe you. Here comes other reck'nings.
Which is the lady I must seize upon?

⌈ANTONIO⌉

This same is she, and I do give you her.

CLAUDIO

Why then, she's mine. Sweet, let me see your face.   55

39.1] THEOBALD; *not in* Q   51.1–2 SD] *after* Q *(Enter brother, Hero, Beatrice, Margaret,
Ursula.); the ladies masked*] THEOBALD (*subs.*)   54 ANTONIO] THEOBALD; *Leo.* Q, MARES

---

41 **February face** frowns. Benedick still
has questions about the conduct of
Don Pedro and Claudio.

43 **savage bull** This alludes to the classical
myth in which Jove in the shape of a
bull carried off the beautiful princess
Europa.

45, 46 **Europa** The first refers to the con-
tinent; the second, italicized in F, refers to the princess.

48–51 **Bull . . . bleat** Presumably rhyme

and an air of improvisation relieve
some of the old-joke quality of this
speech.

52 **reck'nings** matters that remain to be
settled. The spelling suggests colloquial
pronunciation.

54 **This . . . her** Q attributes this speech to
Leonato; most editors follow Theobald
in assigning it to Antonio, who carries
out his promise in 14–16.

LEONATO

No, that you shall not till you take her hand
Before this Friar and swear to marry her.

CLAUDIO *(to Hero)*

Give me your hand before this holy friar.
I am your˙husband, if you like of me.

HERO *(unmasking)*

And when I lived I was your other wife;   60
And when you loved, you were my other husband.

CLAUDIO

Another Hero!

HERO   Nothing certainer.

One Hero died defiled, but I do live,
And surely as I live, I am a maid.

DON PEDRO

The former Hero, Hero that is dead!   65

LEONATO

She died, my lord, but whiles her slander lived.

FRIAR

All this amazement can I qualify.
When after that the holy rites are ended
I'll tell you largely of fair Hero's death.
Meantime let wonder seem familiar,   70
And to the chapel let us presently.

BENEDICK

Soft and fair, Friar; which is Beatrice?

BEATRICE *(unmasking)*

I answer to that name. What is your will?

BENEDICK

Do not you love me?

BEATRICE   Why no, no more than reason.

BENEDICK

Why then, your uncle and the Prince and Claudio   75
Have been deceived. They swore you did.

60 *unmasking*] ROWE *(after* 'wife'); *not in* Q   73 *unmasking*] CAPELL *(after* 'name'); *not in* Q   82 me?] F; me. Q

59 **like of** like. See Abbott 177 on this
    idiom.
67 **qualify** moderate
69 **largely** fully

70 **wonder . . . familiar** the amazing seem
    commonplace
72 **Soft and fair** take it easy

BEATRICE
Do not you love me?
BENEDICK   Troth no, no more than reason.
BEATRICE
Why then, my cousin, Margaret, and Ursula
Are much deceived, for they did swear you did.
BENEDICK
They swore that you were almost sick for me.   80
BEATRICE
They swore that you were well nigh dead for me.
BENEDICK
'Tis no such matter. Then you do not love me?
BEATRICE
No, truly, but in friendly recompense.
LEONATO
Come, cousin, I am sure you love the gentleman.
CLAUDIO
And I'll be sworn upon't that he loves her,   85
For here's a paper written in his hand,
A halting sonnet of his own pure brain,
Fashioned to Beatrice.
HERO   And here's another,
Writ in my cousin's hand, stol'n from her pocket,
Containing her affection unto Benedick.   90
BENEDICK A miracle! Here's our own hands against our
hearts. Come, I will have thee. But by this light, I
take thee for pity.
BEATRICE I would not deny you. But by this good day,
I yield upon great persuasion, and partly to save your   95
life, for I was told you were in a consumption.
BENEDICK (*kissing her*) Peace, I will stop your mouth.
DON PEDRO How dost thou, 'Benedick the married
man'?
BENEDICK I'll tell thee what, Prince: a college of wit-   100
crackers cannot flout me out of my humour. Dost

97 BENEDICK] THEOBALD; *Leon.* Q   97 *kissing her*] THEOBALD; *not in* Q

83 **friendly recompense** mutuality
87 **halting** metrically awkward
97 **Peace . . . mouth** Q assigns this line to
   Leonato, but it comes more appropriately from Benedick.
100–1 **college of wit-crackers** a whole
   club of smart alecs (like Don Pedro in
   the previous line)

thou think I care for a satire or an epigram? No, if a man will be beaten with brains, a shall wear nothing handsome about him. In brief, since I do purpose to marry, I will think nothing to any purpose   105
that the world can say against it. And therefore never flout at me for what I have said against it. For man is a giddy thing, and this is my conclusion. For thy part, Claudio, I did think to have beaten thee, but in that thou art like to be my kinsman, live un-   110
bruised, and love my cousin.

CLAUDIO I had well hoped thou wouldst have denied Beatrice, that I might have cudgelled thee out of thy single life to make thee a double dealer, which out of question thou wilt be, if my cousin do not look   115
exceeding narrowly to thee.

BENEDICK Come, come, we are friends. Let's have a dance ere we are married, that we may lighten our own hearts and our wives' heels.

LEONATO We'll have dancing afterward.   120

BENEDICK First, of my word! Therefore play, music. (*To Don Pedro*) Prince, thou art sad. Get thee a wife, get thee a wife. There is no staff more reverend than one tipped with horn.

Enter Messenger

123 reverend] F; reuerent Q

101, 107 **flout** mock
101 **humour** here a happy mood
102 **a satire or an epigram** Both forms were extremely popular at the turn of the century. John Hall, claiming to be the first English satirist, began publishing both 'toothless' and 'biting' satires in 1597.
102–4 **No . . . him** Contemporary fashions were a prime subject for satire; hence, according to Benedick, even the merely well dressed were at risk if they feared mockery.
108 **giddy** inconstant
110–11 **kinsman . . . cousin** The juxtaposition makes clear the sentimental rather than formal relationship implied in 'cousin'.
114 **double dealer** humorously, an unfaithful husband, since 'men were de-

ceivers ever'. Here and through 122 the speeches are a coda of the play's themes of sexual infidelity and the risks of marriage.
119 **wives' heels** lighter for dancing, but also a bawdy allusion; see 3.4.44–5. This, as much as his determination to see the marriage completed as soon as possible, may explain Leonato's starchy response in the next speech.
121 **of** by
122–4 **sad . . . horn** The seriousness of Don Pedro recalls the isolation of Antonio at the end of *The Merchant of Venice*. Benedick's advice is bittersweet: there is honour in marriage although the staff of rule (here male domination) may also be a symbol of betrayal, i.e. tipped with horn rather than gold.

MESSENGER
   My lord, your brother John is ta'en in flight,   125
   And brought with armèd men back to Messina.
BENEDICK Think not on him till tomorrow. I'll devise
   thee brave punishments for him. Strike up, pipers.
                                        Dance, and exeunt

128.1 *and exeunt] not in* Q

128 **brave** fine

APPENDIX

MUSIC, SONG, AND DANCE

IN few other plays does Shakespeare employ music, dance, and song so extensively or with such significance. Since *Much Ado* represents courtship among Messina's gilded youth, we should expect formal dance and singing; the play does not disappoint. As F. W. Sternfeld points out, Shakespeare was mastering the integration of song and script by the time he came to write *Much Ado*;[1] the introduction of song is far more arbitrary in, for example, *Romeo and Juliet*.

In *Much Ado* Shakespeare uses the 'arts of the theatre' as structure as well as atmosphere. The masked ball of 2.1 summarizes the relations between masters and servants, wooers and wooed, which are in turn resolved in the wedding dance that ends the play. In addition, dance and song in *Much Ado* convey the play's pervasive ideas. Masked balls suggest the problematics of courtship, of knowing and not quite knowing one's partners; formal dance suggests the interacting harmonies of the Two and the Many, of lovers and society.

Yet Shakespeare goes further. Beatrice's (and the play's) rueful view of 'the woe that is in marriage' turns dance to metaphor, predicting the devolution of marital relations from the newly-weds' sprightly (and suggestively earthy) jig to the depressingly named but actually lively cinquepace which Beatrice puns into a term (sink-apace) for dull connubial coping. Equally significant is the refrain 'men were deceivers ever' in Balthasar's song in 2.3. The song expresses a point of view that qualifies the strain of misogyny underlying Claudio's too ready accusations of Hero and their quick acceptance by Don Pedro and Leonato. In view of male deception, the song's advice is hardly reassuring counsel. It is wonderfully irrelevant to the circumstances of *Much Ado* to be told that women ought to leave lamentation over male infidelity and sing songs of 'hey nonny, nonny', presumably songs of flirtation. Such sauce for the gander is simply not available in *Much Ado*, unthinkable for either a Hero or a Beatrice. So the song functions as one of the play's rueful perspectives, a glance at the possibilities open perhaps to a Margaret but not to women with the virtue or sensibility of Shakespeare's heroines. It suggests also the self-serving nature of male counsel: that women reconcile themselves to playing in an

---

[1] F. W. Sternfeld, *Music in Shakespearian Tragedy* (1963), 105.

unfair game, even as it blandly owns up to male unfairness. Together, Beatrice's dance-metaphors and Balthasar's song offer some of the dark reflections on courtship and marriage that distinguish *Much Ado* from the romantic comedies. Finally, Benedick's change from a preference for martial music to romantic song is an obvious sign of his capitulation to his feelings for Beatrice.

Even when Shakespeare is apparently most conventional, as in ending the play with a wedding dance, he manages to tease a further significance from the convention. Benedick overrules Leonato's stuffy insistence that the wedding ceremony take place before the dance. This is amusing as realistic tug-of-war between senex and suitor. But it also queries the conventional symbolism of the dance as a union validated by religious ceremony. Benedick's reversal of priorities carries forward the undercurrent in the play of the specifically sexual force that now at last triumphs over Beatrice's humiliations and Benedick's fears.

Some of the problems of original music commissioned for the play are interestingly discussed by Virgil Thomson.[1] For modern productions the choice and performance of music can be crucial in establishing the balance between romance and realism. The scene of Claudio's formal repentance at Hero's supposed shrine is a case in point. Its frequent omission, along with its solemn music, leaves *Much Ado* and its characterization of Claudio tougher-minded and less congenial. Another opportunity for controlling the 'romantic' effects of music is provided by Balthasar's singing. A case is made in the Introduction (page 44) that Balthasar's vocal abilities are limited indeed; if this is correct his performance can neutralize the emotional power of song that Noel Coward so memorably identified, and may even emphasize the limitations of the advice in the lyrics.

Yet if Balthasar is so poor a singer as Benedick thinks, why did the company trouble to import an apparently professional musician for the role, specifically the Jack Wilson of the speech-prefixes about whom so much is conjectured? Wilson has been variously identified with an Oxford Professor of Music, a dinner guest at Edward Alleyn's 28th wedding anniversary[2]—possibly both the same person—and by Halliwell and Greg[3] with the son of a Nicholas Wilson; this Jack Wilson was christened at St Bartholomew the Less and was a long-time resident of the parish. None of these candidates convinces: the dates (1595–1674) are wrong for the first and possibly the

---

[1] V. Thomson, 'Music for *Much Ado About Nothing*', *Theatre Arts* (June 1959), 14–19.

[2] W. Young, *History of Dulwich College* (1889), ii. 192.

[3] *The Shakespeare First Folio* (Oxford, 1955), 280.

second. John Manifold finds the style of the second possible Wilson's song settings more 'Davenantian', that is later, than Shakespearian, and the son of Nicholas is a shadow.[1]

Yet a professional was needed. Bad singing—not mediocre but truly outrageous singing—is an art akin to travesty, as the careers of Anna Russell and others attest. Artfully bad song is the province of the cultivated voice: hence Jack Wilson. In any case, Wilson would have exercised his proper talents in 5.7, singing 'Pardon, goddess of the night,' though not necessarily in the person of Balthasar.

In addition to the high musical culture of a Thomas Tallis and a William Byrd and the elegant song collections of a John Dowland and a Thomas Campion, Elizabethan England produced an intensely participatory popular musical culture. Song and ballad celebrated the commonplace and the extraordinary, natural disasters and martial triumphs, and the perennial turns of criminal and amatory behaviour. Lyrics to familiar settings were sold as broadside ballads by the likes of Autolycus, marvelled at, bought, and sung by shepherds and citizens.

The vitality of this popular musical culture is preserved in Francis Beaumont's *Knight of the Burning Pestle*, in which ballad adaptations accompany much of the action and an obligatory song by all is necessary for their forgiveness as the play ends. Evidently such popular tunes as 'Fortune, My Foe' with its interminable lyrics were known even to the play's Venturewell, the most staid of entrepreneurs.

That Shakespeare employs a popular song like William Elderton's 'God of Love' is typical of contemporary practice in the theatre. Most of the audience would have known it, but we should probably trace its evocative power to its popularity rather than—to recall Noel Coward again—to its being 'cheap music'.

THE SONGS

1. *'Sigh no more, ladies'*: 2.3

We have no contemporary setting for 'Sigh no more, ladies'. Peter Seng concludes that the setting by Thomas Ford (1580?–1648) in a Christ Church, Oxford, MS published in 1925 by Peter Warlock in *Four English Songs of the Early Seventeenth Century* was probably not sung in the original production of *Much Ado*.[2] Only the first stanza

---

[1] J. Manifold, *Music in the English Drama: From Shakespeare to Purcell* (1956), 40.

[2] P. Seng, *The Vocal Songs of the Plays of Shakespeare: A Critical History* (Cambridge, Mass., 1967), 58–60.

of three matches Shakespeare's text, and Ford has an additional rhyming line after the first line in each stanza. John Manifold[1] suggests that Thomas Morley's wordless air for three voices, one of the sight-reading exercises in *A Plain and Easy Introduction to Practical Music* (1577), could be used as a setting in modern productions.

2. 'The God of love': 5.2

In 1958 James Osborn published in *The Times* of 17 November (p. 11) a modernization of these lines from a song printed in 1562 by the actor William Elderton, which had escaped notice until Osborn's discovery. Elderton's lament of the pitiful lover was extremely popular and much imitated. Its currency would have helped convey the irony of its being sung by Benedick. Seng[2] cites a version in the University of Nottingham's *Francis Willoughby Song Book*. Other versions survive in library collections elsewhere. Elderton's stanzas have little to recommend them as verse: more likely the musical setting, based on the well-known dance tune 'Turkeyloney',[3] resulted in the popularity of the song.

3. 'Pardon, goddess of the night': 5.3

As John Long observes, this song may ironically answer Don Pedro's request in 2.3 for a serenade. Jack Wilson and perhaps other singers (note the plural pronouns in the lyrics) could here have redeemed the play's singing from Balthasar's travesty and Benedick's presumably ordinary vocal talent. No contemporary setting of the lines is known. But John Payne Collier asserts that 'This was a well known tune of "Heavily, heavily" and probably the above [song] was sung to it.'[4] Collier refers to volume 2 of *The British Bibliographer*,[5] which mentions a black-letter ballad miscellany with the title of The World's Folly; this miscellany included a song, 'Oaken leaves begin to wither' sung to the tune of 'Heauille, heauilie', of which we learn no more. Even setting aside the issue of Collier's reliability, we are left with a will-o-the-wisp. The likelihood is that Shakespeare was using a familiar ballad, but precisely which ballad and which tune is unclear.

---

[1] *Music in the English Drama*, 163.
[2] *Vocal Songs*, 63.
[3] Ibid, 62–3.
[4] J. P. Collier, *Notes and Emendations to the Text of Shakespeare's Plays from Early Manuscript Corrections in a Copy of the Folio in the Possession of John Payne Collier, Esq. FSA* (1853), 72.
[5] (1812), 559–60, compiled by Sir Egerton Brydges and Joseph Haslewood.

INDEX

THIS is a selective guide to points in the Introduction and Commentary of more than routine note. Biblical illustrations are grouped together; so are proverbial parallels.

Index

Index

Index

Rossiter, A. P., pp. 36, 75, 77
Rowe, Nicholas, p. 82

salved, 1.1.304
satire, 5.4.102
Saturn, pp. 3, 45; 1.3.11
Saviolo, Vincentio, 5.1.75
scab, 3.3.98–9
scambling, 5.1.94
scarf, lieutenant's, 2.1.191
scenes, pp. 50–1, 52–6
scholarship, recent, 75–8
Scott, Mary Augusta, p. 13
scruple, 5.1.93
Seacoal, Francis (character),
  3.5.55–6
second (v.), 5.1.2
Sexton (speech-prefix), p. 82;
  4.2.2
Shakespeare, William: All's Well
  That Ends Well, pp. 4, 14, 16,
  24, 43–4, 54; As You Like It,
  pp. 1, 3, 5, 14, 15, 60; Hamlet,
  p. 15; 1 Henry IV, pp. 5, 10,
  18, 39; Henry V, pp. 6, 26, 79;
  King Lear, pp. 18, 32; Love's
  Labour's Lost, pp. 5, 13, 30, 60;
  Measure for Measure, 4, 14, 23,
  25, 26; The Merchant of Venice,
  p. 4; 3.3 108; A Midsummer
  Night's Dream, pp. 1, 2, 3, 60;
  Richard II, pp. 19, 38; Romeo
  and Juliet, pp. 2, 5, 58; The Taming of the Shrew, pp. 4, 21, 29,
  58; 5.2.42–6; Twelfth Night,
  pp. 1, 2, 3, 4, 14, 15, 43–4,
  60; Two Gentlemen of Verona, p. 9
Shaw, George Bernard, pp. 63
shift, 3.3.141
Sigh no more, ladies (song), pp. 44,
  71; 2.3.43.1; Appendix
Simmes, Valentine, pp. 79, 80
Sinden, Donald, pp. 34–5, 66, 72
sing, p. 40
sink-apace, 2.1.71–2; Appendix
sirrah, 4.2.13
skin between his brows, 3.5.12
sleeves, 3.4.19
Smith, John Hazel, p. 80
smock, 2.3.136
society, pp. 1–2, 2–3, 4, 10, 16,
  44–5, 45, 47, 49, 51, 74, 77–8
son, eldest, 2.1.9

songs, Appendix; see also 'god of
  love, The'; 'Light o'love'; 'Pardon, goddess of the night'; 'Sigh
  no more, ladies'
sores, strange, 4.1.252
sort (sb.), 1.1.7; 1.1.32
sources, pp. 4, 6–14, 52–3
Spedding, James, pp. 50–1
speech-prefixes, pp. 80, 81, 82–5,
  86; 3.3.11; 4.2.1; 4.2.67–8;
  5.3.3
speeds, 5.3.32
Spenser, Edmund; Faerie Queen,
  p. 12; 2.1.254; 4.1.254
spirits, 4.1.111
squarer, young, p. 24; 1.1.77–8
squire, 1.3.50
stables, 3.4.45–6
staff, 5.1.136
stage directions, pp. 80, 85–6;
  1.1.0; 1.2.21; 2.1.216–17;
  2.3.43.1
stage history, pp. 58–70, 70–1
stage sets, p. 63
staging, problems of, pp. 72–4
stalk, 2.3.97
stamp, 1.2.6–7
Stanislavski, p. 69
start-up, pp. 10, 23; 1.3.63
Stationers' Register, pp. 5, 79;
  2.1.317
statutes, 3.3.78
staying, p. 79
Sternfeld, F. W.; Appendix
Stoker, Bram, p. 30
stomach, 1.1.50; 2.1.379;
  2.3.253
stops, 3.2.55–6
strain, 2.1.375; 5.1.12
Stratford (Ontario), Canada, p. 69
Stratford, Connecticut, USA, p. 68
study of imagination, 4.1.225
stuffed, 1.1.54; 1.1.56–7; 3.2.44;
  3.4.62
style, 5.1.37; 5.2.6
subdued, 1.3.69
success, 4.1.234
suffer, 5.2.64
suit, out of, 2.1.347
suited, 5.1.220
sunburnt, p. 31; 2.1.315–16
sword, 5.2.18–19; by my s.,
  4.1.274; eat the s., 4.1.275